Henri Forneron

Louise de Keroualle, duchess of Portsmouth, 1649-1734 : society in the court of Charles II.

Compiled from state papers preserved in the archives of the French foreign office

Henri Forneron

Louise de Keroualle, duchess of Portsmouth, 1649-1734 : society in the court of Charles II.
Compiled from state papers preserved in the archives of the French foreign office

ISBN/EAN: 9783337156756

Printed in Europe, USA, Canada, Australia, Japan

Cover: Foto ©ninafisch / pixelio.de

More available books at **www.hansebooks.com**

LOUISE DE KEROUALLE,

Duchess of Portsmouth,

1649-1734:

SOCIETY IN THE COURT OF CHARLES II.

COMPILED FROM STATE PAPERS PRESERVED IN THE ARCHIVES OF THE FRENCH FOREIGN OFFICE BY H. FORNERON.

With Portraits, Facsimile Letter, etc., and a

PREFACE BY MRS. G. M. CRAWFORD.

THIRD   EDITION.

LONDON:
SWAN SONNENSCHEIN, LOWREY & CO.,
PATERNOSTER SQUARE.
1888.

*Butler & Tanner,
The Selwood Printing Works,
Frome, and London.*

DEDICATION.

THIS translation of the true story of the origin of pension of the ducal family of Richmond, is respectfully dedicated to the ladies of the Primrose League, who will see in it the beauty of their theory of Crown and Constitution, when consistently applied. It is also dedicated to Mr. Henry Labouchere, who has shown such fine trust in common sense, in his war against time-honoured abuses—arrogant giants that ought to be slain, and the tyranny of follies which put on the mask of "ancestral wisdom." The Translator owes the idea of translating this truthful (no pun meant) little book, to a question vainly put by Mr. Labouchere in the House of Commons, and hopes that a perusal of Louise de Keroualle's progress at Whitehall may embolden him to again ask why the Duke of Richmond is a great pensioner of England.

PREFACE BY MRS. G. M. CRAWFORD.

On the stormy 3rd of September, 1658, the soul of that master-man Cromwell, which had so often undergone gloomy eclipses, lay in deep darkness. The throes of death were on the Protector, and black presentiments took hold of his mind. One of the causes of his anguish was leaving behind him an unfinished work. This, to a man of his genius and disposition, was like leaving in hard times an infant child to buffet alone with the troubles of life. Limp and gritless, Richard Cromwell was no meet guardian for such a ward as the young Commonwealth of England; and which of the Major-Generals could better assume the office? In the broken phrases the Protector uttered, he showed a foreboding of the decadence into which his nation was to fall, and of the moral crisis through which, like a drunken Bacchante, she was to reel and stagger with a merry monarch at her head, and a crew of greedy and sensual nobles—arrant knaves and rascals for the most part—at his heels.

Cromwell, it being no use to take thought for the morrow and the days after, did what it was best under the circumstances to do. He ended by leaving the whole matter for his disquietude to God. Oppressed with the feeling that he was a "miserable worm" and "a poor, foolish creature," he took his stand on the Covenant of Grace, and in his quaint Puritan speech, supplicated on behalf of the people he had led, for higher guidance. He was an affectionate kinsman, and his heart habitually went out to his children. But on that stormy September day, which brought back memories of his greatest victories, and placed him face to face with death, he was so absorbed in patriotic anxiousness that, said one who watched beside him, "He forgot to entreat God for his own family."

"However, Lord," cried the dying hero, "Thou do dispose of me, do good for Thy people. Give them consistency of judgment, and go to deliver them with the work of reformation."

"With the work of reformation!" Think of that, all honest Britons, whether Tory or Primrose Leaguer, for this book is not intended to point a moral for the teaching of the dishonest, they being unteachable.

If God's mill grinds fine, the grinding process is—when men and women do not keep up a good supply of grist—so slow as to be imperceptible, unless we look to the work it does in the long course of generations. Cromwell's prayer was answered, but in a way that neither he himself nor those around him could have looked forward to. The tale this volume furnishes, of a French harlot's progress at Whitehall, and of the solid anchorage (£19,000 a year for ever!) which a supine nation allowed to her offspring, would not on the first blush seem to justify this view. What would any old Ironside have thought of the power of a good man's prayer, were Harvey, at the time of the Rye-House Plot convictions and executions, to have told him what he overheard Cromwell utter when the shadow of death was upon him? It would not have occurred to him that the slow grinding mill was grinding at all. Nor was it, in a general way in England, where the supply of grist was too miserably stinted for the millstones not to grind each other out, if they did long and strong spells of work. Here and there, there was a soul in touch with Heaven. But persecution was the lot of such. One of them, the tinker Bunyan, escaped from a jail-bird's noisome sufferings by a flight into Dreamland. He dreamed day-dreams, in which the vulgar facts of life—the heart-wringings that sprang from inability to protect his dear blind little child—the slips, the falls, and the hindrances to moral growth, were transmuted into the circumstances of an epic poem. We find in his Dream counterparts of Louise de Keroualle and her Court of Whitehall rivals, in Madam Bubble, Mrs. Lechery, Mrs. Batseyes, and Mrs. Filth. Fashion travelled slowly in those times—but it travelled. The titled demi-reps who formed the *cortége* of the Merry Monarch had, we may rest assured, their copyists in the low-lying social strata which the tinker was only able to observe.

. Among the phenomena of nervous diseases there are none more curious than susceptibility to "suggestion" and anesthesia or transfer of vital force from one member of the body to another.

In the one case a human being can be directed by the expressed—or, what is more noteworthy, the verbally unuttered—will of a strong-minded person in full health. Hypnotic patients of Doctor Charcot have afforded instances of this strange susceptibility. In the lives of nations we often see collective maladies similar to those which trouble individuals. England, after Cromwell's death, was like a machine going at full speed, when it loses the fly-wheel. She fell into a state of nervous unbalancement and then moral inertia. There were times when, acting under—as it is shown by the author of " Louise de Keroualle,"—the " suggestions " of a French faction, secretly organized in London to work her ruin, she was as one demented. This faction, was managed dexterously by French ambassadors, and through Louise de Keroualle it held the Crown. Indeed, all the disposing and directing powers of the nation were exercised according to orders or suggestions from Versailles. England had no more volition of her own than an hypnotic patient of Doctor Charcot. Her condition was closely watched and reported on by the agents of Louis to that monarch, and worked upon for the furtherance of a great political scheme, which was a feasible one. This plan of policy broke down chiefly because the legitimate offspring of the Grand Monarch had all bad constitutions, and died early. In consequence, the French crown passed, at the beginning of the eighteenth century, to a child of no natural political ability and of vicious instincts, who was placed under the tutelage of a voluptuary. England had under Charles become so deranged in mind as to justify a French diplomatist writing to his King that if a thing was irrational and absurd, it was the more certain for that reason to succeed among the English. Yet there was no lack of cleverness, and fine talents cropped up in literature and science. But these various gifts and capacities did not make for the general weal. The aristocracy were profligate and knavish, and, according to their degree, their leading men as much the pensioners of Louis as their monarch. In their orgies, they kept their eyes well fixed on the main chances of their class. Their wits were successfully employed in throwing off the military burdens with which their broad estates were charged, and shifting them to the shoulders of mercantile lacklands. So far as the middle and lower middle class went, there was a clear case of anesthesia, as shown in the transfer of reforming power and self-governing will to New England.

When Louise de Keroualle was above the crowned Queen at Whitehall, that New England territory was the sparsely colonized fringe of the wildest and biggest wilderness in the world. Its colonists were "the people," to whom by early associations and Puritan breeding Cromwell belonged and gave his last thoughts. God's mill was then grinding fast and fine among them, because the supply of grist was plentiful. But New England was out of the sight and mind of old England, which was supine and inert, when she was not either carousing, attacked with nervous convulsions, or a prey to wild panics, got up by agents of the Prince of Orange and limbs of the French faction. These scares are known to us as the Papist and the Rye-House Plots. Hitherto their causes have remained in semi-obscurity. In " Louise de Keroualle " they are brought into a light, full and clear to fierceness.

It has been a subject of anxiety to the translator, whether he should tone down what might appear to many well-meaning persons the too crisp scandals of the Court of Whitehall, which fill so large a place in the letters of French ambassadors to their king and his secretary for foreign affairs. Happily he has been induced not to Bowdlerize. This book is for the information of men and women who like to see the facts of history divested of conventional forms, and allowed to speak for themselves, in their own way. So the letter and the spirit are adhered to of the documents to which we owe this new vista on the wildly dissipated court of Charles II. Nothing is watered; nor would morality be served by a watering process. There are great lessons to be deduced from the piquant gossip in which this volume abounds. They would miss their mark were the translator to have toned them down. M. Forneron's book came out in Paris a few years ago, when the Duke of Richmond was in the enjoyment of an hereditary annuity of £19,000 a year. The last edition of the *Financial Reform Almanac* states that his pension has been commuted by a sum of nearly half a million sterling. It is to be supposed that this arrangement was hastened forward and quietly got through because the publication of "Louise de Keroualle" was expected in England, and a foretaste of it given in the House of Commons in a question put by Mr. Labouchere. Nobody who has any share in bringing this book before the English public harbours any sort of grudge against the ducal family of Richmond. At the same time, it is hard to conceive anything more monstrous than the commutation of the pension originally granted to Louise de Keroualle. Its enormity must come home to all who read in this volume the story of her aims and efforts. We have to go back three thousand years, to the Valley of Sorek, to find a wanton who was a match for her in cold-blooded astuteness. There is a good deal to be forgiven to a Magdalen who loves much, even though she has loved often. But the woman who plans betrayal while bewitching with her caresses, deserves outlawry. This was what Louise de Keroualle did.

However, there was a sound spot in her. Though gorged with English money (and indeed Irish money too), and always expectant of, and hungering for more, her allegiance to her own king was never shaken. She was born.

lived, and died a Frenchwoman. Under all circumstances, and in every case, she was a leal and intelligent agent of Louis the Fourteenth in London; and she won every wage he paid her, by consciously trying to bring England into subjection to France. She all but succeeded. Unfortunately for her and the King of France, the means they took defeated their object. Charles's vices being overstimulated and overdone, he died before his time, and then a new chapter of history was opened. Had he lived a few years more, the work of reformation on which Cromwell set his heart, and which after his time went on so well across the Atlantic, must have been nipped in the bud. It is in general idle to speculate upon "what might have been." But it is easy to say what, under given circumstances, could not have been. Thus, if Louise de Keroualle had remained effective queen at Whitehall for a few years more, that Greater Britain, wherein the Irish Celt has full play for his tumultuous activities and the Anglo-Saxon all the personal liberty he wants, must have fallen into the limbo of the could-not-have-beens. It was a part of the French scheme to edge

England out of North America. Seeing that France held Canada and the Mississippi Valley, was herself a great naval power, the greatest existing military power, and had her hand on Holland, the design was essentially practicable. Its success must have relegated the Boston Harbour tea fight to the could-not-have-beens; and we know that out of that event arose, not only a fresh order of things in the New World, but in the Old World too. It was the people with whom Cromwell was in his last hour in heart and thought, who settled around Boston Harbour. The changes to which the tea fray led in Europe brought about the suppression— and without commutation!—of the ducal fief of Aubigny in France, which was granted to Louise de Keroualle and her heirs, for her secret services in England.[1] But the perpetual wages which the Merry Monarch granted her out of

---

[1] I am told, but have as yet been unable to obtain documentary evidence, that the late Duke, in the reign of Charles X., put in, as disestablished lord of Aubigny, a claim for a slice of the £10,000,000 sterling indemnity voted to the *émigrés* of the French aristocracy by "la Chambre introuvable."

his lackland subjects' pockets, for the means she took to render these services to her own king, continue to gild the ducal coronet of Richmond.

I wish it were otherwise, for the sake of the readers who like to see, in novels and at the close of the play, vice well whipped and virtue triumphant. But history evolves itself independently of our likings or dislikings; and all that historians should do is to record, to seek for missing links, to connect them, when found, with the rest of the chain, and to leave their narrative to point its own moral.

CONTENTS.

CHAPTER I.

ENGLAND AND THE POLICY OF LOUIS XIV.

Indebtedness of France to Louise de Keroualle.—French ingratitude for services rendered by her at the Court of Whitehall.—Pedigree of Louise.—Her early life.—Adventures at the French court.—Libels and lampoons.—Ambitious policy of Louis the Fourteenth.—England the main obstacle to its accomplishment.—Charles II. his disposition and vices.—Henrietta Maria, her intrigues and secret marriage.—Catherine of Braganza, her ugliness and incapacity to become a useful tool of France.—Her bridal humiliations.—Her displeasure at Lady Castlemaine's supremacy at Whitehall.—The beautiful Lady Castlemaine.—Her truculence and triumph over the Queen.—Presents sent her by the King of France.—Inconstancy of Charles II.—The lovely and vacuous Miss Stuart.—Nelly Gwynn, her theatrical career, jests, and frolics.—Arlington and Buckingham, their foreign intrigues.—Sir Samuel Morland, his life and adventures.—French noblemen at Whitehall.—French diplomatists, diplomatic wires and wire pullers.—Manœuvres to hold Charles.—The Italian astrologer, his erroneous forecasts of the Newmarket races and his recall to France 1

CHAPTER II.

MADAME HENRIETTE.

Buckingham's suspicions of Henriette, Duchess of Orleans and Princess of England.—Influence of the Duchess with Charles II.—Her intervention in the French intrigues at Whitehall advised by Colbert.—The Countess of Shrewsbury's relations with Buckingham and complicity in Killegrew's murder.—Charles's greed for French gold.—He proposes a secret league to Louis XIV.—Its un-English purport.—Holland to be sacrificed.—Hitch on the French side about Hamburg.—Henriette's dexterity.—Her visit to England decided upon.—Choice by her of Louise de Keroualle to attend her there.—Meeting of Charles and Henriette.—Betrayal of England by her King.—Louis, at Dunkirk, watches the progress of negociations at Dover.—Henriette returns to France.—Her sudden death, and suspicion that she was poisoned.—Louise de Keroualle sent to London to console and manage Charles.—His susceptibility to her charms.—Lady Castlemaine's jealousy.—The Royal bastards.—Louise's adroitness.—Public suspicions of her and the Cabal.—Her close game and affected coyness. . . 47

CHAPTER III.

ACCESSION OF LOUISE DE KEROUALLE.

Louise pursues her close game.—She remains coy.—Uneasiness thereat of the French Embassy.—Fury of the Duchess of Cleveland.—The King's fancy for Louise.—Her soft graces and refinement.—Lady Arlington's plot to break down her supposed scruples.—Euston Hall.—The King goes to Euston from Newmarket.—Louise fetched to meet him.—Mock marriage of Charles and the French beauty at Euston Hall.—France, through her ambassador, congratulates the pseudo bride, and turns her new position to diplomatic account. —Charles declares war on Holland.—Louis conquers Flanders.—Attempts to make Charles declare himself a Catholic.—The Duke of York. —Intrigues to bring him to propose for the Duchess of Guise 64

CHAPTER IV.
THE RIVALS.

The Dangers which beset Louise.—The Queen's bad health.—The French favourite aims at the Crown.—Catherine's Doctors and their prognostics.—A Royal divorce mooted.—The King's new amours.—Their cost to the nation.—The Duchess of Cleveland's four sons.—The three rival beauties. —English·taste for boisterous fun.—The Queen's jollifications.—Her Majesty's adventure at Saffron Walden fair.—Actresses under Charles II.—Mary Davies.—Louise holding ground against Court and people.—Her tact.—Refuses to urge the Conversion of Charles.—Her match-making scheme for the Duke of York.—His uxoriousness.—He stands out for a pretty wife.—A princess of Wurtemburg offered.—Louise gets her set aside.—The Duke of York marries Mary Beatrice of Este.—Louise enters the peerage as Baroness of Peterfield, Countess of Farnham, Duchess of Pendennis, and Duchess of Portsmouth. She aspires to a French Duchy.—Obstacles to her ambition.—Charles II. solicits for her the Ducal fief of Aubigny which she desires.—Its Royal Stuart associations.—French nobles at Whitehall.—Duras created Earl of Feversham.—The Frenchmen of Buckingham's set.—Saint Evremond.—The Marquis de Sessac.—His gambling gains.—Buckingham a secret service agent of France.—His plan to buy M.P.'s for Louis.—De Ruvigny's mission, his honourable life.—His Protestantism and relationship to the Russells.—His secret mission to London.—Is instructed to purchase King and Parliament.—France stretches her Frontiers.—Louis feels England slipping from him.—Alarm given to France by the Comte D'Estrades.—Tide of public hatred turning against Roman Catholicism and France.—Charles is given a bribe of eight millions of francs.—Buckingham curries popular favour, reforms his life and goes to church.—Peace with Holland 79

CHAPTER V.

THE DUCHESS OF PORTSMOUTH'S FIRST CHECK.

Plain Speech the rule at the polished Court of Versailles.—Prudish niceness unknown there.—The sins of Charles and Louise find them out.—Ruvigny's letters about Charles.—Louise seeks a cure at Tunbridge Wells.—Derision of the Marchioness of Worcester.—The Household

guard escorts Louise from the Wells to Windsor.
—The King's doctor treats her.—Henriette her
sister comes to England and marries Lord Pembroke.—Louise still solicits a French Duchy.—
Nell Gwynn derides her for her oft vaunted high
connections.—Versailles finds matter for amusement in her progress at Whitehall.—Madame de
Sévigné's jests.—Her sketch of Nell Gwynn.—
Queen Catherine's card table.—Hierarchy of the
King's Seraglio.—Louise's son created Duke of
Richmond.—Maternal tricks to secure him precedence over the King's other progeny.—Their
success.—The Dukes of Grafton and St. Albans.—
A Scotch Countess named governess to Louise's
son.—Pensions and emoluments granted to the
Duchesses of the Seraglio and to their heirs.—
The fair favourites fleece the exchequer.—The
French favourite's passion for gaming.—Her
sumptuous lodgings a cause of envy.—The contempt in which the English held her.—Advent
of the Duchess Mazarin 107

CHAPTER VI.

THE DUCHESS MAZARIN.

Close of a great era.—The Congress of Nimeguen.
—Danby gained for Louis by Louise.—French
subsidy of two millions of francs for Charles.
—Parliament prorogued for fifteen months.—
Charles's old passion for the Duchess Mazarin
revived.—Her story, domestic misery, fanatical
husband, imprisonments in convents, flight to
Italy, subsequent adventures and Roman style of

beauty.—Triumphant reception at Whitehall.—She is welcomed by English rivals of Louise.—Struggle between the three Duchesses. — The Duchess of Cleveland retires to France.—Louise's new cares.—Her jealousy and altered looks.—Pecuniary troubles. — The Duchess of York's friendship for the Duchess Mazarin.—Monetary straits of the latter.—De Ruvigny unable to manage Charles and the Seraglio.—He is superseded by Courtin. 123

CHAPTER VII.

COURTIN.

Courtin's career.—His honourable name.—His relations in London with the Duchess Mazarin.—Asks her husband to increase her allowance, and advises Louis XIV. to make him do so.—Liaison of the Duchess with the Abbé St. Réal.—The Duchess of Portsmouth tries the Bath waters, and halts at Windsor on her way back to London.—Her dinner to the Comte and Comtesse de Ruvigny, and dejected manner.—Louvois.—Laughter at her lachrymosity.—Courtin hides her decline in Royal favour from the other ambassadors.—He advises her to conceal mortification.—Passes his evenings at the Duchess Mazarin's.—The Countess of Sussex.—Beauteous and well-bred Mrs. Middleton.—A moonlight walk in St. James's Park.—A fête given to the Court belles at the French Embassy.—Card parties at Madame Mazarin's. — Her library, bright wit, companions, and care to preserve appearances.—Courtin on Englishwomen's feet, and their smart shoes, stockings, and garters.— His gossip about Charles II. and his Court.— The romping games of Lady Sussex and the Duchess Mazarin.—John Churchill.—Louis the Fourteenth declines to give him a regiment.— His attachment to Miss Jennings, and refusal to marry an ugly heiress.—Is discredited in France for having plundered the Duchess of Cleveland. —Further decline of the Duchess of Portsmouth's influence.—Suppers at Nell Gwynn's.—Charles's nocturnal visits to the Duchess Mazarin.—His day visits to the Duchess of Portsmouth.—Haste of Louis XIV. to work whatever power remains to Louise.—He forces the Prince of Orange to raise the siege of Maestricht.—Sullen hatred of the English people to France.—Charles's autograph receipts for French bribes.—The opposition in the Commons.—Courtin told to ascertain what members are purchasable.—Importuned for bribes by Lord Berkshire.—Knavery of that nobleman.—English lords and commoners willing to pocket French money, but afraid to keep to their bargains with France.—The Duke and Duchess of Lauderdale.—The canny prudence of the Duchess, and her fear of compromising her husband.—Presents of French wines to incorruptible Englishmen.—Their liking for champagne.—A dinner at the Duchess of Portsmouth's.—Courtin patches up a peace between the ladies of the Seraglio.—Lady Hervey and Nell Gwynn at the Duchess of Mazarin's.—Nell bids for the post of agent to King Louis.—She

shows her petticoats to the company.—Lady
Hervey's mental gifts and vices.—Parallel between the belles of Versailles and the beauties of
Whitehall.—The Duchess of Mazarin's style of
living.—Chiffinch.—War between Parliament and
Palace.—Union of all the ladies deemed necessary by the French party.—Outcry against the
French intrigues at Court.—Louis takes Valenciennes, St. Omer, and Cambray.—French bribes
paid to Charles in 1677.—Welsh flannel worn by
the King.—The Duchess of Portsmouth regains
her looks at Bath. — Lord Ibrickan.—Courtin
retires from diplomacy.—Barrillon succeeds him   139

CHAPTER VIII.

BARRILLON.

Barrillon's qualifications for his mission to London.—
His professional unscrupulousness.—His friendship with Madame de Sévigné.—He enters into
close relations with corrupt English politicians.
—Meets with a check.—The Prince of Orange
visits London.—He wins the Princess Mary.—
Their marriage.—National joy.—Dangerous illness of the Duchess of Portsmouth. — Her
struggles with new rivals. — Disgrace of the
Duchess of Cleveland.—The King's passion
abates for the Duchess Mazarin.—Louise regains
influence.—The Marquise de Courcelles.—Her
set on Charles. — Her adventures. — Romping
games at the Duchess of York's.—Cabal there
against the Duchess of Portsmouth.—The Duke
of York's duplicity.—Louise plays into Barrillon's

hand.—She persuades Charles that he is devoted to him. — Her courtiers. — Sunderland. — The Countess of Sunderland's animosity to the French jade.—Louise as an Exchequer horse-leech.—Her traffic in Royal pardons.—Her profits in the sale of convicts to West India planters.—A London mercer's bill for finery supplied her.—Male attire the fashion for ladies.—The lump sums and annuities paid to the King's concubines, and to purveyors to his Seraglio.—Barrillon's account books.—The political men in his pay.—Austere Puritans corrupted.—Sir John Baber, Poole, Littleton.—Fifteen thousand guineas for Montagu.—His sudden pretended change of front.—Denounces Danby as having, when talking loudest against France, been its agent.—Double games of Montagu, Danby, and Barrillon.—Barrillon's mission to keep England divided.—Danby deserts France.—He concludes a treaty with Holland and makes up the breach between King and Commons.—Energetic campaign of Louis in Flanders.—Ghent, Ypres, and Mons fall into his hands.—Holland crippled.—Anti-Catholic frenzy of England.—Shaftesbury profits by the fury of the nation, to ruin Danby and humiliate Charles.—The Popish Plot.—Coleman's knavery and trial.—Oates' perjuries.—Terror of Charles and his ladies.—The Duchess of Portsmouth wants to retire to France.—The Duke of York leaves England.—Strafford tried and executed.—Shaftesbury's preponderance.—He discards the Prince of Orange to set up Monmouth as heir to the Crown.—The King's embarrassment.—He sends for Barrillon, expresses fear of a republic, and conjures Louis to make England dependent on him.—Monmouth's fabulous maternal pedigree.—English taste for romantic improbability.—Louis stops the subsidies to Charles.—No serious services, no more money.—Louis advances 500,000 francs to prevent Parliament meeting.—The Duchess of Portsmouth pleads at the French Embassy for Charles to be kept supplied.—His secret meetings with Barrillon revealed by Lady Sunderland.—Louise's dexterity.—She courts Monmouth, and is lampooned.—Charles attacked with fever.—Political effects of his illness.—Monmouth sent from London.—France secretly stirs up a quarrel between Charles and the Country Party.—Monmouth comes back.—His intimacy with Nell Gwynn.—Nell sets up to head the Protestant party.—Parliament demands the banishment of Louise de Keroualle.—Her trial and execution agitated for.—Parliament prorogued 193

CHAPTER IX.

SUNDERLAND AND SHAFTESBURY.

English hatred to France grows hotter.—It threatens the Duchess of Portsmouth.—The King finds a new and noble mistress.—Politic game of the Duchess.—She tries to keep friends and avoid exasperating foes.—Allies herself with Sunderland.—They play Monmouth against the Prince of Orange and the Duke of York.—Louise declares for the Prince of Orange.—The seeming

sincerity of this declaration ruffles Barrillon.—
He ceases to deem her services important.— Her
further campaign of corruption.—Lady Hervey's
rapacity. — French bribes for Nonconformist
ministers.—Lords and members of the House of
Commons proposed for bribery by Barrillon.—
Barrillon's political indifference.—His plan of
setting all English parties by the ears.—His
relations with Sidney.—His relations with Presbyterians and popular preachers.—Nell Gwynn's
eldest son dies.—The Duchess of Portsmouth
rears the daughter of Mary Davis.—The Duchess
suffers the King to show attention to the Queen.
—Parliament meets.— Bill to exclude the Duke
of York.— Barrillon's secret efforts against the
Prince of Orange.—Montagu, Herbert, Sidney,
Hampden, Baber, and Lady Hervey, usefullest
allies of Barrillon.—France finds it cheaper to
bribe the Opposition than the King.—Louise de
Keroualle urges Charles to prorogue indefinitely.
—Her ignorance of Barrillon's relations with
Republicans and Nonconformists.—Her astonishment at being thwarted by Barrillon.—He prefers
bribery to intrigue.—Her consummate address.—
She makes for the Duke of York's friendship.—
She gets a percentage on Irish taxes.—Webs of
intrigue woven round Charles.—His utter subjection to Louis.—Parliament indefinitely prorogued.—Louise recovers mental serenity.—Her
portrait by Gascar.—Count Kœnigsmarck prosecuted for murder.—Louis intervenes to stop
prosecution.—The Kœnigsmarck scandal.—The
heiress of the Earl of Northumberland.—The

girl-wife and widow of Lord Ogle.—Her abduction and marriage with Thynne. — Thynne's assassination.—Her third marriage at fifteen with the Duke of Somerset.—Apparent accomplishment of Louis the Fourteenth's scheme.—Louise de Keroualle becomes the direct link between him and Charles.—She keeps England in subjection to France.—She longs to revisit Versailles . 234

CHAPTER X.
RETURN TO FRANCE.

Charles goes to Newmarket and Louise visits France.—She draws her pension in advance.—The letters of recommendation that she takes to Louis XIV.—By his command she is received as a sovereign.—Her visit to the Capucines in the Rue St. Honoré.—The Duke of York's French investments.—The Duchess of Portsmouth triumphs in France.—Her success there dazzles the English.—She returns to London.—Her undisputed power there.—She takes offence at the Dutch minister.—He humbles himself before her.—The Queen deferential towards her.—The Duchess Mazarin accepts Louise de Keroualle's supremacy.—Gallants and courtiers of the Duchess Mazarin.—Her nephew, Prince Eugene, of Savoy.—She captivates him.—Her daughters.—One of them elopes from a convent. The fugitive's adventures and marriage.—The gloom and sadness of the Duchess Mazarin.—She kills care in drink and gambling.—Her antique vices.—How she lived at Newmarket.—Her court of ladies 253

CHAPTER XI.

END OF THE REIGN.

Louise de Keroualle's love affair with the Grand Prior of France. — Love makes her imprudent. — Charles takes umbrage, but puts up with his rival.—Louise receives fresh tokens of regard from Louis.—Charles jealous but unnerved.—Barrillon comes to his aid.—The Grand Prior has to leave England.—Louise fears her new lover's indiscreet tongue.—Louis orders him to keep silence.—The Grand Prior recalled to Versailles. —Charles's French annuity of £60,000. — Rochester and Louise alone know of it.—They both direct the whole Royal family.—Louise is consulted about the proposed match of Princess Anne and Prince George of Demark.—She sends her miniature to the King of Denmark.—She receives ambassadors in state.—She settles international broils.—She represents France at the marriage of the Princess Anne.—Indignation of the old Ironsides.—Charles in their eyes "the Man of Sin."—Marks of God's displeasure at his profligacy.—The Rye House Plot.—Executions of Sidney and Lord Grey.—Charles pities Lord Grey's children. — Louise hardens his heart against them.—She obtains their father's confiscated estate for herself and Rochester.—Subjection to her of Rochester and Godolphin.— Barrillon chafes at her yoke.—Louis goes on supporting her.—Charles's distress.—He grants her fresh privileges.—Her French Duchy to revert to her son.—Her scandalous luxury.—

Her sumptuous rooms at Whitehall.—A suggestive haberdasher's bill.—The spoils Louise's sister took to France.—Voluptuousness of the Court.—The Breton favourite is the Government of England.—Louis on the point of complete success.—The death of Charles II.—Confusion of the courtiers.—Louise alone shows presence of mind.—She comes out as a good Catholic.—James II. promises her his friendship.—His base motives.—The young Duke of Richmond ceases to be Grand Equerry.—Louise aims at securing £19,000 a year.—James grants her £3,000 a year.—£2,000 a year granted to the Duke of Richmond.—Louise claims £30,000 a year out of the Irish taxes.—She misses this mark.—What she can take to France.—James visits her.—She leaves England 264

CHAPTER XII.

IN RETIREMENT.

Those whom the Duchess of Portsmouth survived.—Her sister's private marriage.—The Duke of Richmond. — He openly enters the Catholic Church.—His subsequent relapse into Protestantism.—His debauchery.—Louise visits England.—Courtin prevents Louis XIV. from exiling her.—Her obligatory relations with England.—Her niece marries Judge Jeffrey's son.—Louise is suspected in France of being a spy of England. She and her son pay court to William III — Her English annuity suspended.—Her furniture destroyed in the fire at Whitehall.—The Duke of Richmond becomes an Orangist.—He cuts his French connections.—Louis transfers his pension to Louise.—Her portraits.—Her pecuniary troubles.—Her creditors.—French orders of Council to stay their executions.—Louise's appetite for French public money.—Her claims on the French Crown.—Impoverishment of the French Exchequer.—Louise's begging petitions to the Regent.—Their success.—Death of Louise's sister and son.—Louise devotes herself to piety and charity.—Her death and burial.—Her neglected tomb.—Her French duchy and château. —Her descendants. — England pays for the services rendered to ungrateful France . . 292

Letters of the Duchess of Portsmouth . . . 309

LOUISE DE KEROUALLE.

CHAPTER I.

ENGLAND AND THE POLICY OF LOUIS XIV.

LOUISE DE KEROUALLE was the pretty Breton who became, at the court of Charles II., the pivot on which the ambitious and wide-reaching policy of Louis XIV. turned. To her, more than to any statesman, France is indebted for French Flanders, the Franche Comté, her twice secular possession of Alsace, her old ownership of the valley of the Mississippi and Canada, and her lately revived claim on Madagascar. One owes the sacrifice of everything save honour to one's country; but Louise abandoned fair fame, and—although her posterity still fatten on her ill-gotten gains at the expense of the country on which she saddled them—her memory rots in England. Englishmen go on paying the tribute she extracted from them, without looking into its origin. But can they ever pardon her for having during fifteen years held Great Britain in her delicate little hand, and manipulated its king and statesmen as dexterously as she might have done her fan? She made that country a tool of Louis XIV.'s policy, and enabled him, by the fineness of her diplomatic art, to consolidate the geographical unity of France. The French nation has forgotten this Agnes Sorel, who undertook to seduce, get round, and hold a monarch whom she never loved, and who, when she undertook to make his conquest, was prematurely old from profligacy. She is so utterly fallen into oblivion, that her countrymen do not know how to write her name.[1] The same forgetfulness extends to the name of her family estate. Even Louise de Perrencour de Kéroualle's descendants suffer the *Peerage*,[2] that

[1] The English call her Querouailles, and the French genealogists Kéroual. Colbert de Croissy wrote her name Queroul; in the charter of donation to her of the lands of Aubigny, it is Kéroël. I write Keroualle, after old family papers in the *Archives Nationales*, J. 152; 6. (*Author's Note.*)

[2] BURKE: *Dictionary of the Peerage*, under the heading of "Richmond." gives as the root of the ducal house of

Golden Book of the English nobility, to state that they are descended from the daughter of a certain Guillaume de Penencourt. Yet these Perrencours were not a family to be denied, even by such high-placed descendants as the Dukes of Richmond. The following is a sketch of their ancestry.

François de Penhoët married Jeanne, Lady of Keroualle de Penancoët, on 10th May, 1330. The Penhoëts were one of the great families of the bishopric of Léon, of whom it was said, "The Penhoëts for antiquity, the Kermans for riches, and the De Kergournadecs for chivalry." The children of this marriage, took the maternal name, with its coat of arms. One of their descendants, Guillamue de Penancour, married, in 1645, Marie de Plœuc de Timeur, daughter of Marie de Rieux; and one of their children was Louise, Duchess of Pendennis and Portsmouth, in England, and of Aubigny, in France.[1]

Richmond, "Louise Renee de Perrencourt"; under the heading of "Aubigny" (*foreign titles*), he puts ."Louise Rénée de Penencourt de Quenouaille, Duchess of Portsmouth in England, daughter of Guillaume de Penencourt."

[1] *Bibliothèque Nationale, Cabinet des Titres*, No. 50,417. (*Author's Note.*)

It does not count for much in our time to be a De Rieux, or to have a forefather so renowned for bravery in the 14th century, as the fair Louise was for her cold-blooded gallantries in the 17th century; but these facts of race and blazon explain the circumstances of her youth, and enable us to understand how she was able to become a maid of honour to Henrietta of England, Duchess of Orleans. They also set at naught the ridiculous stories of the adventures in which, according to some lampoonists and pamphleteers, her early years were spent.

The most widely known of the libellous fictions published in England against her, is *The Secret History of the Duchess of Portsmouth.* An English edition and two French ones, as well as a large number of manuscript copies,[1] of this *factum* were circulated. According to it, Mademoiselle de Keroualle fled from the house of an aunt living in Paris, disguised as a page, and accompanied the Duc de Beaufort

[1] I have in my possession one of these manuscripts; but I have not been able to find at the *Bibliothèque Nationale* either the English edition of 1690 of *The Secret History of the Duchess of Portsmouth*, the French editions of 1690, or the *Mémoires Secrets de la Duchesse de Portsmouth*, by Jacques Lacombe, 2 vols., 12mo; Paris, 1805. (*Author's Note.*)

in the expedition to Candia, which lasted from 5th June until 10th October, 1669. Now during that time she was under the eyes of the whole Court, serving as maid of honour to Henrietta, Duchess of Orleans. The calumny must have originated in the part taken by Louise's brother Sebastien in the unfortunate Beaufort expedition. He died on his return from Candia, a few days after he landed in Provence.[1] The mourning into which his family were thrown was distorted by the libeller into a burlesque fiction. Most of the episodes of Louise's life were malignantly twisted in the same way. The so-called biographer knew enough about her early life to give an air of truth to his cruel inventions.[2]

It was in the year in which Sebastien died in the Duc de Beaufort's service that Louise

[1] Of the three children, only the daughters, Louise and Henriette, survived.
[2] There were many other publications of this kind: *Memoirs of the Court of England*, by the Countess Dunois, 1708; *The Secret History of the Reigns of King Charles II. and James II.*, s.l. 1690. There is a French translation of the latter, Cologne, 1690, and also a refutation, *The Blatant Beast Muzzl'd*, s.l., 1691. (*Author's Note.*)

made the acquaintance of the Comte de Sault.

This gentleman was son of the Duc de Lesdiguières, and was chief victor in the famous jousts which were held in 1662, under the windows of Tuileries, and gave their name to the Place de Carrousel. Father Anselmo tells us that he passed for being in love with a maid of honour of Henrietta of England,[1] or Madame Henriette, as she was called in France. Thirteen years later a haughty English nobleman insultingly reminded Louise de Keroualle[2] of this early attachment.

However innocent may have been the flirtations, in a dissipated court, of a girl of rank who was poor, and impatient to find a husband, it is certain that the fair fame of the Bretonne was tarnished. Madame de Sévigné and Louvois speak slightingly and pitilessly of her relations with De Sault. Saint Simon[3] charges her parents with having aimed at throwing her in the king's way, in the hope that he might

[1] Père Anselme.
[2] MS. *Affaires Etrangères, Angleterre*, tome cxiv., fol. 119, du 6 Août, 1674.
[3] Hachette: *Ecrits inédits de Saint Simon*, t. iv., p. 485.

cast her his pocket-handkerchief, and to further this mode of obtaining a settlement for her, got her into the household of his sister-in-law, who was then suspected of being his mistress. Unfortunately for Mademoiselle de Keroualle, Louise de la Vallière was also a maid of honour to that princess; and the king fell in love with her soft eyes, which only spoke of tender, devoted love. If this Louise had little cleverness, "she was gentle, good-natured, and obliging, and made herself liked at court." Without believing the calumnious pamphlets, it may be supposed that, whether owing to imprudent talk or to ambitious avowals, Louise passed for aspiring to the situation of king's favourite.

Before Louis XIV. tried what might be effected through women, in preserving the alliance, or at least the neutrality, of England, he had had recourse to means which were not sanctioned by diplomatic usage.

The great French statesmen who preceded him never risked an important foreign enterprise without first securing an ally. Richelieu entered into an understanding with Gustavus Adolphus, and Mazarin with Cromwell. Union with Great Britain was all the more necessary during the youth of Louis XIV., because the frontiers of his kingdom tended to advance into Flanders, a country linked with England by the proximity of their coasts and by trade relations, which had gone on for several hundred years.

It would be unjust to suppose that the only sentiment which alienated England from France in the 17th century, was jealousy at seeing the extension of French influence and commerce in Flanders. The Protestant passions of the people, and the Liberal ideas of the aristocracy, inevitably placed England in conflict with an absolute, and a Catholic king. Political interests became intertwined with religious feeling to such a point, that public opinion in England was led into reversing against the Court the foreign policy of Cromwell by supporting Spain, the most ardent foe of the Reformation, against Louis XIV.

Whilst the posterity of Philip II. was falling into decrepitude, and slowly dying out at the Escurial, each of the powers watched for an opportunity to snatch a part of its heritage. Louis wanted to seize on all Flanders. He saw that, to be able to strike his blow at an opportune moment, the agreement of England was necessary. Now, towards the close of Charles II.'s reign, the hatred in which the English held Louis was not doubtful. There was no reliance to be placed in the unstable-minded British monarch. And yet it was on Charles II. that the entire efforts of French diplomacy were of necessity concentrated. He was the only possible ally. With his connivance in the projects of the Court of Versailles, the animosity of England—the nation—would not matter. His complicity was the one condition of success. Without it, every chance must be given up of preponderance in Europe, and of the happy execution of a grand scheme of colonial aggrandisement. France might, if she held Charles, do as she pleased, not only in Flanders, but, with the aid of the Jesuits, all the world over. The diplomatists of Louis XIV., seeing what frontier extension, and indeed wide-world expansion, was to be obtained, came to the conclusion that all scruples should be laid aside.

But there never was a harder man to hold than Charles II., whose will was singularly unsteady, and whose mind was the most versatile, bright, shifty, and frivolous of any prince in Europe. When young, he was voluptuous, loquacious, easy to captivate, and charitable towards intriguers of every sort, because he held a low opinion of human nature, and felt that he set an example himself of lax morals and had mire-ward proclivities. He put on with smiling grace a show of elegance, affected sensibility, and made prodigality pass for the outcome of generous impulse. In many respects he was like Henri III., he being profuse, a connoisseur of art, easy going with those around him, insincere, without respect for his engagements, incurably apt to confound knavery with statecraft, and so fond of lapdogs as to turn his apartments into a disgusting kennel. They bred about on his sofas, and even in his bed. In the bottom of his heart he was a Catholic, at the time when he became head of the Anglican Church. He understood the power of quinine to check ague and other fevers; dabbled in alchemy and vivisection, gave a fillip to the study of natural philosophy, was free from prejudices, devoid of principle, and was an amiable epicurean, so entirely without backbone that he went so far in cowardly meanness as to deny his own father.[1] This degrading denial took place when Charles I. was hemmed in by fanatical Scotch Puritans. It was given the specious name of "The Prince of Wales's Declaration." In it he "humbled himself before Almighty God because of the complacency with which his father had hearkened unto evil counsels, because of his opposition to the Covenant, and likewise because of the blood of the Lord's people which he had shed. The Prince of Wales also confessed his own manifold sins and the sins of his father's house." He was wholly devoid of moral sense, and never rose to a perception of the social use of honour.

Such was the man whom it was the task of French diplomacy to hold. His mother herself, it was remembered at Versailles, could exert no durable authority over his vacillating will and versatile spirit. In appearing to yield, he was always ready to slide away. He was only a liar under pressure, but he was as slippery as an eel, and as fond of the mud.

Henrietta Maria, daughter of Henri IV., had ruled her husband, Charles I. Miss Strickland and some of Vandyke's portraits make her out

[1] WALKER: *Historical Discourses*, p. 170.

a beauty. She probably had when young the comeliness of youth; but after the Restoration she was a little, vulgar-looking, and very commonplace woman. As a child, she was the most petted member of her family; and the person on whom she doubtless unconsciously modelled herself, was her mother's arrogant and domineering foster-sister, favourite, and general directress, Léonore de Galigai, wife of Concini, Maréchal d'Ancre, also a favourite of Marie de Medici, and suspected, with too good reason, of having plotted the assassination of Henri IV.[1] Henrietta Maria behaved on the throne like a spoiled child and shrew. She does not seem to have had any plan of conduct or principle of government, beyond doing just as she pleased, and imposing on her husband the notion which happened to be uppermost in her mind. He was uxorious, and obeyed her. The beginning

[1] The Grand Duke of Florence, father of Marie de Medici, said to his daughter, when she was setting out as a proxy-married bride for France: "Above all things, make haste to have an heir." He sent with her three gallants whom Henry IV. tolerated. They were Virginio and Paolo Orsini, and Concini, afterwards the Maréchal d'Ancre, whose assassination by De Luynes released Louis XIII. from the thraldom in which his mother's favourite held him.

of his misfortunes was his acquiescence in her order, to go to the House of Commons, and bring her "by the ears" the five members who stood out against his exorbitant prerogatives. She called them "those five crop-headed rogues."

The tragedies in which this queen was involved, her terrible reverses of fortune, and the oratorical genius of Bossuet, who preached her funeral sermon, surrounded her, in the eyes of those who did not study her life, with the nimbus of a martyr. Her contemporaries judged her severely, and wasted but small sympathy on her. She was held in slight esteem at the Court of France, when she returned to Paris a widow and a proscript. Her apologists, past and present, have tried to explain away the sarcasms of those Englishmen of her time and circle who noticed her fondness for Lord Jermyn and submission to him, her fear of giving him offence, his meddling and overbearing interference in all her concerns, and his masterful tone in speaking to her.[1] They

---

[1] SIR JOHN RERESBY: *Memoirs*, p. 4. "Lord Jermyn had the queen greatly in awe of him, and indeed it was obvious that he had uncommon interest in her and her concerns;

have tried to disprove that she had a daughter, the issue of a secret marriage with him. However, he and she were inseparable, and she braved public opinion in going, accompanied with him, to pay visits of ceremony.[1] Colbert de Croissy[2] and her nephew Louis XIV. himself[3] are crushing witnesses against her. The but that he . . . had children by her I did not then believe, though the thing was certainly so." Her own son, James II., did not dare in terms to contradict this fact, so evident was it to his contemporaries. In his reply (*The Blatant Beast Muzzl'd*) to the pamphleteers, he replied mildly and in a propitiating tone to those who charged his mother with being the mistress and then the wife of Lord Jermyn, whilst he refuted with passionate virulence all the other attacks on his family. He merely said in reply to the former accusations, "They must pardon me if I don't believe them."

[1] EVELYN: *Diary*, Aug. 14, 1662. Hamilton, always so well informed, speaks of this union. See the anonymous author of the curious *Relation d'Angleterre*, which is in *Les Cinq Cents de Colbert*, tome iv. p. 78 : "Le Comte de St. Jermyn est toujours attaché à ses intérests." (*Translator's Note*.)

[2] MS. *Affaires Etrangères, Angleterre*, tome xciii., fol. 181, du 28 Nov., 1668.

[3] Colber de Croissy was a brother of the great minister Colbert, and for some time ambassador of Louis XIV. to Whitehall. He was sent on other embassies. In negotiating with men, he showed great ability; but he did not understand how to utilize women. On his recall from England he was named Secretary for Foreign Affairs.

former, in writing from London to Versailles just after the formation of the Cabal, says: "The Duke of Buckingham takes for granted the necessity of an impossible thing, when he speaks of a secret imparted to the queen-dowager of England not coming to Lord St. Albans' (Jermyn's) knowledge. It would be the sheerest self-deception to hope that this might be done."

In counting, therefore, on Henrietta Maria, the Court of Versailles would have had to reckon on St. Albans. Those who had hoped otherwise were nursing an illusion. The king of France therefore sought to find a wife for Charles soon after the Restoration had been effected. It being useless to try and hold him by means of the queen-dowager, he tried to influence him through a queen-consort.

Spain being an adversary of France, it was among her most bitter foes that Louis sought a wife for the restored monarch. He chose a Portuguese princess, in doing which he made a blunder. The Portuguese then, like the Moors, kept their women in ignorance and seclusion. Instead of a princess used to the intrigues and complexities of Court life, and able to domineer a rakish husband, Charles II. was mated to a swarthy dwarf of twenty-four, who, when she arrived in England, had never in her life spoken to a man, even during the voyage. Her sedentary habits had made her obese; and this defect was thrown into relief by her curious mode of dressing. She was of a squat figure and a brown complexion; her teeth were so badly set as to be a deformity.[1] "There really is nothing in her face to inspire positive disgust," said Charles mournfully, after the first interview.[2] He was mightily pleased, when the wedding ceremony was over, that she was too tired after her voyage not to wish to be left entirely alone.[3] The Portuguese ladies who came with her were not seductive,[4] and wore monstrous hoops, which followed the waddling

[1] According to Lord Dartmouth, "her fore teeth stood out so as to shorten her upper lip." Evelyn makes the same remark: "Her teeth wrongeth her mouth by sticking out too far." These defects are artistically slurred over by Sir Peter Lely.

[2] Letter of Clarendon, cited by Miss Strickland, viii., p. 304.

[3] The king to Clarendon, May 21, 1662, published from the MS. of the British Museum by Fellowes (*Historical Sketches*).

[4] EVELYN: *Diary*, May 30, 1662.

movement of their gait. These farthingales were called by them *gardes-infantes*. Their headgears were as funny, to English and French eyes, as their skirts; and the skins of all were of a deep olive. Charles wished for more pleasing objects. Instead of retaining them in his wife's service, he drew up a list of bedchamber ladies, at the head of which he placed the Countess of Castlemaine.

Ignorant as the new queen was, she uttered a cry of protest when she heard of this bedchamber nomination.

Lady Castlemaine had, as Mrs. Palmer, engaged in an amorous intrigue with Charles soon after the Restoration.[1] He, the Duke of York, and young sparks in their suites made up to her to infuriate her husband and enjoy the game of making him justly jealous. The Duke of York, to keep his mind from absorbing the heretical Anglican service which he had to attend at the Chapel Royal, used to draw aside the curtains of the royal pew to ogle Mrs. Palmer, who performed her devotions in the one next to it. She appears, however, to have soon dropped the heir presumptive, to become

[1] PEPYS: *Diary*, 13th July, 1660.

publicly the king's favourite. At the time of the formation of the Cabal, she was in all the pride of her beauty, which was splendidly attractive. If her nose was slightly turned up,[1] it gave her a sauciness that was piquant. Her figure was tall, and of a rich, harmonious outline. The eyes and hair were dark, and her skin glowed with health and life. Her lips were cherry red, and her bust,—which, in the fashion of the day, her loose and falling upper garments and thin smocks did not hide,—was white as snow. The eyes, if not large, were lively and bright. They spared none of their artillery to conquer, and promised everything to retain the captive. Nor did the lady disappoint the hopes she thus excited. There must have been something very taking in her appearance, which enabled her to face the London populace in its den. Lady Castlemaine was fond of going to see the puppets at St. Bartholomew's fair. The common people, hearing that she was there, collected round the show to hoot "the king's miss." But the sight of her lovely face disarmed them, and she was allowed to go quietly to her carriage, and ride off.

[1] *Relation d'Angleterre. Cinq Cents de Colbert*, t. v., p. 478.

Lady Castlemaine did not long hold her ground against Louise de Keroualle, when that charming French beauty entered the arena against her; but she had an easy triumph over Queen Catherine, who pricked[1] her name from the king's list of bedchamber women, and who, when she saw her husband lead the beautiful mistress in to her by the hand, was seized with convulsions and got black in the face. This was taken as an affront by Lady Castlemaine, who meant to lie in at Hampton Court, and demanded an apology. Charles thought the queen should humble herself before the favourite, and wrote to say so to the Chancellor Clarendon, who was trying to make peace between the royal couple. The mistress flared up at his daring to meddle in the matter, and put the king on to resent his interference. "Nobody," he wrote to Clarendon, "shall presume to meddle in the affairs of the Countess of Castlemaine. Whoever dares to do so, will have cause to repent it to the last moment of his life. Nothing will shake the resolution I have taken with regard to her; and I shall consent to be miserable in this world and the

[1] See Clarendon, Fellowes, Miss Strickland.

next, if I yield in my decision, which is, that she continue a bedchamber lady to the queen. I shall, to the last hour of my life, regard any one who opposes me in this as my enemy; and whosoever shows himself hostile to the Countess will, I swear by my honour, earn my undying displeasure."

The queen remained inflexible for some weeks, and was open in her anger. She then let herself be coaxed round. The citizens of London were treated to the sight of wife and concubine driving through the streets, in grand array, in the same carriage,[1] along with young Crofts,[2] the son of a former mistress, and the darling of the queen, the queen-dowager, and of Lady Castlemaine.

After yielding, Catherine made up her mind to struggle no more, and to lead an easy life by shutting her eyes to her husband's vices. She put up with the companionship of his favourite, and even showed a greater liking for her than for any other lady at court. The English esteemed the queen a good wife, who bore

---

[1] PEPYS: *Diary*, 7th September, 1662.
[2] Afterwards Duke of Monmouth.

herself meekly when her patience was most severely tried.

Catherine was avenged on her husband by the shrewish temper of her rival. Charles was constantly the object of Lady Castlemaine's truculent abuse. He often returned from her house overpowered by it. Every one knew she played him false. If he dared show jealousy, he was soon reduced to beg pardon on his knees, and swear that he would never again harbour insulting suspicions about her conduct.[1] When he caught her in John Churchill's arms, he only showed his resentment by saying to the young man that, as he had become her lover to escape from starving, he forgave him.[2]

Lady Castlemaine was ready to accept overtures from France, and to support the policy of Louis XIV., as Colbert de Croissy soon informed him.

"The king," wrote in answer Secretary

---

[1] PEPYS : *Diary*, 7th August, 1667.
[2] MS. *Affaires Étrangères, Angleterre*, tome cxxxvii., fol. 400. *Relation de la Cour d'Angleterre*. See also, on this subject, the letter of the ambassador Courtin to the minister Louvois, *ibid.*, tome cxx., C, fol. 206, Nov. 16, 1676.

Lionne,[1] "thinks well of your efforts to obtain the help of the Countess of Castlemaine, and read with interest of her point-blank way of telling you how King Charles[2] had confided to her that Lord Arlington would not hear of an alliance with France. His majesty hopes that you will profit by this good beginning, and he authorizes you, if you judge well, to let her know that you have reported what she said to his majesty, who charges you to offer her his warmest thanks. In this order of ideas, the king has directed your brother, the Treasurer, to send her a handsome present, which you can give her as if from yourself. Ladies are fond of such keepsakes, whatever may be their breeding or disposition; and a nice little present can in any case do no harm."

Lionne[3] renewed his instructions a few days later in these terms: "His majesty attaches great importance to all you can say about Lady

---

[1] In all the diplomatic French despatches *the king* is Louis XIV. To every other king the name of the country over which he reigns is added. It is however impossible to cling to this formula in all the extracts from official papers.

[2] MS. *Affaires Etrangères*, 3 Avril, 1667.

[3] April 20, 1669.

Castlemaine. You can, if you think fit, agree with your brother touching the present the king intends to make this lady. . . . His majesty warmly approves your idea of getting her to put into the King of England's head that the Presbyterians and Nonconformists are ill affected towards monarchy."[1]

But Madam Castlemaine was not the kind of secret service agent the king of France wanted. Not that she was insensible to nice little presents, or that she was not in constant need of money. Her hatred of every curb to her luxurious caprices, and her prodigality, drew her into expenses which astonished the Court. Whitehall wondered at the fineness of her cambric shifts; at her smocks and linen petticoats frilled with the richest lace, and at her costly furniture and plate. But an ambassador could not rely on her support, because she gave herself up completely to the passion of the moment, whether it was an amorous one or arose from ardent rivalry with some other lady of the Court. Her quarrels with the beauties of easy virtue who surrounded Charles II. were as much (if not more)

[1] April 23, 1669.

the object of deep concern to the King of France, as the military evolutions of Turenne and Condé. A war with England depended on the humour of an actress or a bedchamber woman. The Treasurer, Colbert, wrote in these terms to his brother, the Marquis Colbert de Croissy,[1] to London : " I think it would please the king if you were to send M. de Lionne gossiping letters about everything that happens in the private life of the king of England, and in what is known as the inner circle of his Court." "As you have not," returned M. de Croissy,[2] "thought amiss that I should keep you informed about the squabbles of these ladies, which are often as much a cause of deep concern to the King of England as the most serious business, I shall continue to write about them." " I have," wrote Louis XIV. himself to M. Colbert de Croissy,[3] "heard read with great pleasure the curious details you have written to M. de Lionne about the intrigues of the English Court, and the broils of the ladies who are the chief personages there."

[1] MS. *Affaires Etrangères*, 20 Janvier, 1669.
[2] *Ibid.*, 31 Janvier, 1669.
[3] *Ibid.*, 9 Février, 1669.

"I shall take more pains than ever," replied Colbert,[1] to ascertain what goes on among the ladies, since you do not think it beneath you to show an interest in their quarrels, and the king himself deigns to wish for information in those little affairs, on which great events so often hinge." Colbert de Croissy thinks well to make a fresh present to Madam Castlemaine. He says,[2] "I have given away all that I brought from France, not excepting the skirts and smocks made up for my wife, and I have not money enough to go on at this rate. Nor do I see the use of going to much expense, in satisfying the greed of the women here for rich keepsakes. The king often says,[3] that the only woman who has really a hold on him, is his sister, the Duchess of Orleans. If handsome gifts are lavished on Madam Castlemaine, his majesty may think that, in spite of his assertions to the contrary, we fancy that she rules him, and take it in bad part. I should therefore advise giving her only such trifling tokens as a pair of French gloves, ribands, a

---

[1] MS. *Affaires Etrangères*, 14 Jan., 1669.
[2] *Ibid.*, 7 Février, 1669.
[3] *Ibid.*, 14 Février, 1669.

Parisian undress gown, or some little object of finery."[1]

A graver matter than bedizenments for Madam Castlemaine was dealt with, at this juncture, in the correspondence of M. Colbert de Croissy. He was struck with the sadness of the King of England's manner, his constant depression, and his aversion to chat about European affairs, which used to be one of his favourite topics.[2] "The gloom which the king's face and manner betray has been such, that it was impossible not to feel there was some great cause for it. After seeking on all sides for a reason, I discovered that it sprang from an amour with a young girl in Madam Castlemaine's household, whose grace and beauty made, when she served the king, the impression that might be expected on a prince who is fond of change. As she thought it her duty not to stand out against his desire, her mistress was so vexed, that she turned her into the street at midnight. But this amour does not prevent Madam Castlemaine from being as powerful as ever."

[1] This present was sent by the minister Colbert, on May 8, 1669.
[2] Colbert de Croissy à Lionne, 28 Février, 1669.

Barbara Villiers had already been the victim of her fancy to be surrounded by the handsomest damsels she could find. The most adulated beauties were glad to be in her train. The proud Lady Sandwich humbly spoke of Barbara as her Queen of Beauty.[1] Madam Castlemaine had also among her maids of honour Frances Stuart, known as the beautiful Miss Stuart, whom she often kept to sleep in her rooms at Whitehall, and slightingly spoke of as her little Stuart.[2] The king, who seldom failed to visit Barbara before she got up in the morning, saw Miss Stuart in the bed beside her. It was not possible to unite greater beauty and more dulness than were to be found in this young belle. All her features were of perfect regularity. She was of an erect carriage, and above the common height. We still are able to judge of the Grecian regularity of her visage, and of the outlines of her figure, which would have been faultless, were her waist less high and her carriage less stiff.[3] Miss Stuart served

[1] PEPYS, July 26, 1662.
[2] PEPYS, March 23, 1663; HAMILTON: *Mémoires de Gramont.*
[3] *Relation d'Angleterre,* MS. Bibl. Nat., Fonds Colbert, 478.

as a model for the Britannia which is on the copper coins of England. The engraver, Philip de Rothier,[1] reproduced her on the public medals struck by the English mint in his day; and all his successors have copied her effigy. The face and form of Miss Stuart are therefore the most widely known of any beauty that ever lived. "She had,"[2] said a diplomatic despatch, "a leg so admirably shaped that an ambassador, on arriving in England and calling on her, begged her as a favour to let him see almost up to her knee, so as to be able to write to his master to confirm what he had heard about the perfection of her calf and ankle.[3] Miss Stuart was not rapacious. She was satisfied with a pension of £700 a year, which Charles granted her, and only asked him for £6000 worth of jewels when she was

[1] The three brothers Rothier were French, and were employed to design medals at the English mint, from 1661. See Redington's *Calendar of Treasury Papers*, preface, p. 16. The two youngest, Joseph and Philip, took the direction of the Paris and Brussels mints; John, the eldest, remained alone in England. He lost his right hand in 1689, and was replaced by his son James.

[2] *Relation d'Angleterre*, MS. *Affaires Etrangères*, tome cxxxvii., fol. 400.

[3] *Ibid.*

engaged to be married to the Duke of Richmond, whom she persuaded that, notwithstanding her four years' intimacy with the king and Lady Castlemaine, she was as virtuous as no matter what pure English girl.[1] She went on receiving the king's visits after her marriage. But he only called on her at night, and unattended by his gentlemen, or by an escort. "Sometimes he stole down the river stairs at Somerset House, and sculled himself in a punt to Richmond House, landing beneath a low wall which he climbed over." The French ambassador was not so unaccustomed to the manners of the Court of England as to think that a middle-aged king who acted thus was a disgrace to monarchy. The lovely Stuart was destined to be arrayed among the enemies of Louise Keroualle, pitted with smallpox and blind of an eye.[2]

In the Cytherean anarchy which preceded the reign of Louise Keroualle, the woman in whom she was to find her most formidable rival began to fix attention. She was an orange girl of such a finely-wrought physique

[1] PEPYS, April, 1667.
[2] She was a widow in 1672, and died in 1702.

that professional vice, to which she was reared, and every sort of hardship could not spoil her body nor depress her spirits. This wench was witty and pretty, had a comic genius, grace, brass, mirth; and, albeit goodnatured, her tongue was cutting. Her figure was so elegantly feminine that she could wear man's clothes with advantage. She had risen from the pit of the King's Theatre, in which she sold oranges, to the stage, and drew all the Court in the "Vagaries of Flora," in which she was the goddess of flowers; in the "Maiden Queen," in which she was "Florimell," a gay young spark; and in Dryden's "Conquest of Grenada," in which she played the part of "Queen Almahide" in a jauntily-set broad-brimmed hat. Her name was Gwynn, and she was a powerful stimulant to the over-raked Court. Originally, she was, it was said, a dancing-girl in a show. Nell Gwynn had simultaneously for lovers the Earl of Dorset, whom she called her "Charles I."; Hart, the actor, who was her "Charles II."; and the king, who was her "Old Rowley." In her company, whatever moral soundness had remained to Charles soon died out. His will got emasculated from his own vices and pleasurable contact with the vices of all nations. Italian eunuchs came to sing to him in his green chamber. The wife of his valet, Chaffinch, fetched him from theatres Nelly Gwynn, Peg Hughes, and other actresses. His inseparable boon companion in his life of sensuality, was one of the most happily-gifted, and yet most despicable, men of the period—the Duke of Buckingham.

Buckingham was as skilled in seducing a woman as in gaining a popular assembly. He was married to a niece of Cromwell, but never troubled his head about her, unless to wish for her death. Prompt to undertake no matter what, and incapable to realize any of his schemes, he was credulous with charlatans, open to great thoughts, servile, insolent, and the slave of each whim that held his fancy. Out of hatred to his rival, Arlington, who was bribed by Spain, he threw himself entirely on the French side.

Arlington and Buckingham thought alike on one point only. They were both afraid of the return of Clarendon, whom their Cabal had exiled. "Arlington is fond of luxury and amusement,"[1] wrote M. de Croissy. "If he were in less close relations with Spain, he would have to live savingly. He has the mark of a sword-cut across his nose, which, as it does not heal, he covers with a bit of lozenge-shaped sticking-plaister. So far from being a disfigurement, it gives him an air of manly seriousness foreign to his nature."[2] The Marquis de Ruvigny informed the Court of Versailles that "Arlington would sell his soul to the devil to worst an enemy."[3]

Each of these English noblemen had an agent who secretly took charge of his interests at the French Court. Buckingham's agent was one Leyton, a sharp, vulgar, and grasping London tradesman. Williamson, who served Arlington, was disinterested and close-mouthed. Louis XIV. was not ignorant of their political relations, and thus spoke of them in an autograph letter to Colbert de Croissy:[4] "Leyton for Buckingham, and Williamson for Arlington his

[1] *Relation d'Angleterre.* MS. *Bibl. Nat., Fonds Colbert*, 478.
[2] Ruvigny à Pomponne. MS. *Aff. Etr., Angleterre*, tome cxvii. fol. 57, Nov. 4, 1675.
[3] Le Roi à Colbert de Croissy. *Ibid.*, tome xciii. fol. 164, Nov. 7, 1668.
[4] *Ibid.*

master, try to make you believe they can soon bring about a close union between me and the King of England, provided you play into their hands and no longer try to get the Chancellor recalled from exile. Arlington does not act towards me in a way to make me desire the continuance of his influence. You are to make both one and the other think the re-call of the said Chancellor possible, and even probable, if I support him. If they engage to effect the union between me and their king, you can give all the sureties they ask, that I will make use of any means they suggest to block every road by which Clarendon can go back. But I see very well that I shall make no real progress so long as I have not gained the Duke and Arlington by forwarding their separate interests. If each has a strong motive for helping me, they will both, however they may detest each other, plot for a common object. Hints may be held out to Leyton and Williamson, that they are to receive some gifts from me. I prefer that it should be in money. When they have received payment of this kind, I shall in a degree have the advantage of them; and it seems to me, that when they are thus in my power, you can without danger use plain speech with them. Let me know what sums should be offered to the two agents, as well as to the Duke and to Lord Arlington. The affair is so important that I am willing to make any sacrifice of money, provided that payment of the gross amount is stayed, until after the blow is struck."

Leyton did not stand out for a high price. He was bought for four hundred pistoles. "But," said Louis in another autograph letter,[1] "do not stop at that, if more is wanted. Seeing how irresolute the King of England is, do not neglect to gain Arlington. I would willingly spend on him twenty thousand gold pieces. You must take care not to frighten the king by letting him feel that I am seeking to draw him into a war with Holland."

Williamson[2] remained incorruptible. Leyton, on the contrary, came to France to pay his court to Louis. "I have treated him (*régalé*) to a ring worth four hundred pistoles,"[3]

[1] MS. *Aff. Etr.*, *Angleterre*, *Le Roi à Colbert*, Nov. 24, 1668.
[2] Letter of Nov. 28, 1668.
[3] *Le Roi au Colbert*, Dec. 12, 1668. This was an extra present.

wrote that sovereign, "and admitted him to converse twice with me." Some months later he was granted a French pension of three hundred *jacobus*[1] and the promise of a handsome present. "We know," remarked the French ambassador in a despatch to Lionne, "what a knave he is.[2] Nevertheless, he is active, pushing, and intriguing; and as he has the ear of the king, rubs shoulders with the highest men at Court, and is a leading member of the Merchant Taylors' Company and of the Corporation of the City of London, I believe he can keep us well informed." So his Most Christian Majesty went on granting him audiences and treating him as a person of rare distinction.

Louis did not wholly trust to the two great members of the Cabal. He worked many other secret springs with which Charles was surrounded. He had notoriously with him the famous Samuel Morland, and found an agent in every Frenchman settled in London.

Lionne was instructed by Colbert de Croissy never to mention Morland's name, but to speak

[1] *Lettre du* 27 *Mars*, 1669, tome xciv., fol. 287.
[2] *Lettre du* 25 *Fév.*, 1669, *ibid.*, tome xciv.

of him as "our secret manager."[1] Morland
was a scholar and scientist, who ruined himself
in trying to work his inventions, and then resorted to fraudulent expedients to get out of
trouble. One of his inventions was the parent
of the steam engine. He constructed hydraulic
wheels, curiously combined. When secretary
to Thurlow, the chief minister of Cromwell, he
got hold of State secrets, and with so much art
and secresy delivered them to the banished
Stuarts, that the Englishmen who shared their
exile were astounded when he was one of the
first to present himself to Charles II. on his
restoration, and to be knighted by him. He
was overwhelmed with places and pensions,
and being unable to ask for more at Whitehall,
he intrigued for the King of France. His
wife, Susan de Milleville, was French. He
sold his pensions and privileges to build a
château in France, and the château to pursue
his scientific and industrial experiments. When
a widower, and ruined, he was harassed by
creditors. An adventure then befell him more
incredible than any that was ever invented by

---

[1] *Lionne à Colbert*, 26 Août, 1668, tome xciii., fol. 94.

an author of the romances of his day.¹ A man whom in the heyday of prosperity he had saved from hunger came to propose to him a marriage which would relieve him from his embarrassments. "A lady, virtuous, pious, of an amiable disposition, having an estate of £500 a year, £4,000 in gold, and furniture, plate, and jewels," was prepared to take him for her husband. He married her, and a fortnight later discovered that she had not a shilling, was a coachman's daughter, and would in a few months give the king another subject. Morland brought a suit in the Ecclesiastical Court to set aside the marriage, but lost it. His creditors pursuing him, he did not dare to quit the lodging where he was hiding. On the advice of a Nonconformist minister, he was going to be reconciled to his wife, when he heard that during the suit she lived with Sir Gilbert Gerrard. So he attacked her for adultery, obtained a divorce, and married a third time.²

[1] See Defoe's *Moll of Flanders* and Smollett's *Roderick Random*. There are letters of Morland, in his Appendix to Pepys' *Diary*.

[2] A quay in Paris is still called after Morland, in whose fertile brain the idea first originated of raising water to the royal gardens at Marly by means of the great hydraulic wheel on the Seine.

Real life was reflected in the plays and novels which show that in England, under the reign of Charles II., depravity was universal. It is only just to condemn the profligacy of the Court, but it would be ridiculous to ignore it. Indeed, to understand the history of European politics in the second half of the seventeenth century, it is necessary to discard all prudery, and to unveil the private lives of Charles and his courtiers. These dishonoured dead will teach no useful lesson if we do not study the vices and the passions to which they were the slaves when living. It is not the business of the historian to evoke unsubstantial phantoms on a fancifully-decorated stage, but to raise bodies from the grave, make them again the temples of the souls which have flown from them, place them in the surroundings in which they lived, and analyse their hidden motives, good, bad, and indifferent.

The French in London, by the propriety of their manners, contrasted with the English. Notable among them was Saint Evremont, a general of distinction, who had learned the art of war under the great Condé, and who is only, now, remembered as an elegant writer and an epicurean wit. He was disgraced after the battle of the Pyrenees, and retired to London, where his tact, the dignity of his life, and the charm of his mind and conversation assured him an important place. He devoted all his advantages to the consolidation of the French alliance, and to the procuring of valuable information for the ambassadors of Louis XIV. His company was sought for by men of intellect, birth, and position.[1] The venerable Marquis de Rouvigny, father-in-law of Lord William Russell, and head of the French Protestants in England, passed several months in London every year, and was universally respected. Louis XIV., observing the esteem in which he was held, eventually utilized him in his diplomacy. The most noisy of these Frenchmen, and, thanks to the *chef d'œuvre* of Hamilton, the most celebrated, was the Chevalier de Gramont.

The French in London were nearly all connected with the Court. The few tradespeople had also a special influence, by which Louis knew how to profit. A Paris milliner,[2] Madame

[1] SAINT SIMON. EVELYN.
[2] EVELYN : *Diary*, March 1, 1667.

Desborde, governed Queen Catherine. She
decided with sovereign authority in all that
related to petticoats, smocks, laces, stomachers,
fans, frills, furbelows, and other French baga-
telles for ladies' wear. The wine merchant to
the king was a M. de Pontac,[1] of Château
Pontac and Château O'Brien, in the Gironde,
a Gascon whose high spirits and voluble tongue
amused the silent English, while the wine de-
canter, at after-dinner bouts, was being passed
round the table.

But these diplomatic threads, which were
woven into a web by such a powerful will,
rotted as time flew on. Charles was always
promising to join with France against Europe,
and was always ready to join with Holland
against France. Every month that sped weak-
ened the secret springs which Louis directed,
and new combinations had to be resorted to.
In the first nine years of his reign Charles II.
had twice abandoned Louis XIV.[2] There was
nothing in the situation of England to impose
on him a French alliance. On the contrary,

[1] EVELYN: *Diary*, July 13, 1683.
[2] See MIGNON: *Négociations relatives à la Succession d'Espagne;* and CAMILLE ROUSSET: *Histoire de Louvois.*

the interests of his people and a care for his popularity should have made him resist Louis's attempts to seize on the mouths of the Scheldt and Rhine. His changing humour and his duty both drew him from the French king, who, to soften the animosity of the English and give a sop to their traders, devised a sham treaty which would lead them to hope for many commercial advantages. Colbert de Croissy, the Intendant of Paris, was charged, in July, 1668, to negotiate this instrument, the basis of which was drawn up in the king's handwriting.

"The negotiations confided to you are the most important of all Europe,"[1] said the minister Colbert, in a memorandum addressed to his brother the ambassador.[2] "The treaty of commerce is only to throw dust in the eyes of the trading class in England; and you are to make it drag under all the pretexts which

[1] MS. *Affaires Etrangères*, 14 Septembre, 1668.
[2] From October 1, 1668, the French who went to England affected a deep interest in horse-racing, and were reported to know nothing about it. The brilliant de Gramont had no eye for a good horse, if we can believe Algernon Sydney. "He's such a proud ass that he neither knows what's good and won't believe any one else." See, also, Algernon Sydney's letters to Henry Saville.

may suggest themselves to you. It should also afford you pretexts and occasions to strengthen political ties, and widen your relations with political men." When Charles II. went to Newmarket, Lionne wrote to Colbert de Croissy:[1] "Were I *in your place, I should also set out in two or three days*,[2] so as to have an excuse 'for settling all when you come back;' but I should never go away, finding always some pretext for staying, such as a cold or an attack of illness in the house."

After long searching for an agent who might be able to hold the volatile Charles, Louis, in 1668, at length thought he had found the man he wanted. It was at the time that Charles usually went to Newmarket. The King of France noticed this passage in one of his ambassador's gossipping letters: "The King of England, who is so inconstant in most things, shows in one respect fixity of application. Come what may, he spends daily a part of his

[1] *Lionne à Colbert*, 23 *Février*, 1669.
[2] The italics are in the original. As the secretaries of Louis Quatorze were clear in their instructions, and assumed intelligent attention on the part of their agents, they only underlined when there was not time for the latter to give mature consideration to despatches. (*Translator's Note.*)

time in a laboratory making chemical experiments." Since the attempt to govern him through Madam Castlemaine had not succeeded, why not try to manage him through the laboratory for which he clearly had a passion? At this juncture Louis had at his call an Italian monk, named Pregnani, who dazzled the Electress of Bavaria with his knowledge of judicial astrology. After taking him from his convent she recommended him to the King of France, whom she asked to get him made an abbé.[1] "He understands," wrote her Serene Highness, "how to blow a bellows and use crucibles according to the rules of alchemy, has infinite cleverness, marvellous suppleness and dexterity in attaining his ends." But how bring Pregnani into the Court circle without exciting suspicion? The vehicle chosen was the Duke of Monmouth, the eldest of the King's bastards, who was weak-minded and credulous, and the best-beloved son of his Royal sire. At a supper where he met different members of the French embassy, his curiosity was adroitly excited by tales of the wonderful transmutations Pregnani could operate, and the horoscopes

[1] *Lionne à Colbert*, 23 *Février*, 1669.

he cast. Monmouth secretly wished to know whether the heavenly bodies favoured his pretensions to the Crown of England. He invited Pregnani to London. The abbé hastened there. He went at night to see Colbert de Croissy; for Louis XIV., whose sense of what he owed to the dignity of the crown he wore never failed him, in the midst of the lowest intrigues, was half-ashamed to be in any degree represented by a charlatan, and wished the mission to remain secret. The abbé Pregnani followed the Court to Newmarket.[1] The means which he made use of to arouse the interest of the king and fix his attention, were very droll. The Duke of Monmouth being in love with a girl of some beauty, to whom he thought the king, his father, and his uncle, the Duke of York, were both making advances, had the curiosity to ask the abbé which of the three would obtain her the first. The soothsayer, without having seen her, described her face, her humour and inclinations, and said what her past was and what her future would be. He was so circumstantial that the king was informed of the matter by the duke, and wished to have his

---

[1] *Colbert à Lionne*, 18 *Mars*, 1669.

own horoscope drawn. The abbé was commanded to meet the king's desire by fetching his astrological books to Newmarket. "Such, Monsieur, is the beginning of the business. If it ends well, I shall apprise you; and I believe I shall have queer things to tell you of before long."

The cunning Italian [1] was able, without referring to his books, to read the disposition of Charles; but he was careful to hide his game, and took nobody, unless Colbert de Croissy, into his confidence.

"He (the abbé) does not think much of the King of England's mind, which he says is prone to busy itself with amusing trifles, to the exclusion of what is serious. He has an unconquerable aversion to sustained effort, and recoils from every sort of business. The abbé, however, hopes that he will be able to overcome his taste for mental trifling, and to bring him to take a good resolution by forecasting in his horoscope impending disasters. I wish I could be confident on this point, because the king said to me, on arriving from Newmarket, that the abbé's predictions about the races

[1] *Colbert à Lionne*, 1 *Avril*, 1669.

there were wrong in every single case; and that his errors had caused great loss to the Duke of Monmouth's servants, who regulated their bets according to his forecasts. Certain gain had been promised to them all. The King of England has since puzzled the abbé about his misleading prognostics; but as his majesty's curiosity is great, perhaps he will resort in private to what he affects to laugh at in public."

This unfortunate application of sorcery to horse-racing caused the disgrace of the presumptuous abbé at Versailles. Lionne some days later wrote:[1] "As to the Pregnani, since he has been unable to gain ground with the king by his astrology and chemical tricks, it is not probable that he can be of future use to us. Take means to send him back to France, where we can have him under finger and thumb. To prevent him refusing to leave England, where he might get in our way, affect to send him with a confidential message to Versailles."

[1] *Lionne à Colbert de Croissy*, 4 *Mai*, 1669.

CHAPTER II.

MADAME HENRIETTE.

THE Duke of Buckingham alone suspected that an intrigue was hidden beneath the astrologer's predictions. But he was far from supposing that Louis XIV., Colbert, and Lionne were mixed up with a low cunning charlatan. What he thought was, that Henrietta, or Henriette, Duchess of Orleans, was afraid her hold on Charles might relax because of her enforced absence from England, and sought to maintain it by the agency of the Italian priest. As Buckingham set up to be her lover, and to govern the king vicariously for her, he was angry at the fancied substitution for him of the abbé. "She sends," he complained to Leyton,[1] "a humbugging astrologer, who flatters himself that I am his dupe in love and politics, and who makes me a

[1] Colbert's despatch to Louis XIV. on March 14, 1669, giving an account of a conversation with Leyton.

laughing-stock for Monmouth and Hamilton." "He shows all the fury," added Colbert de Croissy, "of a too enterprising gallant, who is vexed at finding himself an object of mirth. Perhaps the best thing to do would be to send over Madame[1] herself, to keep alive her brother's tenderness, and heal the wounded vanity of Buckingham, which may breed hatred where love was." The ambassador knew that the French Court had been reflecting on the expediency of bringing the influence of Madame Henriette to bear upon her brother. One of the Frenchmen who was most often at the Court of Charles, the Marquis de Flammerens, some months previously had spoken to Colbert about charging the Duchess of Orleans with a mission to England.[2]

Madame Henriette, youngest sister of Charles II. and wife of the French king's only brother, had the charming liveliness of her grandfather,

[1] The king's brother was, at the Court of Versailles, given the title of "Monsieur," without any other qualification, when he was spoken of or spoken to. His wife was "Madame." She was sometimes familiarly called Madame Henriette, to distinguish her from the widow of Gaston, Duc d'Orléans, her aunt-in-law. (*Translator's Note.*)

[2] MS. *Aff. Etr. Angleterre*, vol. xciii., fol. 174.

Henri IV. She was slender, white-skinned, and delicate and small. The two kings were equally fond of her. But her influence with both was the cause of bitter and violent jealousies, and her intervention would only be too patent so as perhaps to defeat its object. Apart from the suspicions of Buckingham, who kept Henriette informed, through his confidant Leyton,[1] with what went on in England, there was Lady Castlemaine to be humoured. That self-willed beauty hated "foreign meddlers." "The Countess of Castlemaine," wrote Colbert de Croissy to Louis, "has given me in my wife's presence a piece of her mind on many subjects, into which I propose to go for your Majesty's information. This lady having said that she had had a letter from Madame, who advised her strongly to make up her quarrel with Buckingham, and that she was puzzled to think why Madame was so anxious for a reconciliation, my wife observed that union with France depended on the agreement of all the favourites with each other."[2]

[1] Colbert to Lionne, relating conversations with Leyton, Feb. 13 and March 9, 1669.
[2] Despatch of Colbert to Lionne, May 13, 1669.

Happily for France, Buckingham and Lady Castlemaine had each their cares and troubles, and did not, after Pregnani was shipped back to France, dare to show themselves exacting. Buckingham was dominated by the Countess of Shrewsbury, a woman of a violent temper, who had just got into a dangerous scrape.

"Infuriated against Killegrew," writes Colbert de Croissy,[1] "because he boasted that she had denied him no favour, she nursed her anger against him until she could wreak vengeance. She was able to do this yesterday. Killegrew had arranged to visit her at her house, which is six miles from London. He went alone in a coach, and on the way fell asleep. He was awoke by the thrust of a sword which pierced his neck, and came out at the shoulder. Before he could cry out, he was flung from the vehicle, and stabbed in three other places by varlets of the Countess. The lady herself looked on from her own coach and six, in which she was with her three daughters, and cried out to the assassins to 'kill the villain.' Nor did she drive off until he was thought dead. He was but badly

[1] Colbert to Lionne, May 20, 1669.

wounded, and has sworn informations. You may fancy the noise the attempt to murder him causes, and the worry and anxiety of the Duke of Buckingham, who is still passionately in love with this virago, whose husband he killed in a duel for having resisted her brow-beatings."

As to Lady Castlemaine, she was not in such a humour as the French ambassador, to laugh at the "buffooneries" of Nell Gwynn,[1] or at the pleasure the king took in them. The orange girl had the charm of novelty; and if her tongue was coarse, her wit was glancing and her laughter was gay and stimulating to the over-raked Charles. He could not help yawning when he was with Lady Castlemaine; but his spirits rose in the company of the jocular Nell.

Charles suddenly made up his mind to have an interview with his sister. He told Colbert de Croissy[2] that he passionately desired to see and converse with her. "I was greatly surprised," adds the ambassador, "at the intimation and I lose no time in sending you an ex

[1] Colbert to Lionne, Nov. 17, 1669, and Jan. 26 1670.
[2] Colbert to Louis XIV., Jan. 2, 1670.

press to say that this is a case, if ever there was one, in which the iron should be hammered while it is hot." The conditions which the King of England hoped by his sister's advocacy to bring Louis to adopt, show more greed for money than statescraft. They were as follows:—

"The league between the King of Great Britain and the Most Christian King, shall be so durable that nothing in the world shall henceforth divide their majesties. The King of Great Britain being convinced of the truth of the Catholic religion, and resolved to declare himself a Catholic, and to be reconciled to the Church of Rome, believes that, for the fulfilment of this design, the aid of the Most Christian King will be needed."[1]

This was written in 1669, more than fifteen years previous to the death of Charles II.; and during these fifteen years a prince so convinced and resolved simulated the Protestant faith, remained the protector of the Episcopal Anglican Church, took part in its services and ceremonies, and went on appointing bishops.

Charles also agreed to connive at the seizure by Louis XIV. of any countries which it

[1] MS. *Aff. Etr. Angleterre*, tome xcv., fol. 235.

might suit him to annex to his monarchy, whether to the detriment of Spain or the United Provinces. But, in return, Louis engaged to pay him £200,000 sterling, plus the cost of any English troops engaged in helping him. This cost was to be rated at a minimum of £3 16s. a day per soldier, and £800,000 a month while the campaign lasted. The King of France was to cede to England, out of the common conquests, the Isle of Minorca and the port of Ostend, and all the countries and strongholds in America under Spanish rule. The king's nephew, the Prince of Orange, was to receive compensation for his losses, but in what form was not stipulated. As the Senate and Republic of Hamburg were bound by ties of interest with the United Provinces, war was to be declared on them."

These crude and incoherent proposals came suddenly on Louis, who had been long studying how to carry out the well elaborated schemes of Mazarin, by securing the inaction of England. "The most odious of the clauses," observed Colbert de Croissy,[1] "is the one binding us to attack Hamburg, without any given

[1] Colbert to the King of France, Dec. 19, 1669.

motive or plausible excuse. To do so would be to foolishly bring down on our backs the Hanseatic towns and the princes of the German Empire."[1]

It was high time for Madame Henriette to come forward and negotiate. She began by writing to her brother[2] that Louis XIV. was shocked at the demand to attack Hamburg, which had never given any one cause for complaint; and she insisted that Arlington should be forced to modify the proposed basis for negotiation. Arlington at bottom was a Roman Catholic, and would not like Charles to have haggled about the sum of money that he was to pocket as a premium for going over to Rome. "The King of England," he notified to Louis, "will not hear of the sums which your Majesty agrees to let him have, in consideration of his change of religion, being made payable in Paris.[3] I think, I own, it very hard

---

[1] Colbert wanted to bring the Hanse towns as shareholders, into his two great organizations for establishing a French Colonial Empire; *viz.*, the chartered Company of the East, or East India Company, and the chartered Company of the West, or American Company. (*Translator's Note.*)

[2] Colbert to the King of France, Jan. 29, 1670.

[3] *Ibid.*, May 15, 1670.

on your Majesty, that the money promised for a declaration of Catholicity should be transported at your Majesty's expense to London." Arlington seems to have been disinterested for the time and Court in which he lived. His wife had begged Madame Colbert[1] "to send her from Paris enough of the finest Venice brocatelle to make hangings for an anteroom, and covers for twelve chairs; bed curtains in green damask, and covering of the same stuff for a sofa a set of chairs and fauteuils in another chamber. "If the king thinks it for the good of his service to make this present, it would, I fancy, much gratify the lady." The stuff and furniture were sent from Paris; but Lady Arlington frequently, in the course of a few months, offered to pay for them.

Little by little, difficulties began to vanish under the dexterous manipulation of Madame Henriette. She got a draft treaty prepared, which left the King of France full liberty to conquer in the North, and bound Charles to

[1] Colbert to the King of France, February 24, 1670. Madame Colbert was a daughter of a bourgeois of Lyons, who made a fortune in the manufacture of French half-farthings, or *liards*. She was mother of the Marquis Colbert de Torcy.

declare himself a Roman Catholic, in return for a subvention payable in London. To overcome every remaining difficulty, the Duchess of Orleans set out for England, after arranging to meet Charles at Dover.

Madame Henriette had the happy thought, in choosing the maids of honour who were to attend her to England, to select Louise de Keroualle. It is hardly probable that she designed increasing her own power over her brother by taking with her this young girl, whose baby face, melancholy eyes, and languid walk did not indicate an adroit diplomatic agent.[1] But it is certain that Louise was present at the interviews between Charles and his sister, and made a deep impression on him. He was tired of the furious temper of his dark Castlemaine, and of the vulgarity of Nell Gwynn. The conversation of the Breton blonde, who appeared sad and gentle, interested him. She had also the charming freshness of twenty, and the high delicate breeding which

---

[1] A mistake. A languid manner, when not arising from ill health, often goes with falsity, and gains time for deliberation. Frankness is direct, and does not loiter. (*Translator's Note.*)

distinguished the Court of Louis XIV. before that monarch's illegitimate children grew up.

Whether to prolong the enjoyment of spending quiet evenings with his sister, or to keep the pretty Louise some time longer in England, Charles insisted on Madame Henriette delaying her return to France. This treaty, he argued, is an affair of the highest importance, and should be discussed maturely. My subjects hate the French. The pains they are now at to create a great trade, and to become a maritime power will sharpen their jealousy.[1] The King of France wants to hold all the great ports of the Continent, and bring under his sway a maritime people which have been the main rivals of England on sea and in the colonial trade. I must therefore be very wary, and not show my hand too soon. Madame Henriette did not easily obtain a prolonged leave of absence at Dover. She had a husband whom she always treated as an inferior being, which his effeminacy and base, false nature justified her in doing. He was jealous of her, and saw with umbrage the importance

[1] See Mignet's *Négociations relatives à la Succession d'Espagne*, tome iii., p. 50.

she was obtaining by the political part she played in England. Louis XIV., who was at Dunkirk, watching anxiously the progress of the negotiations, had to command his brother not to be an obstacle to the conclusion of a State affair of the greatest importance. He wrote to Colbert de Croissy:[1]

"I send you this to inform you that my brother has consented to let Madame remain ten or twelve days longer at Dover. You can exaggerate to King Charles the efforts we make, and points we stretch to be agreeable to him. Let him feel how much obliged he should be to us, so that when we make demands, he will be in a humour to yield."

A month later, Madame Henriette died. It was rumoured that she was poisoned.[2] The Court of England appeared to believe that she was. The diplomatic web she had helped to weave seemed ravelled.

[1] The original autograph letter is in the archives of the Ministry for Foreign Affairs, English section, vol. xcvii., folio 257, May 31, 1670.

[2] Littré seemed to have established that she died a natural death. He drew this conclusion from the medical report on her *post mortem* examination. M. Lair has, however, taken up the old theory, that her death was caused by poison.

"*Must we abandon* the great affair?" asked Colbert de Croissy of Lionne. "It is to be feared [1] that the grief of the King of England, which is deeper than can be imagined, and the malevolent talk and rumours of our enemies, will spoil everything."

The enemies of France were not the only ones to attack her. Buckingham turned against the French alliance. Colbert de Croissy informed Lionne that, had it been possible, Buckingham would have picked a quarrel with France, if only to win popularity.[2]

Louis despatched Marshal de Bellefonds to present his official condolence to Charles on his sister's death. The Marshal was a very fine gentleman, had bland manners, and was skilled in smoothing down angles.

"When do they intend to let the Chevalier de Lorraine back to Court?" asked the King of England, with a rudeness foreign to his manners and disposition.

"I replied," said the Marshal, "that I did

---

[1] Colbert to Lionne, July 2, 1670.
[2] Original autograph letter of Marshal Bellefonds to the King of France. *Affr. Etr. Angleterre*, tome xcviii., fol. 35, du 10 Juillet, 1670.

not know; that it was not easy to divine the thoughts of your Majesty on such a trifling subject; and that none of your servants would take the liberty of conversing about it, unless your Majesty first broached the matter."

It was feared that Charles and his Court had slipped from the grasp of Louis. A last resource was to be tried. Louise de Keroualle, whom Charles in his interview with de Bellefonds associated, with apparent tenderness, with the memory of his sister, was packed off in all haste to Calais, to be at his beck and call. Apprised of this attention, Charles sent a yacht to take her across to Dover. He wept, and fell into a sentimental mood on meeting her, and named her maid of honour to his patient wife. Her presence assuaged his grief. Relations with France grew less ticklish.

But man walketh in a vain show, truly! In the funeral oration in honour of Madame Henriette, Bossuet said: "The worthy link which bound the two greatest monarchs of the earth was broken, but now is soldered up again.[1] Their noble desires win confidence of

---

[1] BOSSUET: *Oraison Funèbre de Madame.*

their peoples, and virtue henceforth shall be the only mediator between them." [1]

It was not hard to regain Buckingham. The French ambassador apprised Lionne that in obtaining a pension for the Countess of Shrewsbury, he would make the Duke his obedient servant. The pension was fixed at 10,000 livres, and faithfully paid. Colbert de Croissy was not slow to perceive the spell in which Louise de Keroualle held Charles, and the advantages to be obtained therefrom.

"The king is always finding opportunities to talk with this beauty in the queen's room. But he has not, contrary to what is reported, gone yet to chat with her in her own room,[1] contrary to what has been said here."

Lady Castlemaine prepared to make war on the French charmer. She demanded the title of Duchess of Cleveland, and looked for support to the Spanish faction.[2] She made believe that she still reigned over the king, by getting royal favours heaped upon herself. Her patent of duchess was scarcely made out, when she exacted for her eldest son the title of

[1] Colbert to Lionne, August 28 and Sept. 10, 1670.
[2] *Ibid.*, Dec. 15, 1670.

Marquis of Southampton, and for the second that of Earl of Northumberland.

"In a few years," cried a malcontent, "England will be so happy as to see a House of Peers extracted out of the blood Royal."

These evidences of victory caused sharper rivalry. Louise de Keroualle began seriously to study her game, and to play it with no light purpose at the balls given in December, 1670, at Whitehall. "The fashion of masquerading, introduced this winter," wrote Colbert de Croissy, "is a source of great diversion to persons of quality." The treaty of Madame was defended by Louise, who had not yet sacrificed honour to her country. On the other hand, public feeling weighed on the statesmen of the Cabal. The English people had a true instinct of their maritime future, and of the great hidden danger that faced it. They cried out for the king to support Protestant Holland, and even Catholic Spain,[1] against the King of

[1] In this, popular feeling was wiser than Cromwell, great statesman though he was, had shown himself, twelve years earlier, in allowing Mazarin to circumvent him and to lead him into prostrating the naval power of Spain, which, in the Protector's time, had almost fallen into a decrepit state. (*Translator's Note.*)

France. It had an uneasy feeling that a great conspiracy was being hatched, but was ignorant of its nature. The brooding suspicions came to a head, when England got into a state of frenzy about the Popish Plot.

Louise was not sure of her empire, and found herself an object of ill-will to the English. Her only chance, she saw, was in the discomfiture of the Duchess of Cleveland, to bring about which she seemed inclined to yield to Charles, and yet, when pressed too closely, slipped away from him. In the close game of the masquerading winter, her affected coyness was ill-understood by her ally, the French ambassador, who, not venturing to believe in her full success, and fearing a return of the vindictive Duchess of Cleveland, wrote to Louis, "I think it safe, while undermining that lady, to keep her on our side by appearing to be with her."[1]

[1] Colbert to the King of France, Dec. 12, 1670.

CHAPTER III.

ACCESSION OF LOUISE DE KEROUALLE.

"I NOW also saw that famous beauty, but in my opinion of a childish simple baby face, Mademoiselle Querouaille, maid of honour to Madame, and now to be so to the Queen," Evelyn jotted in his *Diary*. The baby face was a deceptive one; and the simplicity was a mask for transcendent art in finessing. "How long," asked Louis XIV., Louvois, Lionne Colbert, and the Court of Louis XIV., "will the resistance of this childish-looking girl be carried on?"

Meanwhile, the Court of Whitehall noted the furious tantrums of the Duchess of Cleveland, and other signs of her disgrace. "The influence of the Duchess," reported the French ambassador,[1] "visibly wanes. The trouble and expense which the Conde Molina has been at to get her round to the Spanish side, have been thrown away. While she loses favour,

[1] Colbert to Louvois, Sept. 21, 1671.

the King of England's fancy for Mademoiselle de Kerouaile grows stronger. The attacks of nausea she had yesterday, when dining with me, makes me hope I shall find in her a useful ally as long as my embassy lasts."[1]

This attack of nausea was a cause of delight to the Court of France. "The King was greatly pleased," wrote Louvois, "to hear in what manner Mademoiselle Keroualle suffered when dining the other day at the French embassy. There was nothing in her conduct since she left France, to lead us to expect that such a piece of good fortune was going so soon to befall her. His Majesty is anxious to be informed of what may grow out of this situation, and of the terms on which she and the King have come to stand mutually."[2] But the rejoicing was premature, and the sickness recorded in the diplomatic paper had not the cause suspected. Louise continued to blow hot and cold at King Charles. She seemed to make light of the great interests which her coyness might damage. Her re-

[1] Colbert to Louvois, Sept. 21, 1671.
[2] Louvois to Colbert de Croissy, in original autograph, Sept. 29, 1671, *Aff. Etr., Angleterre*, tome cii., fol. 283.

F

sistance alarmed the Court of Versailles. Doubtless, Charles found pleasure in her society only. But he was not a man to suffer a prude long to reign over him. Was it not to be feared, that he would console himself for her reserve, with some other beauty?

"It is certain that the King of England shows a warm pássion for Mademoiselle Keroualle; and perhaps you may have heard from other sources, what a finely furnished set of lodgings have been given to her at Whitehall. His Majesty goes to her rooms at nine o'clock every morning, never stays there for less than an hour, and often remains until eleven o'clock. He returns after dinner, and shares at her card-table in all her stakes and losses, never letting her want for anything. All the ministers, therefore, seek her friendship. Milord Arlington said to me quite recently, that he was much pleased at this new attachment of the king; and that although His Majesty never communicated state affairs to ladies, still, as they could whenever they pleased, render ill-services to statesmen, and defeat their plans, it was well for the king's good servants that his majesty should have a fancy for Mademoiselle Keroualle, who was not of an evil disposition, and was a lady. It was better to have dealings with her than with lewd and bouncing orange-girls and actresses, of whom no man of quality could take the measure. She was no termagant or scold; and when the king was with her, persons of breeding could, without loss of dignity, go to her rooms, and pay him and her their court. Milord Arlington told me to advise Mademoiselle Keroualle to cultivate the king's good graces, and to so manage, that he should only find at her lodgings enjoyment, peace, and quietness. He added that, if Lady Arlington took his advice, she would urge the new favourite either to yield unreservedly to the King, or to retire to a French convent. In his opinion, I should also advise her in this sense. I answered jocularly, that I was not such a fool, or so ungrateful to the king, as to tell her to prefer religion to his good graces; that I was persuaded she did not await my advice, but that, nevertheless, I should not spare it upon her, to show how both I and Milord appreciated her influence, and in what esteem he held her. I believe I can assure you that she has so got round King Charles as to be of the greatest service to our sovereign and master, if she only does her duty."[1]

The Countess of Arlington ended by following her husband's advice, and concerted with Colbert de Croissy how to bring about the complete surrender of the young French beauty.

This ambassador had held a high place in the French Judicature as Président à Mortier. "He was a safe and sagacious mediocrity, who, by dint of application and plain common sense, made up for what he spoiled by the coarse manners and self-sufficient disposition of his family." He did not think the tradition of judicial dignity anywise incompatible with ministering to the vicious fancies of Charles, as the ensuing despatch to Lionne shows.

"The king did me yesterday the honour to sup at the Embassy, where he proved to me, by indulging in a gay and unfettered debauch, that he does not mistrust me."[2] Charles

---
[1] Colbert to Louvois, Oct. 8, 1671, tome ci., fol. 167.
[2] January 15, 1671.

was therefore brought, without difficulty, to accept an invitation from the Countess of Arlington, to take Louise Keroualle to her ladyship's seat at Euston, so that he might escape there from his Court, which he had brought to Newmarket, and triumph over her remaining scruples.

"I am going," the ambassador informed Louis, "to the Arlingtons' place at Euston; and as the king's inclination for Mademoiselle Keroualle, who is to go there with me, is rising, I foresee that he will often run across from Newmarket to see her."[1]

The plot was approved of by Louis; but, to save his dignity, when it was a little bruited he affected to treat it as a good practical joke. "His Majesty was vastly amused," Louvois was instructed to say,[2] "with all that was in your letter about Mlle. de Keroualle, and will have pleasure in hearing of the progress she makes in the King's favour. He even jested on the subject, and says that there must either be small love for the mistress or great confi-

---

[1] October 8, 1671.
[2] Oct. 20, 1671. Original autograph, *Affaires Etrangères Angleterre*, tome cii., fol. 290.

•dence felt in you, to suffer you to go to Euston in such jolly company.'

Lady Arlington was a Dutchwoman. Her maiden name was De Brederode, and her grandfather was the illegitimate son of Prince Henry Frederick of Orange. She was fond of luxurious living and sumptuous surroundings, and had been forced by the necessities arising from these tastes, to promise in marriage her only child,—one of the most lovely girls that ever bloomed on English soil,—to the son of the Duchess of Cleveland. She insured herself against the loss of patronage which the disgrace of that mistress would entail, by making her own seat, near Newmarket, the theatre of the French favourite's grand triumph.

Euston is an immense house, built in brick, with two wings and four pavilions. A balustrade crowns the mansion, and is ornamented at equal distances with alternate vases and statues. There was there, in 1672, a picture gallery and billiard room; a chapel, an orangery, and a conservatory adorned with busts of the Cæsars in alabaster. The apartments of each guest were so well isolated, that he, or she, might cut off all communication with the rest of the house, and enjoy an independent establishment. The king's apartments were painted in fresco. All the others were elegantly furnished. There were numerous bath rooms, a pharmacy; and in the poultry yard coops for fattening fowl. The stables contained thirty horses, and the park a thousand deer. No member of the aristocracy had so many coaches in his mews as Lord Arlington. Besides the French party, Lady Arlington had invited the Countess of Sunderland and a large number of members of the Court. The king, who was at Newmarket, came every other day, and often slept at Euston in the month of October.

"The king," wrote Colbert,[1] "comes here for his repasts; and after eating he passes several hours with Mlle. Keroualle. He has already paid her three visits; and he invited us yesterday to Newmarket, to see the races. We went, and were charmingly entertained, and he seemed more than ever solicitous to please Mlle. Keroualle. Those small attentions which denote a great passion were lavished on her; and as she showed by her expressions

[1] Colbert to Louvois, Oct. 22, 1671.

of gratitude that she was not insensible to the kindness of a great king, we hope she will so behave that the attachment will be durable and exclude every other."

It may be, that the Countesses of Arlington and Sunderland, under the pretext of killing the tedium of October evenings in a country house, got up a burlesque wedding in which Louise de Keroualle was the bride and the king the bridegroom, with all the immodest ceremonies which marked, in the good old times, the retirement of the former into her nuptial chamber.

"The events of that night were the talk of the whole Court, and the subject of the pamphlets of the day." These pamphlets, in their sharp precision and directness, bear the stamp of truth. They give in broken English the coy exclamations of Louise, "Me no bad woman. If me taut me was one bad woman, me would cut mine own trote."[1] A guest of

[1] See EVELYN, Oct. 9, 1671; and *The Secret History of the Reigns of Charles II. and James II.* See also *The Blatant Beast.* The English puritans braved modesty when they wanted to defend decency against licence. Their descriptions of "the nights at Euston" are too strong for modern taste to bear. *The Royal Wanton,* and Andrew Marvel's

the Arlingtons, Evelyn, declares that he never saw at Euston a fête such as is described by the pamphleteers. But he adds, that he was only admitted twice to the king's table; and he states that Louise remained in her undress for a whole day, whilst every one was trying to amuse and pet her. At any rate, she had a son exactly nine months after the mock marriage at Euston,[1] and Louis XIV. on being informed of what took place there, ordered his ambassador to present his congratulations to Mlle. de Keroualle. " I have made that young lady joyful," replied Colbert de Croissy, "in assuring her of the pleasure with which his majesty learned of her brilliant conquest. There is every prospect that she will hold long what she has conquered."

The French ladies at Paris and Versailles viewed the intrigue in another light. Mme. de Sévigné wrote to her daughter,[2] " Don't you like to hear that little Keroualle, whose star was divined before she left, has followed

lampoons show how English feeling was in revolt against the French mistress of Charles.
[1] Colbert to Louvois, Nov. 2, 1671.
[2] March 30, 1672.

it faithfully. The King of England, on seeing her, straightway fell in love, and she did not frown at him when he declared his passion. The upshot is, that she is in an interesting state. Is it not all astonishing! Castlemaine is in disgrace. England, truly, is a droll country!"

Yet in that "droll country" Milton had, four years earlier, published his *Paradise Lost*, and Newton in that very year his *Theory of Light*.

Louis at once tried to turn Louise's situation to diplomatic account. Three advantages, he believed, might be derived from the favour she enjoyed: (1) an alliance against Holland; (2) a profession by Charles of the Catholic faith; (3) a match between the king's brother, the Duke of York, and a princess chosen by Louis.

The alliance was soon concluded. In the face of the interests, the prejudices, and the religious feelings of the English, Charles declared war against Holland in March, 1672, in the sixth month of Louise's pregnancy. On the 28th of April of the same year, Louis set out from St. Germain en Laye on his conquering tour in Flanders.

The profession by Charles of the Catholic

faith was not so easy to obtain. He began by objecting that the Pope was too old to bring to a happy conclusion a step of such importance,[1] and that the English Catholics were too weak in numbers, and had too few strong brains among them, to give him good support. Louise and his wife's confessor, Father Patrick, tried to screw his courage up,[2] because the Catholic religion could only be set up again, they argued, through a close union between the Most Christian King and Charles. Father Patrick kept Colbert de Croissy well informed about the king's objections, and everything else that he thought worth reporting. Charles and Arlington more than hinted that it would be gratifying to them were Louis to grant the diplomatic priest an abbey, with a salary of four or five thousand *livres*. This wish was strongly dwelt upon in despatches of Colbert de Croissy, who said that Father Patrick had so brought round Charles that he sent word to the Queen of Spain that he was determined to become a Catholic.[3]

[1] Colbert to Lionne, tome c., fol. 82.
[2] *Ibid.*, March 1, 1672.
[3] Colbert to Pomponne, March 14, 1672. The Queen

Charles's brother had no sort of hesitation to profess his religion. His wife had just died in the Catholic faith, and expressing all the sentiments which a recent conversion might be expected to prompt. His son followed her to the grave a few days later. The Duke of York asked the king's leave to remarry, taking a Catholic wife, and declaring openly his faith. All the belles of the court bedizened themselves in their precious stones and other finery, to make a conquest of the heir presumptive to the throne. The beauty and wealth of the widowed Duchess of Northumberland made her a redoubtable competitor. Lady Falmouth, another widow, was then spoken of.[1] "But," said Colbert, "I doubt whether this Prince's passion for her is so great as to lead him to marry her. He would rather take a French princess, to whom his majesty might give a dowry."[2]

of Spain, placed between her conscience and her political interest, coldly said: "*Me haveis alegrado mucho con la buena neuva de la piadosa intencion del rey vuestro amo. Yo ayudare cumplimiento de todas mis fuercas.*"

[1] Colbert to the King of France, April 13, 1671. Lady Falmouth received immense sums and secret subventions from Charles.   [2] Sept. 29, 1671.

"If the Duke of York," answered Louvois, "wants a wife who is almost certain to bear him children, he can't do better than take Madame de Guise,[1] who laid in thrice in two years, and whose birth, wealth, and hopes of fecundity should make up for her want of beauty."

The Duke of York, meanwhile, sought to console himself for the loss of his wife by giving up Arabella Churchill, and becoming intimate with Miss Sedley, who passed for being a prude.[2] Colbert was therefore puzzled to think how he could draw the Duke into wishing for a marriage between himself and Madame de Guise. He promised Lionne to neglect no opportunity to bring about a match

---

[1] Elizabeth d'Orléans, second daughter of Gaston, brother of Louis XIII., married in 1667 to Louis Joseph, sixth Duc de Guise, a widow in July, 1671; died in 1696. The desirability of a match between the Duke of York and la Grande Mademoiselle was never once discussed, although that Princess said she was asked to marry him.

[2] Miss Sedley had the gift of wit. On coming to the throne, James created her Countess of Dorchester, and when he was dethroned by his daughter Mary, Sir Charles Sedley, who voted for the Prince and Princess of Orange, said: "James made my daughter a Countess, and I now make his daughter a Queen."

with that lady, who, being the second daughter of Gaston, Duc d'Orléans, was a niece of Henrietta Maria, and a first cousin of the Duke of York. On the 23rd of January, 1673, he wrote, "I shall neglect no means to ensure success in this affair, and I hope to triumph over every difficulty through the queen's confessor and the new mistress."

CHAPTER IV.

THE RIVALS.

COLBERT DE CROISSY ignored none of the dangers which beset Louise de Keroualle, who was hated and attacked by such old favourites as the Duchesses of Cleveland and Richmond, and the fresher theatrical ones like Nell Gwynn. In his despatch of December 24th he wrote to Louvois: "The king is going to sup and dance at Lord Arlington's, and I am to be of the party. So also is the Duchess of Richmond. Her great talent is dancing. Mademoiselle de Keroualle may be taken in by all these parties, and all the more so because she does not keep her head sober, since she has got the notion into it that it is possible she may yet be Queen of England. She talks from morning till night of the Queen's ailments as if they were mortal."

The tongues of every one else, it must be owned, ran on the same topic, and each demanded the other when Catherine might be expected to die.

"M. Frazer, the king's physician, has obtained the king's leave to examine into the queen's malady, and has found it to be consumption, which will end her life in two or three months, or, at latest, in a year. I hear it said, that the king was resolved the moment God takes this princess to Himself, not to let a month pass without satisfying the prayers of his subjects. He would choose for his wife some young and beautiful person of high birth capable of bearing him children. The doctors all talk thus to ingratiate themselves with the king."[1]

Catherine, though reputed so feeble and diseased, had a long life before her. She died thirty-two years later. But the theologians came to the help of the doctors, when it was found the latter had excited false hopes. The death of the queen, they said, was not necessary for the king's happiness. He was, as Luther taught in a parallel case, free to take a second wife while the first was living.[2]

[1] Colbert to Louvois, Feb. 20, 1673.
[2] This was the opinion of Gilbert Barnet, the theologian

But as Charles had no fixity of aim, he was led by his pleasures from the idea of a second marriage. Without meaning to afflict the queen, or vex any of his mistresses, he was drawn into fresh amours. In eight months he gave Lady Falmouth seven thousand pounds, and the Duchess of Cleveland more than forty thousand.

The duchess held the king by her four children, of three of whom he thought himself the father. She hectored him into acknowledging himself the parent of the fourth, which she did not deny to be a son of Henry Jermyn, brother of the Queen Dowager's domestic tyrant, and husband, in fact if not in name. Henry himself stood in a similar relation to the Princess Dowager of Orange, born Princess Royal of England. The Duchess of Cleveland, notwithstanding her undisguised passion for him, remained virtual sovereign, not only at the court festivities, but in the queen's bedchamber. Louise de Keroualle was unable

and historian of William of Orange. His famous treatises: *Solution of two Cases of Conscience*, and *The other Devorce, and what Scripture allows in those Cases*, have not been reprinted in the collection of his works, but are to be found in John Mackey's *Court of Great Britain*.

to dislodge her from that position until her Grace had to retire to France to escape from her creditors. The two rivals were, therefore, at the time of Catherine's great illness, face to face. Barbara was a furious scold, and absorbed in amours which could not be termed secret, inasmuch as they were the town talk. Louise was tender, languishing, reticent, and devoted to French interests, or rather to her own interests, which were bound up in those of France. One impudently played the wanton with other men, and the other sold Charles. Barbara scolded, laughed, and swore; Louise pretended to love and languish. Of all the favourites, the only one the English liked was Nelly Gwynn, the gay, piquant orange-girl and actress. Sparks about the Court, and statesmen, took liberties with her, which she sometimes resented in a way that would, were it not for her feminine charm and good temper, have been thought too rough and ready. Colbert de Croissy informed Pomponne [1] that Buckingham, having one morning entered the reserved apartment of the king to talk with him about state affairs, found Nell there, she still having the good

[1] Colbert to Pomponne, Jan. 23, 1672.

fortune to please Charles. The duke pressed her hard to grant him the favours she accorded to his master; and as he rumpled her collar in trying to snatch kisses, she boxed his ears. At least so she said, and those who heard, believed her. Her adventures were the town talk, and amused rather than shocked the good folks of London. It is clear that she was an impudent jade, with irrepressible spirits and romping ways. But the English, under the merry monarch, liked boisterous gaiety and coarse fun. Clarendon's popularity was due to his jollity, frank bluntness, hilarious sensuality, and complete absence of pretension. He let himself be ruined by buffoons and mistresses, and had a joyous disposition of a purely English type, which prevented him taking any pleasure in French fashions and ceremonious festivity. Sympathy with high animal spirits was general at Whitehall in the time of Charles II. Even the poor queen herself was drawn into the torrent of jollification. She did not think it beneath her dignity to disguise herself as a country-woman to mingle in the popular sports at fairs and markets and around Maypoles. When a visitor of the Countess of Suffolk at

Audley End, she in such a disguise started off on a pillion behind old Sir Bernard Gascoigne.[1] The beautiful Frances Stuart, Duchess of Richmond, was in attendance, dressed as a farmer's wife, and also on a pillion behind Mr. Roper. In these travesties they went to the fair of Saffron Walden. The real country folks, taking them for play-actors, mobbed them so roughly that they had to get on horseback and gallop off. A band of well-mounted yeomen rode after them, giving them chase to Audley End, where the porters, when the fugitives dashed into the park, shut the gates in the faces of their pursuers.

Successful actresses, in the reign of Charles, lived in great luxury. Nell Gwynn's bed was adorned with ornaments in carved and *repoussé* silver.[2] She was, in the Royal favour, the suc-

---

[1] A Florentine gentleman, brought into England by Mary de Medici when Queen Dowager of France and mother-in-law of Charles I. Sir Bernard Gascoigne had served in the Royal army in the Civil War.

[2] See the documents that have been preserved at Malvern Wells, at Mr. Francis Hopkinson's. Nell made the Treasury pay for her boxes at the theatres to which she went as a spectator. She saw the "Tempest" four times at the cost of the country; and "Macbeth," "Hamlet,"

cessor of Mary, or Moll Davies, whom the king got Sir Francis Ratcliffe to marry, after she had given birth to a daughter, christened Mary Tudor, to point out that she was of the blood royal.[1] Moll was Welsh, like Nell; and so were the Tudors. In turn, Nell Gwynn was supplanted by a comic actress, named Knight. But she was never wholly abandoned by the king, whose last words were: "Don't let poor Nelly starve." She was popular to the end.

The most hated of all the favourites was Louise de Keroualle, who was thought sly and intriguing, and was regarded as the incarnation of the French king's policy, and the worst enemy of England. Court and people were of one mind about her; and it must be owned that popular instinct roughly, but truly, divined the part she was playing, and the danger there

---

and "Lear," once between September, 1674, and June, 1675. See also the *Commission on Historical Manuscripts*, vol. iii., p. 266; and Pennant's *Account of London*.

[1] This girl was, on growing up, provided with a dowry from the Exchequer, and given in marriage to the Earl of Derwentwater. Her son was the Catholic earl who was implicated in the Jacobite rising against George I., and executed, Feb. 24, 1716.

was, through her toils, of an arrest of the national evolution. It was into her ear, chiefly, that Charles poured his complaints of the rude and restive behaviour of his Parliaments. "The King of England," wrote Colbert de Croissy, on March 9, 1673, "hides his chagrin as well as he can. But I see that he has plenty of it; and, if I can believe Mademoiselle de Keroualle, he told her yesterday that there was no course open to him but to dissolve Parliament. Although such a step would be of the most vital importance to your Majesty's interests, I have not yet ventured to try and obtain from Arlington confirmation of what the new favourite told me."

Louise was very adroit and careful in feeling her way, and keeping within her depth. She abstained from urging anything which might lead to civil war. Seeing it would be fatal to her influence, and to her matrimonial hopes, to force Charles into making a profession of Roman Catholicism, she got the ambassador, Colbert, to inform Louis that, if the King of England once declared himself a Catholic, every one would forsake him. The part of the nation which alone had backbone and stubborn will, was anti-Popish. The Duke of York, by his rash zeal, had made a public reconciliation of his brother with the Church of Rome impossible. There was but a single course to follow. It was by slow degrees to habituate the English to a revival of Catholic ideas, rites, and ceremonies.

On the subject of the Duke of York's second marriage, Louise stood apart from the French embassy. She wanted that prince to marry a daughter of the Duke d'Elbœuf, and not the widow of the Duke de Guise, whom Louvois proposed.

The diplomacy of Louis XIV. had been, up to this juncture, under the direction of Lionne, a man of superior parts, and the greatest of Mazarin's disciples. He died prematurely at the end of 1671. Arnauld de Pomponne, his successor, was remarkable for his native rectitude, his good judgment, and the exquisite keenness of his perceptions. He weighed and did everything with maturity, and yet did not procrastinate needlessly. He was modest and moderate; of beautiful simplicity of life and manners; had a gentle address; and was, in conversation, instructive and of penetrating sweetness and courtesy. But he had not enough of weight or self-assertion to resist Louvois' overbearing temper, was not laborious, and preferred rather to let complex situations work out their own solutions, than to solve difficulties or grapple with them as they arose. Louvois enjoyed tugs of war; Pomponne shrank from them.

It was easy to see from the first that the Duke of York would stand out against a match between himself and Madame de Guise. An unfavourable account of her, given by Madame Henriette, his sister, who disliked her, had left such a strong impression on his mind that he would not listen to anything to her advantage. He said he did not want to be the husband of more than one wife, which was a good reason for insisting on beauty. Charles was at the trouble of explaining to the French ambassador, that his brother had two great weaknesses—one was touching religion, and the other touching marriage. The first had done him a deal of mischief, and he feared the other would have more baleful consequences. Since the death of the Duchess of York, he was agog for making a fool of himself a second time. To prevent him marrying for love alone, all the princesses and great ladies who passed for being devoted to French interests had been proposed, one by one, to him, because it was certain that, with his uxorious and narrowly virtuous disposition, he would be governed by his wife.

But Colbert de Croissy, goaded by Louvois, continued to thwart the Duke of York, who was bent on a love-match, in trying to force him to marry the Duchess de Guise. This was the more ill-judged, because the French court ran the risk of losing all power over him, and throwing him into the arms of some German princess. Louise de Keroualle saw the danger from the beginning, and started the idea of a match with another French lady. She herself insisted, in an interview with Colbert, on the folly of trying to impose a mature and by no means attractive widow on the Duke, who had set his heart upon a saintly life with a young beauty of virginal attractions.

"Mlle. de Keroualle," reported Colbert, in a despatch dated July 24, 1673, "has had the address to get the Princess of Wurtemburg excluded from the list of candidates for matrimony with the Duke of York. But she has shown such ardour in trying to obtain a preference for Mlle. d'Elbœuf, that nobody will now listen to the praises of Madame de Guise. Yesterday Mlle. de Keroualle took me aside in the queen's chamber, to whisper to me that the duke would have preferred Mlle. d'Elbœuf, even had I been colder in speaking of her. She begged me as a great favour not to let it transpire here that it would be disagreeable to your Majesty were that young lady chosen.

Thus, the maid of honour who filled an insignificant place in the household of the Duchess of Orleans, was now able to patronize the proud ladies of the house of Lorraine. The Duchess d'Elbœuf was a daughter of the Duke de Bouillon and sister of Turenne. In suffering Louise to be the patroness of her daughters, she made the world see what a great personage "la petite Keroualle" had become.

Henceforth, the Court of France would have to treat with deference the Breton favourite who took under her protection the Princesses of Lorraine.

The d'Elbœufs were poor. But Louise reckoned on their beauty, and had their portraits hung up in her room, to accustom the Duke of York to their charms. The only fault he found with them was their great youth.

Colbert was annoyed at this stratagem. He informed Arnauld de Pomponne that Mlle. de Keroualle had obtained from the Duchess d'Elbœuf portraits of her daughters, and had done her best to lure the Duke of York into proposing for one of them. She did this, he represented, both out of friendship for their mother, with whom she had kept up a regular correspondence, and to show what power she enjoyed.

M. Colbert de Croissy thought he had destroyed the web she was weaving round the heir presumptive; but he found he was mistaken. However, he hoped it was not too late to defeat her plan.

Colbert de Croissy thus drifted into enmity with Louise. He behaved towards her with his characteristic rudeness, and turned Arlington against her. Both threw in her face the stratagems to which they had stooped, in order to unite her and the king in an amorous *liaison.* " Arlington," de Pomponne was informed, "neither likes nor esteems Mlle. de Keroualle, and reproaches her with having as soon forgotten the obligations he conferred on her, as any of the good dinners she has eaten."

The French ambassador was defeated in this conflict. Louise, it is true, had to give up her *protégées*,[1] who became nuns of the Visitation, and to accept Mary Beatrice of Modena, whom James decided to marry. She next applied her skill to bringing to a happy issue an affair of great importance to herself.

At the end of 1672 Mlle. de Keroualle, through the French Embassy and de Pomponne,[2] petitioned the King of France for leave to become an English subject, and " so

[1] Louis the Fourteenth was formally against the Elbœuf match. "I have reasons," he said, "which would make such a marriage disagreeable to me, and I therefore hope you will adroitly apply yourself to cause hitches so that it will never take place" (the king to Colbert, April 12, 1673). The Duchess d'Elbœuf—*née* Elisabeth de la Tour —was married in 1656, and died in 1688. Françoise Marie, whom Louise de Keroualle wished to be married to the Duke of York, and Marie Eléonore, the two daughters of the duchess, became sisters of the Visitation.

[2] Colbert to Pomponne, Jan. 30, 1673.

benefit by the gifts and honours which King Charles wanted to lavish on her." Soon after, she received the titles of Baroness of Petersfield, Countess of Farnham, and Duchess of Pendennis, a title which—nobody knows why—was immediately changed to that of Duchess of Portsmouth. The promise was given that in a few days she was to be a lady of the bedchamber,[1] and thus rank as high as any of the older mistresses who were duchesses. Her elevation gave umbrage both to Court and town; and she and her strawberry leaves were made the subject of ribald lampoons. But much as she prized an English ducal coronet, she would have valued more a stool, or *tabouret*, of duchess in the presence-chamber at the Court of Versailles, where she had played such a humble part but a few years before.

The *tabouret* was the highest object of a Frenchwoman's ambition in the seventeenth century. Not until Marie d'Arquien, the wife of John Sobieski, had become Queen of Poland, did she cease from striving to obtain a *tabouret* at the Court of the Louvre. "To

[1] Colbert to Pomponne, Aug. 7, 1673.

think," cried her husband,[1] "how she longs for that miserable stool, on which nobody can sit at ease!" When she was queen, she kept soliciting the title of French duke for her father, and by her importunities forced Louis XIV. to say, through his ambassador at Warsaw,[2] that he regretted to be obliged to express his just repugnance to grant the Marquis d'Arquien a dignity which he had so little merited, and that he was astonished at the Queen of Poland continuing to ask it for him.

But if the King of Poland was not an important factor in the policy of Louis, the King of England was such a necessary ally that his favourite was to be regarded as having merited no matter what high dignity. The first step to the *tabouret* would be to obtain the ducal fief of Aubigny. The negotiations on this matter were soon got through.

In July, 1673, Charles spoke to Colbert of "his desire that Mlle. de Kerouaille should be granted the fief, not only for her life, but

[1] Letter of John Sobieski to his wife, May 11, 1668.
[2] The Bishop of Beauvais to the Marquis de Vitry, Dec. 10, 1680.

that she might be able to transmit it to her son.[1] He would take care that it should not pass from her posterity of Stuart blood. Colbert, who was in the thick of the struggle against the Elbœuf ladies, was astounded at this intimation, and exasperated at the impudence of Louise, in demanding a French Crown land. But he felt obliged to communicate what Charles said to him to De Pomponne, and did so in the following terms : " I own I find her on all occasions so ill-disposed for the service of the king, and showing such ill-humour against France (whether because she feels herself despised there, or whether from an effect of caprice), that I really think she deserves no favour of his Majesty. But as the King of England shows her much love, and so visibly likes to please her, his Majesty can judge whether it is best not to treat her according to her merits. An attention paid to her will be taken by the King of England as one paid to himself. I have, however, told him upon what conditions alone the fief could be granted, and what he asks is just the contrary."

[1] Colbert to Pomponne, July 17, 1673.

The estate of Aubigny-sur-Nièvre, in Berri, had been raised to a ducal fief in 1422, by Charles VII., in favour of John Stuart, who served under that king. It was to return to the Crown at the death of the last male heir, who was the Duke of Richmond, husband of the lovely Frances Stuart. This nobleman had just died. Were Aubigny given to the Duchess of Portsmouth, it would be detached afresh from the Crown domain, and go into the possession of her son, who was a year old, and not yet recognised by Charles. Arlington told Colbert that the king, whose fatherhood was multiple, shrank from owning he had another child,[1] and had remarked to the Attorney-General, when he was drawing up the patents of nobility for Louise and for her children, that the boy in existence could not inherit them. Nevertheless Colbert himself hit on a solution. He proposed a donation of Aubigny in favour of the Duchess of Portsmouth, with reversion to any natural child of the king, whom he should appoint to succeed her. In this way she would not become a French duchess, and would simply receive a ducal estate.

[1] Colbert to Pomponne, August 29, 1673.

Colbert's suggestion was in part adopted.[1] But while he was thus obliged to help a woman of whom he had become an enemy to rise in the world, he had to struggle against the influence which the French living in London had gained. He did not know how to make use of them; and as they got in his way, he and they soon became mutually disagreeable. At a time when England and France were combined against Holland, the military Frenchmen at the Court of Whitehall were thought more of than their diplomatic countrymen. Count d'Estrées, who commanded the French fleet, had won the hearts of English sailors. Charles went on board his flag-ship,[2] accompanied by Comte Canaples, to whom he had given a pension of 2000 crowns.

This Canaples had obtained leave to serve in the English army. He was a brother of Marshal de Créquy, and was always an ailing and imbecile courtier. At the age of seventy-

---

[1] The patent of grant is dated December, 1673, and is to be found in the archives *Des Affaires Etrangères, Angleterre*, tome cviii., fol. 234; the patent of erection into a duchy is dated January 1684. It is in the National Archives, reg. o, 1, 28, fol. 18.

[2] BUSSY RABUTIN : *Correspondence* t. ii., p. 257.

six, after he returned to live in France, he married a daughter of Marshal de Vivenne, and astonished all who knew him by his tardily recovered health. "Canaples, who," Madame de Sévigné wrote to her daughter, "had been cut, hacked, and carved up again by the doctors," survived his four brothers and died of old age.

Charles preferred to this valetudinarian a nephew of de Turenne, Louis Duras, whom he created Earl of Feversham, and made his boon companion. Feversham took such a part in his amusements that Colbert warned de Pomponne to keep well with him, because his help could not be dispensed with. His good fortune caused a run of French noblemen on the Court of Whitehall. It became the fashion in Paris to visit London. The Frenchmen of Buckingham's set were of as much importance in the eyes of Louis as of Charles. Since Parliament had grown sullen, Buckingham won popularity by forming a party in the House of Commons to defend the Anglican Church and the Protestant States of Europe. He was too clever to like his new position thus gained, and often went back to his French friends. Saint Evremond did Colbert a service in bringing round the Duke of Buckingham to him, and aided him with much wit and address in keeping them friends. The wit of Saint Evremond was kept bright by the gift of a snuff-box, with the portrait of the King of France on the lid, worth twenty-eight thousand *livres tournois*. To prevent Arlington feeling envious, another snuff-box, to which a diamond ring was added, was sent him.[1] Buckingham was revolving in his head a financial scheme of the greatest consequence, and, encouraged by Louis's bounty and amiable condescension, he had his project submitted to that monarch by the Marquis de Sessac.

The Marquis de Sessac had most of the faults of the Chevalier de Gramont, without his charming wit. He was, like him, rash, presumptuous, and meddling. After he was banished from the Court of France, he took refuge in London, where he attempted, as did Gramont, to make a fortune in gambling. De Sessac had large coffers, which were often suddenly filled with gold, and as frequently

[1] MIGNET: *Négociations de la Succession d'Espagne*, t. iv., p. 48.

emptied in a single night. The Duke of Buckingham struck up a friendship with him, and offered to sell himself and his party to the King of France for a respectable sum. The operation was to be effected unknown to the French embassy, Buckingham having still in him a little of that hypocrisy which is a tribute to virtue. But Colbert de Croissy could not be kept long in ignorance of this bargain, which he was unable to approve. "Votes are only," he wrote,[1] "to be obtained by parading hatred of France. Let us entertain no illusion on that score. It must not be imagined that with two hundred thousand crowns we can bring so great a body to follow a course which reason should alone dictate. As Monsieur de Sessac takes pleasure in big talk about himself, and in giving himself importance, one risks, in drawing close to his friend Buckingham, to offend Arlington."

De Sessac went secretly to Marshal de Bellfonds, at Versailles,[2] to announce to him that he was charged to submit to Louis an affair

---

[1] Colbert to King Louis, Nov. 27, 1673.
[2] In October, 1673. See instructions to De Ruvigny, *Aff. Etr. Angleterre*, tome cx., fol. 127.

of the highest importance for the State, but that he could only communicate it to the king. He refused to see De Pomponne, the Secretary on Foreign Affairs. At length a royal audience was granted him, and he handed Buckingham's letter to the king. The duke, in that paper, said he was ready for everything. But it was essential that he should gain some members of Parliament, and it would be necessary for the King of France to create a fund in London to provide for the expense of buying members of the House of Commons. The opposition of Parliament to the Court presented such dangers, that Louis judged well to enter into the relations with Buckingham, and sent to England, as secret negotiator, the Count de Ruvigny, whom he intended should a few weeks later supersede Colbert. The choice of De Ruvigny was a good one. He was a soldier, elderly, respected, and the recognised chief of the Reformed Church of France, Several marriages had united his family and that of the Russells, who were all-powerful with the English Protestants. His son[1] was

[1] After the revocation of the Edict of Nantes, he was naturalized English, and became Lord Galloway; and,

born in England. Ruvigny was of high birth, but of simple bearing, sagacious, honourable, honest, and singularly clever. He reconciled exceptional uprightness with the greatest shrewdness and fertility of resource and social tact.

Ruvigny was instructed to concert with Colbert and the Marquis de Sessac.[1] He was kept in the dark about the interviews the latter had with the King of France. One of the orders he was given was, to deceive Buckingham in making him believe that Charles knew nothing of his scheme. But Louis judged well, while Buckingham was to think that close secresy was being observed, to inform that monarch of what had been negotiated through De Sessac. The knavery to which Louis resorted was so multiple and shameful, that Ruvigny was to read over and over his instructions, and to make a *précis* of them, to show he understood them, but to be allowed no copy. Louis "thought it too dangerous to let them be taken away to England in writing. His

in the War of the Spanish Succession, commanded the English army which was sent to operate in Portugal.

[1] Tome cx., fol. 127, Nov. 4, 1673.

Majesty wished them only to be well-impressed on Ruvigny's mind, which could be done by reading them many times attentively."

Thus, in the winter which separated the two great campaigns of 1673 and 1674, Louis sought to buy the King of England and the Parliament; the king by the subventions of the secret treaty, and the gift of the estate of Aubigny to the Duchess of Portsmouth; and the Parliament through Buckingham. Ruvigny said of it, that it was "a filthy traffic."[1]

All Europe had turned against France in 1673, even to the Prussians of Brandenburg, who had backed out of an alliance with the Dutch the moment they were attacked.[2] Spain overcame her horror of Protestantism in siding with Holland. Far up in the North, Louis had taken Maestricht,[3] and he was silently preparing to seize on the Franche Comté and the Palatinate. His frontiers were being widened, and his armies increased. Suddenly, at this decisive

[1] Ruvigny expressed, in a letter to King Louis, dated Nov. 27, 1673, disgust at being an agent in such dirty affairs, and seemed to doubt of their eventual success because of their immorality.

[2] See Rousset's *Histoire de Louvois*, t. ii., p. 5.

[3] June 29, 1673.

crisis in his affairs, he felt England beginning to slip from his hands.

The alarm was given by Comte d'Estrades, who wrote from London with a clearness of insight that was truly marvellous:[1] "The English do not think themselves bound by treaties. If they are once leagued with Spain, the Empire, and Holland, nobody of our generation will see the end of this war."

Up to this period of the reign of Charles, the national passions of England had been spending themselves against Roman Catholicism; the Lord Treasurer Clifford and the Duke of York had to resign their offices. When nothing more could be done against the Roman Catholics, the whole tide of hatred flowed against France.

On the day[2] on which Ruvigny succeeded Colbert as ambassador, Charles was paid his bribe of eight millions of *livres*,[3] and he let the regiments which this money was to keep up be disbanded. Buckingham, who wanted to

---

[1] See Rousset's *Histoire de Louvois*, t. ii., p. 278.
[2] Jan. 11, 1674.
[3] MIGNET: *Négociations relatives à la Succession d'Espagne*, t. vi., p. 254.

sell his sovereign at a high price, was, of all the political men of the day, the hardest used by Parliament. Lady Shrewsbury, his Roman Catholic or "Popish" mistress, was thrown in his face; and his Canaanitish vices, his debts, and his dishonesty were all the subject of acrimonious attacks. He bent beneath the blast; and, with the suppleness of a man who has more wit than stoutness of heart or firmness of character, veered round and changed his way of living. He broke with the faithful Countess of Shrewsbury, who retired to a convent at Dunkirk,[1] made up his quarrel with his wife, and adopted the Biblical phraseology and nasal twang of the Puritans. The Protestant De Ruvigny reported the sudden conversion,[2] which was shown in regular attendance at the services of the Episcopal Church with his wife, in his methodic attention to his expenses, in the

[1] Ruvigny to Pomponne, Jan. 29, 1674. Her son, Charles Talbot, Earl of Shrewsbury, became, on the contrary, the idol of the people, because of his manly beauty and Anglican fanaticism. He was created a duke by William III., and led the *coup d'Etat*, when Queen Anne was dying, which secured the throne to the House of Hanover.

[2] *Idem*, Sept. 10, 1674.

payment of debts, and in the order established in his household, all of which made him popular.[1] Charles followed Buckingham in yielding to popular pressure, and concluded a peace with Holland. But he did not yet break with France, and even left King Louis the English regiments which were in his pay, abroad. Still, the situation was most critical. The best agent of the French policy in England, Louise de Keroualle, had been in a single day reduced to impotency.

[1] Ruvigny to Pomponne, Feb. 16, 1674

CHAPTER V.

THE DUCHESS OF PORTSMOUTH'S FIRST CHECK.

In the spring of 1674, just when another French campaign was begun, and a few weeks before the battle of Seneffe, Charles got tired of his French shackles. The cause was well known to his Court; and the austere De Ruvigny said what it was in plain terms. Plain, graphic words were not held vulgar at the Court of Versailles. Madame de Sévigné and the Marshal de Richelieu never muffled up disagreeable things in weak or vague expressions, and were as free from prudish niceness as Molière or Voltaire. It was permissible in good society in the 17th century to quote texually what the Protestant Ruvigny wrote to the Jansenist de Pomponne, in a letter which was to be read by Louis the Fourteenth, whose Court was the most polished and literary in Europe.

"I have a thing to tell you,[1] Monsieur, for the king's information, which should remain secret as long as it pleases his majesty to keep it so, because if it gets out it might be a source of unseemly raillery. Whilst the king[2] was winning provinces, the King of England was catching a malady which he has been at the trouble of communicating to the Duchess of Portsmouth. That prince is nearly cured; but to all appearance the lady will not so soon be rid of the virus. She has been, however, in a degree consoled for such a troublesome present by one more suitable to her charms — a pearl necklace, worth four thousand jacobus, and a diamond worth six thousand, which have so rejoiced her that I should not wonder if, for the price, she were not willing to risk another attack of the disease."

The presents, which came from Louis, must have been useful at a moment when the clerks of the Exchequer refused to pay the favourites' bills.[3] But the forced separation from the

[1] May 14, 1674, fol. 201.
[2] Ruvigny invariably spoke of Louis as "the King," and of Charles as "the King of England."
[3] In a letter of Sir H. Stubbs to Lord Kent, dated Sept. 28, 1673, and preserved in Lord Shaftesbury's library at

king, which the prolonged bad health of the Duchess of Portsmouth occasioned, aroused competition, and spurred on all the rivals to abuse, and try to supersede her. The doctors said she ought to go to Tunbridge[1] for the waters. She hired a house there, but on her arrival found the Marchioness of Worcester settled in it for the season. The Duchess reminded the intruder that the law was against her, and what duty she owed to a lady who was a degree above her in the peerage. Thereupon the Marchioness replied, that the titles women earned by prostitution, had no effect upon persons of quality and sense. She derided the Duchess about her former gallantries with De Sault, and Hamilton. To compensate Louise for this public humiliation, Charles sent a detachment of the Household Guards to escort her in pomp to Windsor, where he placed her under the treatment of his physician Crimp.

Long after a cure was effected, she was

St. Giles, he says: "Neither Madam Kerwell's, nor the Duchess of Cleveland's, nor Nell Gwynn's warrants will be accepted."

[1] Diplomatic note of August 16, 1674, vol. cxiv., fol. 119.

ashamed of the accident, and for years after was in the habit of gently reminding the guilty Charles of the injury and disgrace he had inflicted on her. She made him blush for himself before the different confidential agents whom Louis afterwards sent to England. One of Ruvigny's successors describes a scene in which she raked up the scandal to confound Charles: "I tell you privately, and in the hope that it will not travel further, how three days ago the Duchess of Portsmouth in my presence attacked the king about his infidelities. She did not hide from me what she had suffered two years ago from his misconduct with trulls; and he himself then described to me how his head doctor had prescribed for her."[1]

The Duchess of Portsmouth found some consolation in the arrival of her sister, whom she turned into a means of securing herself English allies. Henriette de Keroualle arrived in London in May, 1674. Ruvigny reported to his Court that she was a young girl of not more than ordinary attractions;[2] that she crossed the sea alone with the gentle-

[1] Courtin to Louvois, Dec. 27, 1674.
[2] Ruvigny to Pomponne, May 12, 1674.

man who was sent in a yacht to fetch her from Brest, and that on landing she was given a pension of six hundred pounds sterling a year. She was not long in finding a noble husband, the Earl of Pembroke, who was, Ruvigny also reported to the Court of Versailles, more ill, and from the same disease, than Charles had been, but who thought himself cured.[1] The king, besides the pension, gave the bride a marriage portion.

Louis did not abandon Louise. She had the address to be reserved in asking him for favours, and went on feeling her way.

Her main desire was, to obtain the *tabouret*, to which the ducal fief of Aubigny would give her a right. But she contrived, with the finest art, to put on Ruvigny to prepare the way for future claims on the generosity of Louis.[2] "I write," he said, "to your Majesty at the prayer of the Duchess of Portsmouth, who is uneasy about a blunder of the Marquis de

[1] Letter, dated Westminster, Dec. 19, 1674, in the possession of Mr. T. Stamford Raffles, 13, Abercromby Street, Liverpool: "Her sister was on Thursday married to the Earl of Pembroke, he being pretty well recovered from his * * *. The king pays the wedding portion."

[2] Ruvigny to Pomponne, March 15, 1674.

Dangeau,[1] which places her in a wrong light. She had besought him, Sire, to convey to you how much she takes to heart the interests of your service; with what zeal she looks after them, and what a passionate desire she has to earn your Majesty's confidence. But instead of that she has been informed by the marquis himself that he merely solicited for her the promise of a *tabouret*, when she would go back to France. She tells me that there is so little chance of this, that she has ceased to hope for it; but that, being in a position still to serve your Majesty, what she would most wish would be to persuade you of the heartfelt passion with which she is moved to accomplish your behests. I pressed her to write herself to express these sentiments, but she answered that she could not dare to do so, because of the profound respect that she entertained for her sovereign and master."[2]

When she thought the time was ripe for making her demand, she still appeared held back by modesty, and always preferred speak-

[1] Dangeau had come to London to fight a duel with Lord Peterborough.
[2] Ruvigny to Pomponne, Oct. 24, 1675.

ing through Charles or the ambassador. Fifteen months after she had expressed through the latter her passionate zeal for the French King's service, the King of England[1] said to Ruvigny that it would give him much satisfaction if Louis would be pleased to bestow the first abbey vacant on an aunt of the Duchess of Portsmouth, Dame Suzanne de Plœuc de Timeur, a professed nun in the Abbey of Lajois at Hennebon, in the Bishopric of Vannes. In conveying this begging message, the ambassador thought it would be politic to accede to it at once, and with a good grace.

In the same despatch,[2] he said that, at the request of the Duchess of Portsmouth, the King of England charged him to recommend to the king her relative, M. Calloët, for the post of Syndic of the States of Brittany. Louis, who did not like this meddling in affairs of his internal administration, inflicted a reproof in making no allusion to M. de Calloët in any of his despatches, but sent by return of post, and silently, a pair of pendant diamond earrings to the favourite. She received them with a show

---

[1] Ruvigny to Pomponne, Jan 21, 1674.
[2] *Idem*, Oct. 24, 1675.

of the deepest respect and gratitude, and renewed her assurances of zeal for her master's interests.

Sometimes her diplomatic tact failed her, and she brought ridicule upon herself by parading her love for France. To make believe that she was a near relative of the De Rohans,[1] she went into deep mourning when the Chevalier de Rohan died. This exposed her to the gibes of Nelly Gwynn. Nell's fun was not the most delicate; and, judging from some of the few witticisms of hers which have come down to us, one wonders how a prince of refined taste could have relished them.[2] One day Charles, at her house, complained of want of money. On hearing him, Nell offered, with a loud laugh, to get it by treating the Parliament to

---

[1] Letter in the Stamford Raffles collection, dated Dec. 19, 1674: "She is in deep mourning for the Chevalier de Rohan, as being forsoothe of kin to that family."

[2] The French hold punning and playing upon words in contempt, and also any sort of witticism that is rudely personal. Nell's *mot* showed cleverness and an intelligent perception of the state of parties. She meant, that, to please Parliament, the king should sacrifice his French miss (the ragout), Lauderdale (the Scotch collops), and Sunderland, whose face resembled a calf's, and who was said to be in the ideas of the late king. (*Translator's Note.*)

a French ragout, Scotch collops, and a calf's head. By which she meant that he was to throw over the Duchess of Portsmouth, Lauderdale, Sunderland, and every one who wished him to revive the policy of the late king his father, the anniversary of whose execution was called by the Puritans "Calves' Head day." Charles laughed, and was well pleased at the joke, and thought it a shrewd one. He was used to her Covent Garden mode of speech; and she was not a woman to watch her words to please him.

The Court of Versailles watched with amusement the French harlot's progress at Whitehall. Madame de Sévigné records some of the echoes of what was said there about her. "Keroualle," she wrote,[1] "saw well her way, and has made everything she wished for come to pass. She wanted to be the mistress of the King of England; and behold, he now shares her couch before the eyes of the whole Court. She wanted to be rich; and she is heaping up treasures, and making herself feared and courted. But she did not foresee that a low actress was to cross her path, and to bewitch

[1] Sept. 11, 1675; t. iv., p. 128.

the king. She is powerless to detach him from this comedian. He divides his money, his time, and his health between the pair. The low actress is as proud as the Duchess of Portsmouth, whom she jeers at, mimics, and makes game of. She braves her to her face, and often takes the king away from her, and boasts that she is the best loved of the two. She is young, of madcap gaiety, bold, brazen, debauched, and ready witted. She sings, dances, and frankly makes love her business. Since Keroualle has become a favourite, Gwynn insists upon the king owning her son as his.[1] This is how she argues: 'That hoity-toity French duchess sets up to be of grand quality. Every one of rank in France is her cousin. The moment some grand lord or lady over there dies, she orders a suit of deep mourning. Well, if she's of such high station, why is she such a jade? She ought to be ashamed of herself! If I were reared to be a lady, I am sure I should blush for *myself*. But it's my trade to be a doxy, and I was never anything

---

[1] Charles Beauclerc, the son of Nelly, was born before the arrival of Louise. He was recognised by Charles, and created Duke of St Albans.

else. The king keeps me; ever since he has done so, I have been true to him. He has had a son by me, and I'm going to make him own the brat, for he is as fond of me as of his French miss.' This creature holds her own in an extraordinary manner, and embarrasses and disconcerts the new-fledged duchess."

The degrading subjection in which Charles was to the actress was a just judgment on him for the humiliations which he inflicted on the queen. Poor Catherine of Portugal had but one consolation, her card-table. The game of basset was her only amusement.[1] In the evening she never left her circle, if the king did not offer her his hand to lead her to her chamber.[2] She was often ailing, and was subject to nervous headaches, so severe as to puzzle the doctors,[3] who so often purged her, that the cure was more perilous than the disease.

The hierarchy in the king's seraglio was

[1] The Duke of York to the Countess of Lichfield, in a letter in the possession of Viscount Dillon at Dytchley.

[2] Ruvigny to King Louis, August 30, 1674. The accounts of the queen, kept from 1679 to 1703 by Sir R. Be'lings, are in the possession of Lord Arundel at Wardour Castle.

[3] Ruvigny to Pomponne, March 28, 1675.

manifested when the children came to be provided for.

The title of Duke of Richmond was rendered vacant by the death, in 1672, of the beautiful Miss Stuart's husband. The Duchess of Portsmouth, who had obtained the fief of Aubigny, asked it for her son Charles. But she was opposed by the Duchess of Cleveland, who wanted the title of Duke of Grafton for her eldest son, and insisted that he should have the precedence of the brat of a French hussy, and that her other son should stand next his brother in the peerage. Charles, who still feared the termagant tongue and temper of her grace of Cleveland, tried to turn the difficulty by making the two sets of bastards dukes simultaneously. But precedence depended on the patent that was first signed. The Duchess of Portsmouth, who was more sly and clever than her rivals, got the Lord Treasurer to receive her attorney at midnight, just as he was stepping into his coach to go to Bath, and affix the seal to the patents of the Duke of Richmond. Next morning the lawyer of the Duchess of Cleveland waited on him, but was told that his lordship had gone to take the waters at Bath. As to the son of Nelly, he was just then only given a pension of four thousand pounds sterling a year. The Duchy of St. Albans was granted later.

Charles, the new Duke of Richmond,[1] was given a Scotchwoman of high quality, the Countess Mareschal, for his governess. She was accorded a salary of two hundred a year. Her youthful pupil was the root of the existing ducal family of Richmond. Besides the grants to their sons, the two duchesses were each given annual pensions of £10,000, reversible to their heirs; that of the Duchess of Portsmouth was to be paid out of the wine licences; Cleveland preferred, as the more secure from

[1] Charles (1672–1723) was a low rake, and slid, with a facility which showed him to be his father's son, from Protestantism to Catholicism and back. He shifted with equal facility his allegiance from Louis Fourteenth and James Second to William Third. He was the first duke of the actual stock of Richmond, and father of Charles, the second Duke (1701–50), whose son Charles (1735–1806) was one of the leading members of the Whig cabinets of the reign of George Third, and uncle of that Charles (1764–1819) who died of a mad dog's bite in Canada. It will thus be seen that the present Duke of Richmond is by no means a remote descendant of "the French hussy" who sold Charles II., her lover, to Louis XIV. (*Translator's Note.*)

parliamentary meddling, a lien on the excise. Both mistresses, having noted a diminution of vitality in Charles, only thought of fleecing the exchequer and investing their hoards in France, where they would be outside the range of English popular tempests. But the Duchess of Portsmouth, who was fond of gambling, lost heavily at the queen's card table, and spent large sums in luxurious furniture. The luxury of her rooms at Whitehall excited general envy at Court; and they were visited by crowds of people, who wanted to feast their eyes on the massy plate, tapestries, and objects of *vertu* they contained.

Louise wished her sister to live also in sumptuous style, and teased the Earl of Pembroke to give her, when she lay in, a present suitable to his wife's high rank. But he resented the interference, and threatened to rid himself of the countess by sending her packing to Whitehall, to Louise's lodgings. All the titles, grants, and luxury did not efface the stigmas that were on the Keroualle sisters. The foul name which Madame de Sévigné called the Duchess of Portsmouth in French, had an equivalent in every English mouth.

When the Count and Countess de Keroualle visited London to see their daughters, they did not stay with either of them, but at Sir Richard Browne's, whom they had known in France as an *émigré* when Cromwell was at Whitehall. Count de Keroualle made a good impression. He had a military air and Breton frankness. His wife still preserved remains of great beauty, and showed a lively mind. They were said never to have derived any profit from the situation of Louise.

When they were in London, another stranger arrived there, whose advent was a cause of sore anxiety to the Duchess of Portsmouth. She felt that a struggle for power was imminent, from the moment when the news was brought to town, that the greatest beauty in Europe, the splendid Duchess Mazarin,—

> "Mazarin, des amours
> Déesse tutélaire," [1]

as La Fontaine qualified her,—had landed at Torbay. This lady soon after made her advent in London, furious against the Court of Versailles, and decked out to conquer.

[1] LA FONTAINE: *Le Renard anglais.*

Ruvigny was not less uneasy than Louise de Keroualle, and sent agents to find out whether the charms for which the new comer was famous, were well preserved. A valet of de Gramont had witnessed her arrival.[1] She had embarked in Holland, and was driven by stress of weather down the Channel to Torbay, whence she rode up to town attired as a gentleman of fashion. She had with her, also on horseback, two women, five men-servants, and a little blackamoor who ate at her table. Arlington and Montagu, who both hated the Duchess of Portsmouth, concerted how to use to her destruction, the powers of the Duchess Mazarin to fascinate and seduce.

[1] Ruvigny to Pomponne, Jan. 2, 1676.

CHAPTER VI.

THE DUCHESS MAZARIN.

THE year 1675 closed a great historical era. The captains and statesmen who in the preceding years had played the chief parts: Condé, Turenne, and Montecuculli; and Lionne, Jean de Witt, and Arlington, were dead, or had retired. Louis XIV. suffered a Congress to meet at Nimeguen[1] and brought within his orbit the new minister of Charles, the Earl of Danby.

Thomas Osborne, Earl of Danby, was, according to Ruvigny's estimate, more afraid of Charles than of Charles's master. But he was so well ensnared in the toils of the Duchess of Portsmouth, and so carefully compromised by Charles,[2] in the secret negotiations with Ver-

---

[1] The members of the Congress were named; but the Congress itself did not meet until the middle of 1676.

[2] MIGNET: *Négociations relatives à la Succession d'Espagne*, tome iv. pp. 354–399.

sailles,[1] that, owing to his struggle against the House of Commons, he found himself, against his will, acting with the French party. Ruvigny spoke incessantly to his Government of the Commons as "the great obstacle;" and he repeated this every time he found the king, Louise, and Danby together. Charles was at length, on the 16th of February, 1676, enabled by a French subsidy of two millions and a half of *livres tournois*, to prorogue for fifteen months. He had thus, as he thought, made sure of a period of quietness, when the Duchess Mazarin arrived, and he was again plunged by her advent into all kinds of embarrassments.

Hortense Mancini, then thirty years old, had, at the time Charles was a refugee in France, captivated him by her beauty. "The destiny" which, she said, "has rendered me the most unhappy of my sex, began by dangling a crown before my eyes.[2] It was notorious that the

---

[1] Ruvigny to Pomponne, August 1, 1675.

[2] It has never been well established whether *Les Mémoires de la Duchesse Mazarin* were by her or St. Real, and in any case they should be mistrusted. But what they say about Charles II.'s attachment when he was in exile, and the offer of marriage that he made to her uncle for her, is confirmed

King of England passionately loved me, and wanted me to be his wife." Her precocious charms inspired the poets who furnished themes for ballets; and when, in 1661, she made her appearance at Fontainebleau in the ballet of the Seasons as a Muse, one of them wrote:—

> "Nulle Muse jamais
> N'eut l'esprit et le sein formés de si bonne heure."

She was given in marriage to the son of Marshal de Meilleraye, who received from the Cardinal the title of Duc Mazarin[1] and a dowry of twenty-eight millions of francs. The fancies and the manias of her husband amused the Court of France for nearly sixty years. He was a man of the brightest wit, was well read, and good company. His manners were gracious, affable, and polite. But excess of religious

by Madame de Motteville, Mlle. de Montpensier, *La Relation du Fonds Colbert*, No. 4782 by Riordan de Muscry.

[1] The nobiliary prefix *de* was not in the ducal patent made out for the husband of Hortense Manchini. When a clerk of the patent office wrote "M. le Duc de Mazarin,' Cardinal Mazarin ran his pen through it. He said, that the *de* would imply a fief of Mazarin, and that he (the Cardinal) in whose honour the ducal standing was granted by the king to M. de Meilleraye, was originally but a mean varlet who had not a patch of ground anywhere, and whose parents owed their graves to their commune.

devotion spoiled his natural gifts; and he became the prey of monks, bigots, and hypocrites, who profited by his weakness to draw upon his millions. He mutilated the finest statues, and bedaubed the rarest pictures, forbade the women and wenches on his estates to milk cows —an employment which he feared might suggest bad thoughts.

The Duc Mazarin wanted to pull out the front teeth of his daughters, who inherited their mother's gift of beauty, to prevent coquettish feeling arising in them. In his letters he only spoke of monks and missionaries[1] who were pouring out spiritual blessings; of designs for church ornaments,[2] of frequently-recurring interventions of Providence in his own personal affairs, and of small miracles. From conscientious scruples, he threw up governorships of provinces and the post of Grand Commander of Artillery. His extravagant actions were innumerable. Though of the brightest intellect, he was a mono-maniac; and his peculiar

---

[1] The Duc Mazarin was probably the original of Orgon in *Tartuffe*. The kind of piety into which he threw himself is ridiculed in that masterpiece of wit, good sense, and satire. (*Translator's Note*.)

[2] See *Mémoires de Mlle. de Montpensier*, tome iv., p. 69.

madness was his wife's best justification. In
the full bloom of matronly loveliness, and
surrounded with young children of whom she
was justly proud, he, for her soul's health,
immured her in a kind of aristocratic Mag-
dalens' Asylum, the convent of Les Filles
de Sainte Marie, in the Rue Saint-Antoine.
The young Duchess became, in her conventual gaol, the friend of another court lady,
the Marquise de Courcelles, who was also
there as an enforced penitent. They both
quarrelled with the nuns for refusing them
water to wash their feet. In their remon-
strance they put forward that they were not
in the nunnery to observe its rules. Both
escaped. The Duchess and her maid Nanon
went to Italy, dressed as men, and escorted
by the Chevalier de Rohan and a gentleman
named Courbeville. The latter so completely
and openly governed her as to scandalize
Italians of her rank. She returned to France,
where her husband succeeded in getting
her confined in the Abbey of Lys, near
Melun. But the king, whose playmate she
was in girlhood, sent a constable with eight
dragoons, to force the convent door and set

the Duchess at liberty.[1] She re-entered Paris triumphantly in the coach of the Treasurer Colbert, and then retired to Provence. The Duchess Mazarin[2] was one of those Roman beauties in whom there is no doll-prettiness, and in whom unaided nature triumphs over all the arts of the coquette. Painters could not say what was the colour of her eyes. They were neither blue, nor grey, nor yet black, nor brown, nor hazel. Nor were they languishing or passionate, as if either demanding to be loved or expressing love. They simply looked as if she had ever basked in love's sunshine. If her mouth was not large, it was not a small one, and was visibly the fit organ for intelligent speech and amiable words. All her motions were charming, in their easy grace and dignity. Her complexion was softly toned, and yet warm and fresh. It was so harmonious, that, though dark, she seemed of beautiful fairness. Her jet-black hair rose in strong waves above her forehead, as if proud to clothe and adorn her splendid head. She never used scents.

[1] DE SÉVIGNÉ, du 12 Août, 1689.—SAINT REAL: *Mémoires*, tome vi., p. 94. DE SÉVIGNÉ, du 6 Février, 1671.

[2] SAINT RÉAL, tome v., p. 79.

At Aix in Provence, the Duchess joined her sister, the Connétable de Colonna, who was of as dazzling beauty as herself. Madame de Grignan met them there, and described them to her mother as divine, and looking like fine pictures. All the ladies were furiously jealous of them, and called them mad-caps, who ought to be locked up, to keep them out of mischief. Madame Scudéry was for whipping them; and the Countess de Soissons and Duchess de Bouillon wanted them to be placed in a lunatic asylum.[1] The town talk at Aix was, that they had come there disguised as men because they

---

[1] These two ladies were the sisters of the runaway Duchess and Connétable. Cardinal Mazarin had five nieces, the daughters of his sister Mancini. They were Laura, Duchess of Mercour; Olympia, Countess of Soissons; Maria, Connétable de Colonna; Hortense, Duchess Mazarin; and Mariana, Duchess de Bouillon. Louis XIV. was successively enamoured of Olympia and Maria, to the latter of whom he promised marriage, and who was passionately attached to him. In obedience to the commands of his mother, and for state reasons pressed upon him by Cardinal Mazarin, he married his first cousin, the Infanta Maria Theresa, in right of whom he claimed Flanders. The Mancini sisters were said to be equally beautiful; they had all a noble style of beauty, and yet they did not resemble each other.

had made an assignation with the Chevalier de Lorraine and the Comte de Marsan.

Be this as it may, their giddy behaviour soon turned the aristocracy of Aix against them, and they had to quit the town suddenly to escape reclusion in a convent. The Duchess Mazarin got away to Savoy, where she spent three years with César Vicard, a gallant who passed himself off as the Abbé de St. Réal, although he was not tonsured, and had no benefice. He was a young man of sparkling conversation, was violently in love with the Duchess, and was of such utter and refined depravity of habits, that Louvois, who was a connoisseur in such things, was horror-stricken when he read his letters, which had been seized and brought to him. They had the effervescence of hot animal spirits, and showed their author to be steeped in the infamous vices which then prevailed in Italy.[1]

The Duchess Mazarin was followed to England by the so-called Abbé. She went to London in the secret hope of reviving the old flame which Charles II. had entertained for

---

[1] Louvois to Courtin, Jan. 3, 1677 ; *Affaires Etrangères, Angleterre*, tome cxxiii.

her. Of the fourteen years which had rolled over her since her marriage, she had spent seven with her husband and her four children. The rest of the time had been passed in convents, on highways, dressed as a man, and in the small courts of Italy, whose lazy tranquillity she disturbed by her adventures. She picked up new vices there, but remained youthful-looking and fresh. Ruvigny, annoyed at the wonderful preservation of her charms, wrote, "She is to all appearance a finely-developed young girl. I never saw any one who so well defies the power of time and vice to disfigure. At the age of fifty she will have the satisfaction of thinking, when she looks at her mirror, that she is as lovely as she ever was in her life."

She was received in London as a triumphant goddess. The Duke of York gave in her honour a rout, at which, through Sunderland, the king presented her his compliments. Every one at Court looked forward to a considerable change there. A lady of her fame and loveliness was sure to carry all before her, and to do something extraordinary. De Gramont, who from the first set up to be her social pilot, was enraptured with her. He had not seen her since she was a bride, and found her altered, but he thought for the better; and told the French ambassador that all the mistresses were eclipsed by her. She entered the Court as Armida entered the camp of Godfrey.[1] Every tongue ran upon her. The men spoke of her to express admiration, and the women to exhale their jealous uneasiness.

Nell Gwynn celebrated the triumph of the Duchess by going into the deepest mourning[2] —for, she said, the eclipsed Duchess of Portsmouth and her dead hopes. The Duchess of Cleveland retired to the country. All the English rivals played into the hands of the new-comer, to get rid the sooner of Keroualle, whose art and diplomacy theretofore had defeated their attacks. They accepted Mazarin as their avenging champion She was at least above-board, and every one knew where to have her. Waller's poem of "The Three Duchesses" is a satire on this struggle.

Ruvigny[3] next warned Pomponne that the Duchess of Cleveland had taken it into her

---

[1] Ruvigny to Pomponne, Jan. 20, 1676.
[2] Ruvigny to King Louis, July 2, 1676.
[3] Ruvigny to Pomponne, Feb. 3, 1676.

head to visit France, with the two young dukes her sons; and he proposed that she should be exempted from custom-house duties of every sort at Calais. She was taking many horses and two carriages. The customs franchise was granted, but in terms which offended the irascible Duchess, who showed the official passport to Charles, and ordered him to complain [1] because she and her sons (who were of the "royal blood") were not styled "cousins" of Louis. He not obeying, she tore up the document, and said she preferred paying any amount of duty, sooner than put up with a snub. She embarked with Gramont.[2] But the French ambassador had taken care to warn the custom-house officers to ask no money and overwhelm her with their civilities, for that such was the king's good pleasure.

The Duchess of Portsmouth stood in need of French support, and was quick to ask it. She was ill and faded. Another pregnancy ended in a premature birth.[3] Jealousy so gnawed her that she was sadly altered, Ru-

[1] Ruvigny to Pomponne, March 19, 1676.
[2] *Ibid.*
[3] Courtin to King Louis, June 8, 1676.

vigny confessed. He remarked, that at the yearly visit of the Court to Newmarket, no lodging was accorded to her by the king, and that she had to hire a house herself in a neighbouring village. This prevented Charles from seeing her as often as she wished. Her money affairs were in disorder, her steward having robbed her of twelve thousand pounds and pawned her jewels, which she had entrusted to him, for an equally large sum.

The pecuniary troubles of the Duchess Mazarin were still greater. This rival was forced, in opening her campaign, to hang out the flag of distress. Charles, whom her loveliness overcame, was melted by the tale of the straits to which she was reduced. With his own hand, he wrote to Louis, asking him to force M. Mazarin to make his wife a suitable allowance; and he charged Ruvigny to say that he would be deeply sensible to this favour, without which it would be impossible for the lady to live.[1] Indeed, he made the affair a personal one, and protested that he could not

[1] Ruvigny to Pomponne, April 16, 1676; and Ruvigny to King Louis, Jan. 30, 1676.

say how deeply obliged he would be were it promptly arranged. Louis was averse always to meddle in family matters, and as he respected the Duc Mazarin, he did not think he could equitably force him to put his wife in a position in which she could more publicly dishonour him at the Court of England. He, himself, wrote to the Duchess to explain why he did not accede to the wish of Charles.[1] Ruvigny handed her the letter, and bore testimony to the great displeasure she showed on reading it, at finding herself abandoned in a Court where money was so necessary. Charles, meanwhile, had given her secretly an order on the keeper of his privy purse for a thousand gold jacobus. A second attack[2] against the husband of the fair fugitive was prepared. Ruvigny thought it "dangerous to vex a woman whose star was in the ascendant, whose importance was fast rising." Every one helped her in the campaign on which she at once entered against the Duchess of Portsmouth. The young Princess of Modena, whom the Duke of York had lately married, was

[1] Ruvigny to Pomponne, Feb. 27, 1676.
[2] *Ibid.*, March 5, 1679.

among the first to side with Hortense Mancini, whom she kept whole days beside her bed, to which the royal lady, being in an interesting situation, was confined. The king went often to the bedroom of his sister-in-law, without appearing to expect to find there the Duchess Mazarin, but on purpose to meet her. She was very natural [1] and open, and did not resort to trick or artifice.[2] It was proposed to give her the suite of rooms of the Duke of York at Whitehall when he moved to St. James's Palace.

The honourable and honest De Ruvigny was sorely embarrassed by these women's quarrels. He lost his way in the labyrinth of intrigues, and owned he had done so. "Sire,"[3] he cried in his distress, "I have just learned that there's certain and secret intelligence between the King of England and the Duchess Mazarin. She carries on her intrigue very quietly with him. Those who hoped to share in the triumph, have not yet had the opportunity they expected." He then urged the expediency of

---

[1] Ruvigny to Pomponne, Jan. 20, 1676.
[2] *Ibid.*, Jan. 27 and 30, 1676.
[3] Ruvigny to the king, March 12, 1676.

obtaining a larger pension for her from her husband. Charles and the Duke of York [1] had been pressing him to represent to Louis their sentiments of old affection, and of pity for Madame Mazarin. Nothing would give them more pleasure than for their good offices on her behalf to be well received at Versailles. They were pained at the refusal of their first intervention, and they hoped to be more fortunate a second time.

"Charles," remarked the ambassador, "shows a deepening interest in the lady; and it may be, that her state of distress will intensify the passion which now, clearly, overmasters him."

Ruvigny was not the person to manage feminine and effeminate souls. Louis sent to reinforce the old Protestant in London,—with the mission to supersede him in a few weeks,— the most wily and refined of his courtiers, and one who, although a favourite of the great king, had always behaved with modesty. The new envoy belonged to the judicature, and had been the intendant of a province under Louvois, and was so highly valued by the king that he was at liberty to appear before him without a court

[1] Ruvigny to King Louis, March 16, 1676.

mantle, and with a cane and councillor's ruffles. His name was Courtin, and he was the only man of his profession who was invited to Marly.

CHAPTER VII.

COURTIN.

HONORÉ COURTIN, Seigneur de Chanteroine,[1] was councillor of the Parliament of Rouen at the age of fourteen. When governor of Picardy, he did not venture to reject an application from the Duke de Chaulnes to exempt several villages on his estate from the payment of the *taille* impost. But on finding that because of this exemption the

---

[1] Born in 1622; died in 1703. Married to Salomé de Beauvers. He came to serve as French ambassador at the Court of Whitehall in May 1676; was author of the *Journal des Entrevues dans l'Isle des Faisans*, describing the interviews between Louis XIV. and Philip IV. and Mazarin and the Conde de Huro, which was published in 1665 as a sequel to *L'Histoire de la Paix des Pyrénées*, de Gualdo Priorato. See also Madame de Sévigné's *Letters*, Capmas, Series II., p. 359; and M. Boisdelisle's notice in his edition of *St. Simon*, tome iii. pp. 279–286. Honoré Courtin, a Norman, should not be confounded with Antoine Courtin, an Auvergnat, who was also in the judicature and an ambassador, and who alone is mentioned in *La Biographie Moneri*.

other villages of the circumscription were weighed down with taxes, he paid, to relieve them, forty thousand livres of his own into the treasury, and resigned his high and lucrative post. He had an amiable and a cheerful disposition,[1] a good judgment, ripeness of mind, a graceful manner, and a bright, delicate wit. Courtin, albeit of diminutive stature, was gallant in his attentions to ladies, had the air and speech of one who had mixed in the best society, and yet without affecting to be above his rank of councillor. Although reticent, he was perfectly sincere; and he had the clean hands of a man of unimpeachable honour.[2]

Before setting out for London, where he had previously been on a diplomatic mission, it occurred to him to obtain information about the town and the Court, from a maid of honour of the Queen of England, who was staying at a convent in the Faubourg St. Germain. He had dined with her at De Gourville's; and he

---

[1] Gourville's *Mémoires*, p. 543; Mignet's *Négociations*, tome iii., p. 347, and t. iv. p. 141; Rousset's *Histoire de Louvois*, t. i. p. 465.
[2] SAINT SIMON.

had heard that she left the Court of Whitehall because she one day, when in the Maids of Honours' waiting-room, gave birth to a child.[1] He also went to see Duke Mazarin,[2] who proposed terms certain not to be accepted. They were, "the retirement of his wife to the Abbey of Montmartre." Courtin, therefore, placed himself on the lady's side when he went to London, and endeavoured to produce on the mind of Louis[3] an impression favourable to her. He mentioned to him, in a letter, how he had seen Madame Mazarin at high mass in the chapel of the Portuguese ambassador; but he could not help noticing that she betrayed disgust at the length of the service. He studied her; he drew the Abbé de St. Réal into talking about her; and the upshot was, uneasiness at her growing influence. The King of France was earnestly advised by him[4] to use his authority

[1] Courtin to Louvois, between May and December, 1665. This was not the young lady whose child, born in the queen's circle, died soon after birth, and was dissected by Charles, who made ribald jests about his supposed paternity of his anatomical subject.
[2] Courtin to King Louis, June 8, 1676.
[3] *Ibid.*, May 25, 1679.
[4] *Ibid.*, June 8, 1676.

in forcing her husband to grant the pension which she demanded. St. Réal had let out that she thought Louis disliked her, and would not be sorry for him to know that it behoved him not to have her against him, since she would, if he went on showing himself against her, use her influence in a way that might not please him.

Had she really influence? Courtin sounded Charles himself on that delicate point; and the King of England told him that he had a real friendship for her, but that he would not suffer any cabal to draw him into a closer relation with her. However, he said, she was a great beauty, and that he found no pleasure equal to that of conversing with her. He also showed that he liked to talk about her and to hear her praised, whereas he appeared indifferent to the Duchess of Portsmouth, who had grown delicate, was somewhat changed, and had only enemies in England. It was to be foreseen that the king would yield to the new temptress, in which case the French ambassador would have uphill work, as he would at the same time have to combat both minister and mistress. Courtin did not see that it mattered to Louis whether the Duchess Ma-. zarin refused conjugal rights to her husband; but that it greatly mattered if the duke went on refusing her the fifty thousand *livres*[1] which she claimed for her necessary expenses, because she might help to keep England from joining with the enemies of his majesty. The English hated the French more than ever. Courtin related how a London crowd were going to throw a Venetian into the Thames because they took him for a Frenchman. At any price, the Duchess Mazarin should be gained, or got out of England. A benefice or an abbey might be promised to S. Réal.[2] It would be a miracle if the King of England did not fall under the empire of the Duchess, because the whole Court was making a set upon him in her behalf.

The situation was so dangerous that the reserved Courtin tried to act on the husband by a letter, which was insolently satirical. The lady, he said, was afraid she might find reclusion at Montmartre irksome; and she did not feel her strength equal to the severe rules of

[1] These were the only conditions she stipulated for.
[2] Courtin to Pomponne, June 8, 1676.

a convent. From a jocular, he went on to a menacing tone. The Duchess took her stand on the conditions which she proposed when Madame de Montespan was at the trouble of endeavouring to make up the breach between her and her husband. She remained determined not to grant him the privileges marriage justifies. But she would be satisfied with a yearly pension of fifty thousand *livres* if her laces, jewels, and precious furniture were given back to her, and if the idea of locking her up in a convent were for ever abandoned. It was not reasonable to suppose that she would consent to such a captivity, she having charming lodgings in St. James's Palace, and handsome furniture belonging to the Crown of England. St. James's was the palace of the Duke of York, who was married to a young Italian princess—an enthusiastic ally of the Duchess Mazarin, who had made up her mind not to reside at Whitehall, where the king lived. She did this from a sense of dignity. If she chose, she would not want for anything, because there were persons at Court who would be glad to aid her in whatever way she wished.

The purblind Duke Mazarin did not see the

irony of Courtin, and wrote to him an unctuous letter of eight pages.[1] He argued like a theologian. The reasons he gave might have told before a conclave of Doctors of Divinity, but they were thrown away on an emancipated beauty, who was breathing with delight the corrupt atmosphere of Whitehall. The husband sent epistle on epistle; and the ambassador continued to treat him as a poor fool. He wrote to Pomponne, that he had had another letter from M. Mazarin which might be used as a sermon.

The Abbé S. Réal was more pliable[2] than his mistress. He was eaten up with jealousy, and would be glad to take her from the temptations of London.[3] He was still very amorous, and promised the ambassador his best services. At this juncture St. Réal suddenly started for Paris. Louvois wrote in October to know the reason of this.[4] He could not imagine why a man so violently enamoured as he by all ac-

---

[1] Courtin to Pomponne, June 22, 1676.
[2] *Ibid.*, July 16, 1676.
[3] *Ibid.*, June 22, 1676.
[4] Louvois to Courtin, Oct. 21, 1676. *Affaires Etrangères, Angleterre*, tome cxx., C., fol. 177.

counts was, should quit in this sudden way the object of his love.

The ambassador had heard, Courtin replied, three weeks before St. Réal's departure, that he meant to go.[1] He was in the position of an unhappy lover, and was wont to sit with a grief-stricken aspect by himself, in the chimney nook of the chamber nearest to the card-room. It was to be surmised that the desire shown by many to keep up the Duchess Mazarin in commodious lodgings, impelled him to take a sudden and violent resolution of which he would probably repent before he got to Dover. The Duchess bore his absence with Roman fortitude, and perhaps thought it a deliverance. Louvois, who had read many of S. Réal's letters, which had been seized in the post-office, opined that his room must be more grateful to her than his company.[2]

The Duchess of Portsmouth, who had been absent forty days from town, to take the waters of Bath,[3] was assailed on her return by the

---

[1] Courtin to Louvois, Jan. 3, 1677.
[2] Louvois to Courtin, Jan. 3, 1677.
[3] She was there from May 25 to July 4. The waters of Bath then began to be the fashion, they being thought

strong jests of Nell Gwynn. The latter armed herself in every possible way, to shelter herself from the resentment Louise might be expected to harbour because of the visits Nell received from the king in her absence. On her way from Bath, the Duchess of Portsmouth halted at Windsor, to dine with Charles. But not being offered a room in the Castle, she had to go on in the evening, to sleep in London.[1] Although still thin and worn, she looked better than when she went to take the waters, and thought herself so restored that she might hope soon to pick up flesh. Three days after, she entertained the Count and Countess de Ruvigny

---

more recuperative and purifying to the blood than those of Tunbridge Wells, of which Hamilton had written a charming discription twelve years previously. To judge from what he said, Tunbridge Pantiles resembled a scene in a comic opera; and English village maids and matrons dressed as tastefully then as Swiss or Breton peasant women still do. He was as much struck as other French gentlemen of his day with the neat feet and dainty shoes and stockings which English women of all classes wore in the time of Charles II. English ladies' feet have now a reputation for being clumsily shod; and the shoes and stockings of lower-order women are of a piece with the rest of their cheap tawdry or slattern dress. (*Translator's Note.*)

[1] Courtin to King Louis, July 6, 1676.

at dinner. The musicians of Louis XIV.'s chamber, who were on a tour in England, played during the repast, and Charles came to hear them. The singers were Giles, Laforest, Godenesche; and Lambert,[1] the father-in-law of Lulli, accompanied them at the spinnet. The hostess asked them to sing, "Mate me con no mirar, mas no me mate con zelos,"[2] and Charles took in good part the laughter caused by her request. He continued to give to Louise, in public, tokens of friendship and regard; but he only saw her in company, and the former intimacy was not renewed. The Duchess Mazarin pleased him more, and he betrayed his passion for her by his efforts to make the Duchess of Portsmouth fancy he was not hot foot after the former. To add to her misfortunes, Louise hurt her eye, which remained black and swollen for many days. The sparks of the Court quizzed her about the accident, and made wretched puns about the ambition shown

---

[1] It was of him that Borlean spoke. Lambert was Director of Chamber Music to Louis XIV., and obtained a copyright in 1658 for the publication of his compositions.—*Archives Nat.* X., 8650. His daughter married Lulli.

[2] "Make me die of grief, but not of jealousy."

in the blackening of her eye to transform herself from a blonde, into a brunette like Madame Mazarin.[1]

The French game seemed to be up. Courtin and Louvois began to neglect Louise, who, after a reign of six years, was apparently about to suffer a final defeat. She, who was so plucky and fertile in resources, began to lose courage; and despair was creeping on her.[2] Courtin wrote to Louis to communicate to him a scene that took place in her lodging. He went to visit her at Whitehall, and found her weeping. She opened her heart to him in the presence of her two French maids, who stood with downcast eyes close to the wall, as if glued to it. Tears flowed from their mistress's eyes; sighs and sobs interrupted her speech. M. Courtin stayed with her until midnight, trying to soothe her wounded spirit, and to persuade her to hide her chagrin, and appear not to mind the king's altered humour. Louvois made fun of her pangs, and coarsely wrote,[3] that the scene of

[1] Courtin to King Louis, July 9, 1676; Courtin to Pomponne, July 16, 1676; *Ibid.*, August 3, 1676.
[2] Courtin to Louvois, August 6, 1676.
[3] Louvois' rough irony was proverbial; and his coarse, arrogant, and overbearing temper made him precipitate

la Signora adolorata had vastly amused his majesty, and that the ambassador must have been the first to laugh at it.

But it was no laughing matter for Louis. If Europe thought the disgrace of Louise imminent, the French plenipotentiaries at Nimeguen would have met with unyielding opposition. It was necessary to keep the foreign envoys there in the belief that the Duchess of Portsmouth was still on the pinnacle of royal favour, and so able to support the policy of France. Courtin wrote to Colbert de Croissy and Count d'Avaux, who represented Louis at the Congress, tnat the Duchess had returned from Bath in better health than when she set out; that the king went to meet her at Windsor and preserved for her the same feelings.[1] Some weeks later, Courtin informed them that the king was frequently at the Duchess of Portsmouth's, where there were card tables for three different games—hombre,

---

France into that war with the German Empire in which the Palatinate was ravaged. The letter cited above was dated August 19, 1676 and is in the records of the *Affaires Etrangères, Angleterre*, tome cxx., A., fol. 260.

[1] July 7, 1676.

basset, and thirty-and-forty; and that he promised to attend her Sunday routs at which she dispensed the most charming hospitality.

While throwing dust in the eyes of the other powers, Courtin sought to make friends with the Duchess Mazarin.

A daughter of the king and Duchess of Cleveland who had been married, almost in childhood, to the Earl of Sussex, formed a tender attachment for the beautiful fugitive, whom Charles arranged to meet at his daughter's apartments. When he was there, nobody was suffered to enter the room where he was. An exception was not even made for the French musicians.[1] The chambers of Lady Sussex were those occupied by her mother when she was in favour, and were above the king's cabinet. He could ascend to them by a private stair, without being seen. Madame Mazarin was always running in from St. James's Palace to Lady Sussex's, and her *têtes-à-tête* with Charles were prolonged far into the night. The French ambassador ingratiated himself with the Countess, and ascertained from her about the, to all

---

[1] Courtin to Pomponne, July 20, 1676

appearance, casual meetings in her rooms of the king and her dear friend the Duchess.

Moved by a less political design, Courtin sought to win the friendship of Mrs. Middleton.

Mrs. Middleton was "that famous, that incomparable beauty," who commanded Gramont's admiration when she made her *début* at Court, and was as much admired twenty-five years later. She was "the belle" of Whitehall, and was formed like a fine statue, was fair haired, fresh complexioned, and had a soft, healthy, milk-white skin. There was something in her manners, and in her carefully chosen diction, that was too nice for the taste of the day. Nor was her indolent languor to the taste of all the gallants of the Court. She painted in oils with talent. Gramont lost his heart on her without obtaining hers in return. Courtin received her at the French embassy, as a sovereign by right of beauty. "If I were younger, or, by not following your example, less wise," he informed Pomponne,[1] "I should be able to lead a pleasant life over here. Madame Mazarin came to dine with me to-day, in company with Lady Sussex. I

[1] July 2, 1676.

had near me at table Mrs. Middleton, who is, without doubt, the English Queen of Beauty. I took them all in the evening to hear the French musicians; and then I went to walk with them by moonlight in St. James's Park. There we met the unfortunate Portuguese ambassador, who is dying for the love of Madame Mazarin."

The ball of dissipation rolled merrily on. Festivity reigned. The only serious man at Whitehall was the French ambassador. He sought, in keeping pace with the amusements of the Court, the means of furthering a great scheme of policy which would have reduced England, the theatre of these junketings, to the position of a satellite of the French Monarchy.

The Duchess of Portsmouth,[1] acting on Courtin's advice, dried her tears, affected indifference to her check, assumed a light-hearted manner, and kept in the stream of dissipation.

"She has just given our Embassy a splendid dinner, to which Mrs. Middleton, the Prince of Monaco, Sunderland, Sessac, and our people were all invited, reported Courtin.[2] "The King

---

[1] Courtin to Pomponne, Sept. 21, 1676.
[2] *Ibid.*

of England, who had dined with the queen, dropped in when we were at table; and I have as good as engaged him to come soon and dine with me. He has also been pleased to say that he will dine next Sunday, with the same company, at the Duchess of Portsmouth's; and, to be in good appetite, he promises not to sup the evening before. The Prince of Monaco cannot complain that every one is not on the alert to find pastimes for him. I had him to dinner early in the week, with the Duchess de Mazarin, and her dear friend, Lady Sussex; and a few days previously he came also to dinner, to meet the Duchess of Portsmouth and Mrs. Middleton. The latter is, of all the English beauties, the one I have most pleasure in seeing. But what a number of watch-dogs surround her!"

Some days later, when writing to Louvois about the balance of funds which remained after the De Sessac mission, Courtin said:[1]

"I should be very glad if you could let me employ this sum in adding a chapel to the buildings of the Embassy, in which prayers would be often offered up for you, and in paying the expenses of a *fête* which I gave the

[1] Sept. 24, 1676.

other evening to the Duchess Mazarin, Lady Sussex, and Mrs. Hamilton's sister, Miss Jennings,[1] who is the most beautiful of all the Duchess of York's maids of honour, and whom the Duke of York is always ogling. I have arranged to give a little ball to amuse these ladies. There is a Secretary of State,[2] whom I knew when I was at Cologne, who means to dance for six hours without resting, in the country dances. Gallants, and young ladies of

---

[1] In the reign of Charles II. it was polite to style a young unmarried lady, who was not a professional beauty, "Mrs." Courtin styles the untitled spinster at Court *Mistress*, and the married lady of every rank *Madame*. To prevent confusion, I adopt the modern fashion. (*Translator's Note.*)

[2] This was evidently Sir Joseph Williamson (1623-1701) who behaved so badly to Arlington, and became Secretary of State when that nobleman retired into private life. Of the other two plenipotentiaries to the Congress of Cologne, Sunderland was not a dancer; and Sir Lioline Jenkins was not a Secretary of State, but Judge of the Prerogative Court and Member for Oxford. Williamson was a Catholic, and persecuted as such. He followed James II. to France, where his descendants now rank with the Fitzjameses, MacMahons, and Dillons, as descendants of "Earl Oillamson," and bear as such the title of Count. Their births, deaths, and marriages are treated as fashionable events by "le High Life" Boulevard journals. (*Translator's Note.*)

condition and note are to be asked; and frolicsome damsels will not be able to say that I do not know how to treat them handsomely. The outer door is to be well shut. I am to play at hombre with the Duchess Mazarin. We both shall leave the young madcaps to skip and dance away to their hearts' content. Don't tell this to M. de Pomponne, or let him know anything about it. He would say that I do not grow wiser as I grow old. But one must be a man of pleasure to get on here; otherwise it is useless to come to England. I can, however, assure you that although I must handle pitch, I am resolved not to be defiled like the other foreign ministers (and among them M. Vanbeuninghen, the Dutch minister), who all keep mistresses. M. Vanbeuninghen[1] is as much enamoured as you were, when you used to go to Chelles. I am going to call on Mrs. Middleton, whom I more than ever regard as the most beautiful and amiable woman at Court. I would give her all your money, if she would listen to overtures from me. But she is not mercenary, and once refused a purse containing fifteen hundred gold angels, which Gramont offered

[1] Ambassador of Holland, who was for peace.

her. Do not, therefore, fear that she will get hold of the balance of the Sessac fund."

"The balance you mention," wrote Louvois,[1] "cannot have the pious use to which you would apply it. We have other things to do, besides building Embassy chapels. However, make use of it until M. Demetz pays you your salary. What you say of the ball you have promised to give, makes me wish to be of the company, although I should not think of dancing down the Secretary of State; and I do not know a single rule of hombre. All I should do would be to feast my eyes on Madame Mazarin, and that I should never stop doing. There is much good now said here about her, which I find hard to believe. You may well imagine that it is not of her beauty the talk is, since she is assuredly the finest woman alive. But it is said that her tongue and disposition, are not so charming as her person. If you were insensible to her, and therefore more free from bias, I should ask you to inform me on these points. I remember having seen M. de Vanbeuninghen at St. Germain with rouge and patches, which the courtesanes of Chatou and Passy had plas-

[1] Oct. 1, 1676.

tered on his cheeks. I don't know whether his London mistress ever sends him to Whitehall so beautified. I have so often heard of the charms of Mrs. Middleton from de Gramont, that I should be glad to have her portrait."

Courtin either did not understand that the drift of this letter was to cajole the Duchess Mazarin by repeating the flattery it contained, or did not see the possibility of getting her over to the French side. He evinced the greatest anxiety to show that he was not subjugated by her. It was not he who was her slave, but the Prince of Monaco,[1] who was always in her company. Courtin supplicated Louvois not to repeat in society the rumour that he was in love with her, because people would say he had avowed it in his despatches, and he would be a subject of raillery. So far, she had not in the least turned his head, and yet there was not a day in which he did not spend several hours in reading in her card room. He often remained thus occupied until midnight. Her house was an agreeable one, and provided with every commodity. Hombre was always

[1] Courtin to Louvois, Oct. 29, 1676.—Autograph minute of Louvois, tome cxx., fol. 186.

going on. Courtin sometimes watched the play, but more often sat in an easy chair, beside the fire, reading a book. S. Réal had got together a good library for the Duchess. The ambassador found in it *Appian*, and the *Annals of Tacitus*, translated by M. d'Ablancourt. The Duchess's conduct towards the ambassador was free from impropriety, of which he was very glad. But he could see that, although she was civil to him, she had something in her mind against him, and was not frank in her dealings with him. He had already informed M. de Pomponne of her annoyance at the intervention of King Charles and the Duke of York in her favour, having had no effect at Versailles. He was half inclined to suspect that she had been sent to London on some intrigue against France. The Duchess of Portsmouth told the French ambassador that she and King Charles had come to some secret understanding. Perhaps this was a jealous fancy; but it was sincerely entertained by her. Courtin complained that his warnings had been neglected as idle, and that his Government haggled about the supplemental pension of eight thousand crowns, which

King Charles asked for Madame Mazarin. He hoped there would be no cause to repent of this; but he knew that the lady was deeply mortified, and that opportunities would arise to enable her to take her revenge. The ambassador entreated Louvois not to treat this as a laughing matter; and, to induce him not to do so, mentioned that the Duchess Mazarin always spoke of him in a friendly manner, and was a woman of very amiable manners. If Louvois had seen her dancing the *furlano*, to the music of a guitar which she thrummed herself, he would have been captivated by her. She had a lady friend of remarkable prettiness always at her side, whose society he would also have enjoyed. Her sallies, and her brightness of fancy and wealth of imagination, which never flagged till midnight,—when the card parties of the Duchess broke up,—would have kept the most tired man from feeling sleepy.[1] The ambassador hoped to be allowed to enjoy this pleasant society, without being set down as a lover of the Duchess. He had sometimes to leave it to go and sup with Mrs. Middleton, who often came to dine with the Duchess of

---

[1] Courtin does not name this *amie*.

Portsmouth at his house, or to spend the evening with Lady Sussex, at whose rooms, as the secret reports to Louvois, Pomponne, and Louis XIV. so often mentioned, kept assignations with the Duchess Mazarin.

In a letter dated November 2, 1676, there is an account of Mrs. Middleton's supper. Courtin began by giving a detailed description, from which he effaced the words: "They wanted to represent after midnight the Newmarket races with the two ladies." He then enters into a curious disquisition on ladies' feet, ankles, shoes, and stockings, which shows that he was not of the priggish school of diplomacy, and thought trifling things worth noting: "I can't endure Paris stockings, or the shoes furnished to our ladies by Madame Desbordes. There is nothing neater than the feet and ankles of the English ladies, in their well-fitting shoes and silk stockings. They wear their skirts short; and I often see legs so well turned that a sculptor would like to mould them. Green silk stockings are modish. The garter, of which glimpses are often afforded, is below the knee, and in black velvet, with diamond buckles. Those who have no silk stockings to wear, show a white skin, smooth as satin. English women prefer being stockingless to wearing clumsy and disfiguring hosiery." Louvois protested that he never thought of laughing at the expense of the Duchess Mazarin,[1] as the ambassador had suspected. On the contrary, he had the greatest regard for her, and always counted her a woman of absolutely peerless beauty.

"The Duchess of Portsmouth,"[2] continued Courtin, "has the king often at her rooms, which are the place where he's seen most publicly. But I have ascertained beyond doubt that he passes nights much less often with her than with Nell Gwynn; and, if I can believe those who are most about with him, his relations with the Duchess of Portsmouth have subsided into a virtuous friendship. As to the Duchess Mazarin, I know he thinks her the finest woman that he ever saw in his life. Although I go every day to her chambers at St. James's palace, I can see that she hides all that she can from me. I am greatly deceived, if she is not intriguing for some of our enemies against us here.

[1] Nov. 2, 1676.   [2] Nov. 12, 1676.

"In general terms I have advised her, that if she wanted to let out, she should do it without causing a scandal, and in a way not to be remarked much, even in London. She finds amusement, she says, in the most innocent diversions. Every evening I witness scenes at her rooms, so astounding that a description of them could not fail to set even a great minister like you laughing. As to Mrs. Middleton, I still hold to the opinion that she's the sweetest woman I ever came across, in any foreign country. She's beautiful, has the air of high breeding, is full of talent, and yet modest and unassuming. Were I no older than you, I should be madly in love with her. But I am forty-nine, and the thick air of London depresses me.[1] Madame Mazarin, after piously attending mass on Sunday, dined with me, and played the rest of the afternoon in my withdrawing-room, at battledore and shuttlecock, with Lady Sussex. She charged me with her compliments for you. I mentioned to Mrs. Middleton your wish to have her portrait, and she answered that she was infinitely obliged to you."

[1] Nov. 23, 1676.

Far from thinking this Court gossip beneath his attention, the great minister Louvois testified to the great pleasure which it afforded him, and hoped that he should be kept informed of what the London ladies were doing.

He was soon informed of the hubbub caused at Whitehall, by the Earl of Sussex trying to force his wife to go and live in the country. She was the inseparable companion of the Duchess Mazarin; and the Duchess of Cleveland had taken it into her head to break up the intimacy. The husband's aunt and mother formed the same design. Though young, the husband was of a morose humour. The Duchess of Portsmouth mortally hated the Countess of Sussex, because she thought she directed the intrigue between the king and the Duchess Mazarin. But Charles was resolved that his new lady-love should not be deprived of the companionship of his romping daughter. The Countess of Sussex was hardly more than a child, and only thought of skipping and dancing, and indulging in games of romps from morning till night; and she was passionately attached to the Duchess Mazarin, who appeared in her young eyes a heroine of romance.

Louvois was enchanted to read about these quarrels and intrigues, and encouraged Courtin not to neglect them in writing to him and the King of France.[1] The statesmen in the employment of Louis the Fourteenth were remarkable for their application and thoroughness. But they were, with the exception of Colbert, free from pomposity, and were above trying to gain prestige by solemn pedantry. However, while they so closely observed the Court, they remained in ignorance of the vital forces and the resources of England. It may be said for them, that a study of the national spirit and energies was not what most concerned them. They had to busy themselves chiefly with the present. To hold England back, through the Court, while the French were conquering on the mouths of the Scheldt and Rhine, in Flanders and the Netherlands, was all they wanted. However, it would have been wise to have tried to understand, if only with the design of preventing their hostility, the men and the forces that were coming up.

[1] Dec. 17, 1676.

In Churchill, the future Duke of Marlborough, Courtin and Louvois did not discern more than a selfish, cool-headed libertine. Churchill asked a regiment of Louis XIV. If he had been accepted, perhaps he would have developed, like his nephew Berwick, into an illustrious French general, and that the reign of the great king would not have had a sombre ending.

When Churchill asked for the French regiment, a correspondence was opened about him.[1] Louvois already knew him, and also much about him that was not to his credit. He had a reputation in London which was not to his advantage, and had traded, in the debauched Court circles in which he mixed, on his fine figure and handsome face. That sort of vice was frequent at the Courts of the Valois kings, where pretty fellows of high birth and light purses received money and jewels, and sometimes estates, from women of wealth and quality. Queen Elizabeth was also generous to the beaux with whom she diverted herself. But the male professional beauty was not a plant of English growth, and was never well

[1] Courtin to Louvois, Nov. 16, 1676.

naturalized in England. It is possible that John Churchill, in seeking a regiment in France, wanted to break with the titled demi-reps to whom he owed what money he possessed and what advancement he had obtained, and desired to lead a virtuous life abroad. He had then formed a pure attachment for Sarah Jennings, the leading belle of the Duchess of York's household. At a ball given by that princess, the lovely Jennings left a dance in which she was engaged, to sit down to weep.[1] Churchill had told her he was menaced with consumption, and ordered by his doctor to go to live in France. She believed him, although he was in perfect health. His father and mother were tormenting him to marry an heiress, ugly to deformity; and he and Sarah Jennings loved each other. Courtin informed Louvois that the beau Churchill had pillaged the Duchess of Cleveland; and that, in one way or another, he had got out of her so much money, that she was obliged to go to France to economize and gain time from her creditors. When the handsome gallant had robbed her, he deserted her.

[1] Courtin, Dec. 7, 1676.

Possibly, if he and she had met in France, they might have been reconciled, and, as he was cool-headed, insinuating, and intriguing, he might have become a valuable instrument of France. Louvois drily objected, that Mr. Churchill was "too fond of pleasure, to discharge well the duties of colonel in the army of the King of France." He had been proposed for the command of the Royal-English regiment, which was in the pay of Louis. But Louvois said he would give "more satisfaction to a rich and faded mistress, than to a monarch who did not want to have dishonourable, and dishonoured, carpet knights in his armies."

Towards the end of 1676, the influence of Louise de Keroualle fell to a low point. Courtin pitied Charles, who wanted to be well with every one[1] — a hard problem to solve, surrounded, as he was, by jealous women. He had to face the anger of the Duchess of Portsmouth for drinking twice in twenty-four hours, to the health of Nell Gwynn, with whom he still often supped, and who still made the Duchess of Portsmouth the butt for her tickling sarcasms. The rakes of the town met

[1] Courtin to Louvois, Dec. 17, 1676.

the king at her supper-table, and said freely before him whatever came uppermost in their heads. As for the Duchess Mazarin, the Court of Versailles was informed by the watchful ambassador that Charles went regularly through the going-to-bed ceremony at Whitehall; and when his gentlemen and servants had left his chamber, he got up, dressed, stole off to St. James's Palace, where he arrived after the Duchess's card-parties were over, and did not return to his palace until after five in the morning. It was evident, then, that he did not spend his nights in the lodging of the Duchess of Portsmouth. He went to see her often in the daytime, when he knew she had company with her; but that was all.

Louis had made haste to profit by what influence remained to the Duchess of Portsmouth, and took Condé, Bouchain, Aire, and Philipsburg. He forced the Prince of Orange to raise the siege of Maestricht, to the great apparent joy of Charles, who cried that that little upsetting gentleman, wanted a whipping to tame his ambition.[1] The irresistible campaign of 1677 was prepared. France, bounded

[1] Courtin to King Louis, Sept. 3, 1676.

by the sea to the west and north-west, by high mountains to the south-west and south-east, and by the Mediterranean to the south, could only extend her frontiers to the north and north-east.[1] The Italian wars were mere showy ones, as the French statesmen began to see in the sixteenth century. Coligny affirmed, with a menace in his eye, that "any one who tried to prevent a war in Flanders was not a good Frenchman, and had a Spanish cross stamped on his heart." The English statesmen, from the time of Queen Elizabeth, understood that France was bound by the fatalities of her geographical position to bear down on Flanders; and as they feared to have a long coast-line to guard, not only in the Channel, but on the German Ocean, into which the Thames flowed, they came to look upon the French as their born enemies. The soldier, the sailor, and the civilian, but particularly in the middle and lower classes, were imbued with hatred for France.[2] Courtin often warned his Government of this deep-rooted animosity,

---

[1] Duc d'Audiffret Pasquier: *Eloge du Maréchal de Berwick*.

[2] Feb. 15, 1677.

which, he said, could not be explained by any freak of fashion, because the Court and courtiers followed the modes of Paris, and the wits of Whitehall took for models the wits of Versailles. Yet they sought pretences for declaring openly their aversion for the French. The king was not only held in French bondage by the Duchess of Portsmouth, but by his personal obligations of an unavowable kind to the King of France, and by his hopes of future pecuniary aids.

In the records of the French Foreign Office there is a paper written by him, in a firm and flowing hand, in which there is no trace of the nervous agitation which shame might cause. It runs thus:—

"I have received from his most Christian Majesty, by the hands of M. Courtin, the sum of a hundred thousand crowns, French money, for the second quarter, ending on the last day of June, and to be deducted from the four hundred thousand crowns payable at the end of this year.

"Given at Whitehall, September 25, 1676.
"CHARLES R."

This paper bears the royal seal. There are two other signed and sealed receipts of the same year, dated October 1st and Dec. 31st.

No formality was left out in delivering them.[1] Charles was not conscious of his ignominy. The four hundred thousand crowns were the price of a prorogation of Parliament, which did not meet in 1676. As he was paid, so he served the King of France. But the day of reckoning was coming round. Parliament was to meet on February 25, 1677, and this caused uneasiness at Versailles, many weeks before the event took place. Courtin was told to neglect no symptom, and to try and see what members of the Opposition were purchasable. He had a very hard card to play, and hid his serious designs under gay attentions to the mistresses and the other ladies about them. He was importuned by the Earl of Berkshire,[2] who had two years previously come begging to De Ruvigny, and complaining that he had lost by his zeal for France a pension he received from Spain.[3]

[1] *Aff. Etr. Angleterre,* tome cxxi., fol. 213, 216, 307.

[2] His name in the foreign archives is spelt Barchis, Bacsha, Barkshe, and Barker. But, as Courtin says this Earl is of the noble house of Howard, he must be the eldest son of Thomas Howard, who in 1625 was created Earl of Berkshire.

[3] Ruvigny to King Louis, March 25, 1674.

Ruvigny, thinking he might be useful, lent him out of his own pocket five hundred Jacobus, which he did not expect to receive again. But he assured Louis that a thousand gold pieces would not have been too much, because at the Court of England, those who did not give high pay were badly served. The King of France ordered the thousand pieces to be given.[1] But they less stimulated the zeal than the cupidity of Lord Berkshire, who wrote to Courtin[2] to know whether he wished to use him as a secret service agent. Courtin, being the soul of probity, recoiled from dealings with Berkshire, who, albeit a scion of the noble house of Howard, was a low knave. He at first merely thanked him; but, as the meeting of Parliament was drawing near, resigned himself to ask if the king would authorize him to let the earl have another thousand Jacobus.[3] Then he promised, then he temporized, and at last gave a quarter in advance, to make sure of a speech against any

---

[1] These five hundred gold pieces are mentioned in *Aff. Etr.*, tome cxii., fol. 199.
[2] Courtin to Pomponne, August, 1676.
[3] Courtin to King Louis, Dec. 21, 1676.

anti-French resolution that might be moved in the House of Lords. There was no lack of men in the House of Commons who would have received money without any sort of scruple from the French Embassy. But it would have been a vain expense to bribe them, because they would not keep any bargain made for the advantage of Louis. The whole House of Commons hated France, and was determined that she should not seize on the Netherlands.[1]

Courtin's repugnance to dirty-handed English noblemen was not taken in good part at Versailles. He was drily reminded that nothing would be thought dirty there, which enabled the king to possess the Rhine and Flanders; and he was commanded to enter into relations with Coleman, a Secretary of State, and favourite of the Duke of York, who was to be bought for three hundred Jacobus.[2] But he found it hard to gain the Duke of Lauderdale, and was instructed to see what he could do through the Duchess. The king of France thought it worth his while to write with his own hand on this subject.

[1] Courtin to Pomponne, March 8, 1677.
[2] *Ibid.*, Dec. 28, 1676.

Courtin replied to Louvois that he owned that the Duchess of Lauderdale ruled her lord. But the Duke having always spoken against men high in the service of the State accepting presents, and his worst enemies admitting that his hands were clean, it was hard to find a way to bribe him. His wife, a cautious woman evidently, was very anxious that he should stand well in the eyes of Parliament, and timorously afraid that he might lose its good opinion. It was not therefore certain that she would listen to proposals from the French embassy; and if overtures were made and rejected, the matter would get noised, and the Parliament would be more dogged than ever in a policy of resistance to France. Nevertheless, as she was extravagant in spending money, and liked to have every nice thing she saw, Courtin thought that Louis might send her a gift of elegant jewellery, to accept which, the ambassador would try to lead her without saying anything that, if repeated, might do mischief.[1]

With Charles there was no need for beating about the bush. It was best to go straight to business with him, and tell him that it

[1] Courtin to Pomponne, Jan. 14, 1677.

depended on himself whether his secret pension was, or was not to be continued. But the statesmen and politicians around him had not got to his degree of easy cynicism. The opposition of those who were above taking money, or ashamed to take it, might be softened by presents of champagne and French liqueurs. It was astonishing, Pomponne was informed, how five or six dozen bottles of that wine, sent at the right moment, softened stiff members of Parliament, because they were in the habit of dining with each other on quitting the House of Commons. All the cabals were formed at these dinners.

Courtin was incurably averse to dishonourable men. He liked better to gossip about the immoral ladies, and related how, at a dinner at the Duchess of Portsmouth's, in company with the beauteous Lady Beauclerc, the king entered as the *entremets* was being served. He coughed a good deal, and, to cure him, the ambassador sent for a bottle of new Canary, which the four emptied, the ladies taking their full share. Courtin made himself useful to Charles in getting, not only the two French Duchesses to live in good intelligence, but the ladies who espoused their quarrels and detested each other. His letters about them are still entertaining, and throw a curious light on the manners and the morals of the English Court, which must have caused them to be read with a deep and amusing interest by the king and ministers for whose eyes they were meant. In one of them the writer relates a diverting scene at which he was present, in the rooms of the Duchess Mazarin. Who should enter but Louise de Keroualle, to pay a visit of ceremony; and, almost at the same moment, Lady Harvey, who hated her worse than any other woman in England. Her ladyship had with her a certain "Miss Nelly," an actress. The comedian had come with Lady Harvey to thank the Duchess Mazarin for the compliments she sent her on the occasion of her son being recognised by King Charles, and given the title of Earl of Brentford. All the thanks and little return speeches passed with gay animation and the utmost civility and good taste; and not a word was dropped to betray the low origin of the actress. But when the Duchess of Portsmouth left, Lady Harvey's fair friend, who was of the bold, laughing sort, turned round to De Courtin and asked why it was that the King of France did not send presents to her, instead of to the weeping willow who had just gone out? She vowed that he would have more profit in doing so, because the King of England was her constant nocturnal companion, and liked her far the best. The other ladies had heard of the luxurious fineness of Miss Nelly's under-clothing, and asked if they could judge of it for themselves. Without more ado she let them raise each petticoat, one by one, and before all in the room examine them on her. "I never in my life," said Courtin, "saw such thorough cleanliness, neatness, and sumptuosity. I should speak of other things that we all were shown if M. de Lionne were still Foreign Secretary. But with you I must be grave and proper; and so, Monsieur, I end my letter."

"Miss Nelly," mother of the Earl of Brentford, was Nell Gwynn; and Lady Harvey, with whom she paid the visit, had just formed a tender friendship for the Duchess Mazarin. She hated the Duchess of Portsmouth, and her hatred was more dangerous than Nell's jests.

Lady Harvey was that sister of Montagu, ambassador of Charles II. to Louis XIV., and was celebrated as a wit[1] among the witty courtiers of the great king. It was of her La Fontaine said, in the fable of *Le Renard Anglais*:—

> "Le bon cœur chez vous, compagnon du bon sens,
>   Avec cent qualités trop long à déduire,
>   Une noblesse d'âme, un talent pour conduire
>   Et les affaires et les gens,
>   Une humeur franche et libre et le don d'être amie
>   Malgré Jupiter même et les temps orageux.

Her animosity towards the Duchess of Cleveland had probably the same cause as her hatred for the Duchess of Portsmouth and her sudden intimacy with the Duchess Mazarin.

Her contemporaries spoke undisguisedly of her vices; and she was brought, by a satirical dramatic author, upon the stage under the name of *Sempronia*.[2] The actress who per-

---

[1] Courtin to Pomponne, July 20, 1676. He often speaks of the brilliant play of her wit in his despatches, and of the bold, gay character of her mind.

[2] Colbert thus gives this threatrical event. "The ways and doings of Lady Harvey have been given undisguisedly (*au naturel*) under the name of *Sempronia*, and with great

formed the part before an applauding house was imprisoned; but when, owing to the Duchess of Castlemaine's intervention, she was released, the king went to see her in the libellous character, which the Duchess of Portsmouth said was only so, because the greater the truth the greater the libel. Colbert de Croissy's letters on this subject have points of resemblance with the Satires of Juvenal on the vices of the patrician ladies of Rome. St. Evremond interpreted, in a letter to Lady Harvey herself, his enthusiasm for Madame Mazarin, according to the light thrown on her manners and her morals in *Sempronia*.[1]

These scandals continued, in 1677, to be treated as State affairs by the Court of Versailles, which was not insensible to their hilarious side. The Foreign Affairs records of that year are full of diverting scenes, in which the British Sultan, his concubines, cour-

applause. Hence the imprisonment of the actress, and her release by Lady Castlemaine's favour." Louis XIV. answered, "I read with much amusement the curious circumstances which you wrote to the Sieur de Lionne, and which he communicated to me yesterday."—*Aff. Etr.*, tome xciii.. fol. 234, Feb. 9, 1669.

[1] *Œuvres*, t. iii. p. 10.

tiers, and the ambassadors accredited to him, are the actors. They are described so vividly, that, although more than two centuries have elapsed since they were described, they seem no mere dry bones, when the dusty records in question are made to give up their secrets. The king's mistresses at Versailles were ladies of high social tone and intellectual acquirements. One of them was renowned for the attic salt of her *mots*. Another could suit her conversation to the pure and elevated tastes of Fénelon and Racine, and eventually became the mother-abbess of the Court. They all had intellect enough, when tired of pleasure, to devote their minds to serious things; and they listened with genuine pleasure to the Advent and Lenten services of Massillon and Bourdaloue. Ninon de Lenclos, who spirited away from Madame de Sévigné her husband, and, later in life, seduced her son, formed a library which,—she having in the eighteenth century bequeathed it to Voltaire,—served as a revolutionary explosive to the world. But, with the exception of Mrs. Middleton, the good and charming Countess of Sunderland, and the shrewish Sarah Jennings, whose virtue turned to vinegar, the ladies of quality at the Court of Charles II. were frivolous and vulgar demi-reps. They had, however, the quality of perfect frankness. One always knew where to have them, and they were as transparent as water. It was therefore impossible to carry on with any of them a long-sustained diplomatic intrigue. Whatever was in their minds they blurted out, often to the confusion of those French diplomatists, who, when new to them, began by trusting them somewhat. In this respect they were at a disadvantage with Louise de Keroualle, who never said anything she did not want to say, and whose reticence, discretion, and secrecy gave her,—until the advent of Madame Mazarin,—the upper hand. This lady, if her life was openly scandalous, had the subtle penetration and diplomatic genius of the Italian; and her English rivals, feeling this, forgot their rivalry while they were trying to detach the king from his French favourite, and destroy her influence. Courtin managed to remain on good terms with the two Duchesses and the English petticoat-party that was behind one of them. His despatches teem with anecdotes illustrative of the difficulty he had in not offending any one. The ambassador had to enter into their amusements without once forgetting that he represented the greatest king in Europe. His gallant and gracious manners, his wit, and probably his broken English, whenever he ventured to talk in that language, greatly helped his address. Even his small stature was an advantage to him at Whitehall and St. James's. The nobly born and ennobled jades there treated him as a charming toy. Meeting him at the theatre, he wrote to Louvois, Lady Harvey and Mrs. Middleton proposed to go and sup three days later at his house, each accompanied by *une de ses amies*. Mrs. Middleton talked of this intended invasion on the French embassy at the Duchess of Portsmouth's, and Lady Harvey at the Duchess Mazarin's. The two duchesses vowed they should join the invaders. Lady Beauclerc was of the party, although she and Lady Harvey were at daggers drawn and could not endure each other. The Duchess Mazarin had always refused to break bread with Louise de Keroualle, or to eat at the same table with her. But Courtin managed to keep all the rivals who were under his roof from breaking the peace, and they enjoyed themselves immensely together. He playfully locked up together in couples in the same rooms the ladies whom he thought the most violently antagonistic; and when he delivered the Duchesses of Portsmouth and Mazarin from this species of imprisonment, they came out hand-in-hand, laughing heartily, and went dancing and jumping down stairs.

This attempt to bring about a reconciliation showed the power of the Duchess Mazarin. As formerly Queen Catherine resigned herself to put up with the power of the Duchess of Cleveland, so the Duchess of Portsmouth learned to stand Nell Gwynn and the other street and stage harlots. She also had to bear the reign of Hortense Mazarin. This reign was no longer a matter of doubt. Hortense's spouse announced her accession to the French, who thought the news of such a rapid victory too marvellous to be true.[1] The discarded lover, St. Réal, talked of Charles like an aggrieved husband to his friends. Courtin was instructed to find out to what extent the reports on the subject were true, and brought his legal

[1] Mdlle. Scudéry's letter to Bussy, July 14th, 1678

acumen to bear in analysing the presumptions which supported the town talk.

He began by summarizing conversations with Louise de Keroualle, who had felt, suspected, and then acquired the certainty, that Madame Mazarin secretly abandoned herself to Charles—not for either love or ambition, but simply because she did not know what in the world else to do for money. If she were sure of not being thrust into a convent, or forced to live with her Tartuffe-ridden husband, she might be easily induced to go back to Paris. She was extravagant in her expenditure, and had the liveries of her men-servants covered with gold lace. The nine different suits for her two porters, six valets, and a page, cost, with the cravats, two thousand six hundred *livres*. Her table was excellent; and the two thousand crowns which she had from her husband went but a short way to cover her ordinary expenses. She had gained in beauty[1] since she came to England. Her success there had lighted up her visage with the most charming expression, and she had picked up flesh just

---

[1] Courtin to Louvois. See copies of Louvois' correspondence at the *Dépôt de la Guerre*, tome dxxxv. fol. 183.

to the right extent. The table that she kept was excellent, and in short her housekeeping expenses alone far exceeded the two thousand crowns that her husband allowed her. If she fed according to the appetite[1] which God had given her, said Courtin, she would eat twice as much as her annuity could buy for her. If her husband knew how good her health and appetite were, he would surely feel the cruelty of not augmenting her pension. It was a puzzle to Courtin to think how she could pay her way if Charles did not serve as her banker. She was as intimate with him as he could wish a woman of her beauty to be. The friendly neutrality of Charles being of the utmost consequence to France, Courtin was unable to think why it was that this mistress was neglected by his Court.[2] She had been with the King of England on the fourth of March from three to seven in the evening, in one of the reserved rooms next to his suite, into which Charles and Chiffinch were the only men who entered. They each had a master key which fitted all the locks to this Cytherean temple.

[1] Courtin to Louvois, fol. 256, Jan. 21, 1677.
[2] Courtin to Pomponne, March 25, 1677.

As Charles liked a gay quiet life, and showed that domestic storms did not suit his epicurean temper, the rivals ended by forming an harmonious group around him. Louise pushed the spirit of conciliation so far as to ask the Duchess Mazarin to dinner[1] and then took her to the Mall in her coach, to the astonishment of all the fine folks of London, who were not less wonderstruck when Lady Harvey appeared in the same company.

In a degree, this general peace in the seraglio was due to Courtin. War between the Palace and the Parliament had waxed so hot, that the union of all the ladies was deemed necessary to keep the indolent monarch in a combative mood. When the Commons assembled,[2] on February 25th, it began by informing the King that it would vote all the funds he wanted, if he lost no time in declaring war on France.

"They will vote anything against us in the House of Commons," wrote Courtin; "and they say, that they are ready to sell their shirts off

---

[1] Courtin to Louvois, March 25, 1677. *Dossiers de la Guerre*, tome dxxxvi., fol. 617.

[2] See Mignet's *Négociations*, t. iv., p. 431.

their backs, to keep the Netherlands from being seized upon by us. These are the very words they make use of:[1] The hubbub in Parliament against us is loud and wild, and will not soon be abated. We fatten, it seems to me, on English curses."

Charles and Louis replied to the Commons each in his own manner—Charles, by proroguing whenever the Lower House menaced; and Louis, by conquering. The first prorogation was from April 24 to May 31, and then from June 7 to July 26. But intermittent sessions growing dangerous, there was a further prorogation to the 13th of December, 1677.

Louis's answer was a sudden attack on Valenciennes; and M. Louvois wrote a boastful letter to London, for the benefit of the English, describing the campaign of 1677; the victory of Mont Cassel; and the sieges of St. Omer and Cambray. "Make haste to conquer what you can," said Courtin in answer, "for it will be impossible for the King of England, unless he chooses to face utter ruin, not to enter into the league against us."

Louis did make haste, and neglected no

[1] Rousett, t. ii., p. 309.

means for securing the silence of the leading members of the House of Commons in debates on foreign affairs. Bribes were again resorted to. The short session of February cost him £2,950, and that of June £550 only. Charles drew at the French Embassy £40,526 between March 1st and September 6th, 1677; and then signed a treaty in which he engaged to remain neutral in return for an annual subvention of £80,000. He congratulated Louis on the severe chastisement he had inflicted on Charles's own nephew, whose father and mother had sheltered him in exile, the Prince of Orange, before Charleroy.[1]

It was not Courtin who transacted these money affairs, but Barrillon, who came to London at the beginning of May, 1677. Louis saw the necessity of having an unscrupulous ambassador in England, and took Courtin at his word, when he complained of suffering from the heavy air of London, and of the injury to his affairs which a prolonged sojourn at such an expensive Court as that of Whitehall occasioned. He owed, he believed, his life to advice given him by Charles, to wear under-

[1] *Dossiers de la Guerre*, tome dxxxvii.

shirts of flannel, "a plain sort of woollen stuff woven in the cottages of Wales. They could," the king told me, "be washed just as linen shirts, and nothing could be more warm, comfortable, or hygiènic." But when Courtin found that Barrillon was coming to supersede him, he repented of his complaints, and tried to show that he preferred the agreeable society of the Court ladies in London, to the profession of law in France. In a post scriptum to a despatch to Pomponne,[1] he said: "Since I had the honour to address to you the above, the Duchess Mazarin has been here to call on me, with the Duchess of Cleveland's eldest daughter, her most intimate friend, who is as fond as she is of amusing herself with dogs and white sparrows. The former lady begged me to offer you a thousand compliments in her name. The Duchess of Portsmouth has returned from taking the waters in sounder health. She is now in good case. Her skin has grown again so fair and fresh that I cannot imagine how King Charles, palled as he is with beauty, will be long in her company without becoming once

---

[1] Courtin to Pomponne, tome cxx., fol. 271, *autograph post scriptum.*

more her slave. She has often with her Catherine Stuart, sister of the Duchess of Richmond, who married Lord Ibrickan, and is one of the most pleasant women here.[1] Her husband sticks to her like her shadow, and is ready to shoot or stab any one who looks at her. He once tried to kill her in a fit of jealousy. I have never been in a country in which women are so prone to backbite each other as in England."

At each prorogation Courtin vainly tried to show what an advantage he had obtained.[2] He at length came to understand that, although he had not displeased Louis, he must retire before Barrillon. Ere he quitted London he presented his successor to the Duchess of Portsmouth,[3] and reminded the King of France of her oft-expressed wish that he should grant an abbey to her aunt, Madame de Tymeur.[4] If Louis granted this favour, he might greatly

---

[1] Lord Ibrickan's family name was O'Brien. Catherine Stuart after his death married Joseph Williamson, his Secretary.
[2] *Dossiers de la Guerre*, tome dxxxviii.
[3] Courtin to Pomponne, Sept. 9, 1677.
[4] *Ibid.*, tome cxxiii., fol. 164.

facilitate Barrillon's mission. There was nothing so essential to the success of French diplomacy in London, as to be able to see the Duchess of Portsmouth every day, and at no matter what hour. Courtin had really spent all his fortune in the service of his king, in London. The following year his daughter, Charlotte Courtin, a tall, handsome woman, of distinguished air and brilliant intellect, married without any dowry a Norman of low birth, named Rocques. But he was very rich, meritorious, and clever; and was authorized to call himself De Varangeville, and named ambassador to Venice. This lady had two daughters who became the wives of Maisons, the Président de Mortier, of the Royal Court of Paris, and of Marshal de Villars. Courtin enjoyed the esteem of Louis to the end of his life. He attended twice a week the king's supper; and from the moment he entered, all the king's conversation was addressed to him until his majesty rose from table. Nevertheless he always remained a simple Councillor of State.

CHAPTER VIII.

BARRILLON.

PAUL BARRILLON D'AMONCOURT,[1] Marquis de Branges, had as much cleverness as Courtin, as delicate taste and tact, and as much address in making his way with ladies. He understood, besides, how to employ money; and he was master in the art of corrupting men, and of hiding his contempt for those whom he corrupted. He kept up towards them a fair and smiling face, and brought about their ruin without any compunction. He resembled those ambassadors of Philip II. who showered doubloons on the Catholic conspirators, affected interest in the democracy of the League, saw their heads fall without a shudder; and when

---

[1] Barrillon was of a legal family. His father was the famous President Barrillon who died a prisoner at Pignerol in 1645. One of his brothers was Bishop of Luçon; the other, Barrillon de Morangis, was a Councillor of State. The private papers of Barrillon are still in the hands of his direct descendants.

the game was lost, prepared coolly for a new one. Cynical, when he was recruiting traitors, Barrillon spoke of their scoundrelism with politeness, and was dry and indifferent when he announced their disgraces or their deaths. He remained haughty and unmoved, in the foul sink of iniquity in which his lot was cast in London. His judgments of his English contemporaries are cold, and his opinions of them rather charitable than otherwise. He only betrays his true feelings, in his indifference to their misfortunes. Nevertheless, he was a pleasant companion and a steady friend. He never stirred, when he was in Paris, from the chimney corner of Madame de Sévigné, to whom he was so attached that he said to her, " Those who like you better than I do, love you far too well." He had also a strong affection for La Fontaine, and had an exquisite feeling for the beauties of his Fables. That poet addressed to him some charming verses, the occasion, of which was Barrillon's mission to England.

There never was such a great diplomatic school as the one formed by Mazarin and Lionne. Their pupils were sufficiently numerous for each to specialize his talents, and to be brought forward as soon as he was wanted. Thus, according to the requirements of the hour, Colbert de Croissy, the austere Ruvigny, and the honourable and polished Courtin were sent to London. When they had taken all soundings, and given faithful pictures of the men and women who had influence at Court and in the House of Commons, the unscrupulous Barrillon was sent to enter into close relation with corrupt politicians, and to bribe them.

Barrillon began with a check. He had hardly taken possession of the French embassy, when the Prince of Orange arrived in London.

William of Nassau, the nephew of Charles, and great-grandson of Henry IV. and Admiral Coligny, was the bitter enemy of Louis XIV. His life passed in a mortal struggle against that king. William was, by reason of his bad lungs, always at death's door, and because of the weakness of his army, always being beaten. But neither ill-health nor defeat wore him out; and he ended by bringing all Europe into a coalition against France, by bringing out great generals, by uniting the Pope and Protestants, and by driving against France all the military and moral forces of the civilized world. He had taken the sudden resolution to go to England, and make a desperate effort to detach Charles from the French alliance, by asking the Princess Mary, daughter of the Duke of York and presumptive heiress to the throne, in marriage. The English people were wild with joy, when they learned of the proposed union between the champion of the Reformation and their possible sovereign. Bonfires were lighted in the most remote villages, when the news arrived. Neither Charles nor his brother dared to struggle against the patriotic and religious impulse of the whole nation. The marriage was suddenly decided upon. Barrillon, feeling that opposition was useless,[1] asked Pomponne whether it would not be good policy to accept the inevitable with a good grace, and compliment the Prince of Orange on the success of his suit, on meeting him in the rooms of the Queen or the Duchess of Portsmouth, where he was to be found every day.

The Duchess of Portsmouth felt, with Barril-

[1] Barrillon to Pomponne, Nov. 1, 1677.

lon, that the Dutch Prince was on the top of such a high and strong wave of public favour, as to render quite vain any opposition she could give to the match. She appeared at the festivities given in honour of the Prince and Princess. But they had hardly sailed for Holland than she fell dangerously ill.[1] Charles continued to visit her, and gave audiences to Barrillon in her room.[2] For six weeks she was confined to her bed.[3] If her illness disturbed the statesmen at Versailles, it set the prudes there smiling. Madame de Scudéry[4] in retailing the gossip of the Court and town to Bussy de Rabutin, Madame de Sévigné's cousin, told him how Kéroualle had, crucifix in hand, been preaching in her bed to the King of England to forsake his mistresses and lead a virtuous life. She was at the last extremity, when a slight change for the better took place, and she got up, had herself dressed, and dragged herself to her Sedan chair, to be car-

[1] Barrillon to Pomponne, Dec. 13, 1677.
[2] *Ibid.*, Dec. 16, 1677.
[3] She took to her bed before Dec. 11, 1677, and was still confined to it on Jan. 20, 1678.
[4] Letter to Bussy Rabutin, May 27, 1678, t. iv., p. 114. It took a long time in those days for news to travel.

ried to the French play, where she had heard the king was to be with Madame Mazarin. The players had come to London for a short time, and Charles attended all their representations. He was sitting as close as he possibly could to the Duchess Mazarin[1] when the Breton came to place herself beside him. She not only wanted to show herself along with her great rival, but to assert her power, and her determination to hold her own against all those who wanted to take her place. She knew she was regarded as a cast off, and that Miss Fraser, daughter of the king's head physician, Mrs. Elliot, and two others, wanted to succeed her. Lastly, she had to defend and help her brother-in-law, Lord Pembroke, who, in one of those orgies into which young English rakes of high family plunged so often in the reign of Charles, had killed a watchman. The Earl was tried by his peers, and only found guilty of manslaughter, to absolve him from the penalty of which, the exercise of the king's prerogative of mercy was required.[2]

[1] Barrillon to Pomponne, Jan. 20, 1678.
[2] *Ibid.*, Jan. 13, 1678.

The struggle between the two chief rivals became less sharp.

The Duchess of Cleveland fell into final disgrace at about this time. She was not able to keep within the bounds of external decency, and her behaviour was a cause of scandal even at Whitehall. Finding herself shunned, she returned to London under the pretext of putting a stop to the too great intimacy between her daughter, the Countess of Suffolk, and the Duchess Mazarin, and to break the matrimonial engagement into which her son, the Duke of Grafton, had entered with Arlington's daughter.[1] But the letters addressed to her by the Chevalier de Chastillon, the lover whom she had left behind her in quitting France, were intercepted in France and shown to Charles, who, wishing to get rid of her, took them in bad part.[2] Chastillon was a captain in the Duc d'Orleans' guard, penniless, without sense or wit, and professionally handsome. He lived on his good looks,[3] nearly every night got implicated in some low brawl, and had a mania[4] for in-

---

[1] Barrillon to Pomponne, Nov. 22, 1677.
[2] Scudèry to Bussy, July 14, 1678.
[3] SAINT-SIMON.   [4] DE SÉVIGNÉ.

dulging in ill-natured practical jokes. The Duchess of Cleveland was not allowed to have her son with her, and had to hasten back to France,[1] where Charles,—he fearing she thirsted for vengeance,—placed a close watch upon her movements.

As to the Duchess Mazarin, she had ceased to be as dangerous as the Duchess of Portsmouth imagined, since the king's lust was no longer stimulated by resistance. Not only did the former Duchess make peace with Louise, but she took care to keep off from the king all aspirants to the rank of favourite, not excepting her own bosom friend, the Marquise de Courcelles, *née* Sidonie de Lénoncourt. This French lady was, in her fifteenth year, given in marriage to the Marquis de Courcelles, who perceived, almost immediately after their nuptials, that Louvois was her lover, and ran the greatest risks to obtain meetings with her. The bride was locked up by her husband in the convent where she met the Duchess Mazarin in the quality of a prisoner. Both captives escaped. When the Marquise was running away, she chanced to fall in with the

[1] Barrillon to Pomponne, Jan. 30, 1678.

Marquis du Boulay,[1] cousin of the Chancellor
Silléry. To see her was to adore her; and he
became her protector and took her to Geneva.
Boulay was as jealous as her husband. "My
poor Boulay," she wrote,[2] "I am dreadfully
afraid of losing patience! The pleasure of remaining innocent does not make up for the pain
of being continually browbeaten and insulted."
If she knew how to analyse her sentiments
with light grace, she was also skilled in the
art of depicting her charms. "I am tall," she
wrote of herself, "and my eyes are anything
but small. But I never open them completely,
which gives them a soft and tender expression. I have a beautifully moulded bust, divine
hands, fairly good arms—that is to say, arms
that are rather thin; but I have a compensation for this misfortune in the pleasure I find
in knowing that my legs are perfect and beat
those of any other woman in existence."
Madame de Courcelles hoped to effect a conquest of Charles when she left Du Boulay, to
make her way to England, which was then,

[1] François Bruslard du Boulay, cousin of the Chancellor
Silléry, and younger brother of the Marquis de Broussin.
[2] MARQUISE DE COURCELLES: *Mémoires*, p. 125.

De Courtin said, the refuge of all the ladies who had quarrelled with their husbands. But the Duchess Mazarin did not believe in the perfect sincerity of her conventual fellow-prisoner, when assured that she merely came to London to have the happiness of seeing the Duchess often. The Marquis de Courcelles dying, Madame Mazarin persuaded the lovely Sidonie to go back to France, and there she met with a young captain, whom she married. She lived miserably with him, and soon died.

But Mesdames Harvey and Middleton were in no humour to put up with the Duchess of Portsmouth, and were indefatigable in goading on the Duchess Mazarin against her. They went so far as to conjure her to get the king "to honour Mrs. Middleton's daughter with his attentions.[1] The Duchess of Portsmouth had caused access to the king's cabinet to be refused to Mrs. Middleton, "who went there with Miss Middleton, intent on pleasing his majesty," a design which, in the eyes of Louise, was nothing short of criminal. Meanwhile the Duchess Mazarin paid assiduous court to the Duchess of York, to whose rooms she

[1] Barrillon to Pomponne, July 25, 1678.

went every day to play at romping games. Lady Hyde, the governess of the Princess Anne,[1] was also intimate with the French Duchess. A cabal against Louise de Keroualle was thus formed. The Duke of York spoke fair to her, but in the bottom of his heart disliked her. She knew this well. Notwithstanding, she kept her head so well above water, after the Orange marriage, as to be respectfully used by the whole Court. The king was regular in his visits; and he spoke to her of everything that was on his mind, and received all her insinuations. The Lord Treasurer Danby made use of her to attain his ends; and she aided the French Embassy, by making Charles think that Barrillon was devoted to him. Secretly, she deplored the danger of a war between England and France. The highest courtiers, Sunderland amongst others, were still her fast friends. But the lovely Countess of Sunderland, who had formerly, at the mock marriage at Euston, undressed the insignificant Breton girl in the king's chamber, and cut up his and her garters, was seized with the most implacable hatred for

[1] Barrillon to Pomponne.

her, and spoke of her as "that abominable harlot and cheat."

Unfortunately, political influence was not the sole object of these feuds. Money was a constant cause of bickering. The Exchequer archives still show the preponderance of Louise as a horseleech. The paymaster's clerk [1] set down in reverential verbiage the sums paid her. Her regular pension was £12,000 sterling a year, which was swollen up by supplements to £40,000 a year. In the year 1681 "the French slut" drew from the Treasury £136,668. She had a business man, one Taylor, who invested for her and gave receipts in her name. One of her hangers-on, a certain Timothy Hall, trafficked for her profit, in royal pardons granted to rich convicts. Poor ones were sold to West India planters.

One of the treasury clerks made an entry in two columns on the same page of the sums paid to "Madam Carwell, now Dutchesse of Portsmouth," and to "Nelly Gwynn." [2] From June 3 to December 30, 1676, the Duchess was paid by this clerk £8,773, and Nell £2,862;

[1] JOHN YONGE AKERMANN: *Moneys received and paid for.*
[2] MS. British Museum addal., 28,094, fol. 54.

in 1677 the Duchess £27,300, and Gwynn only £5,250. But the Duchess grasped and gnawed in many other directions, and was always eating into secret funds, whereas Nell was satisfied with her regular pension. A tradesman's account[1] of bills she ran up at his shop shows that if she clutched at money with one hand, she flung it away with her other like a modern French *demi-mondaine.* This bill contains the following entries:

"Madame Carwell, now Dutchess of Portsmouth,
                                        Dr. to W. Watts :—
"A coat of pigeon-breast and silver brocade; breeches à la rhingrave with canons.[2] A coat faced with white taffety and lined with camlet; breeches also faced at pockets and knees with taffeta; breeches having at the thigh slashed seams, to show red and silver lace, canons *idem, idem* with deep frill of point lace. A coat enriched with plain satin and watered ribbons and red and silver cord with red, silver, and point lace at the cuffs. A linen collar embroidered over with needle open-work; silk pockets of chamois leather for coat and breeches. Six dozen buttons of red and silver cloth; eight ells of taffeta for lining sleeves and breeches. A pair of silk stockings. A belt and embroidered pair of garters. A black beaver hat laced with red and silver."

---

[1] List of assets furnished by the executors of W. Watts, mercer to the Duchess of Portsmouth.

[2] *Canons* were the frills worn at the knees. One still sees them at the *Théâtre Français,* in Molière's *Précieuses Ridicules* and other plays.

Nell Gwynn had had such success on the stage in "Florimel," and other masculine characters, that men's clothes, which in the seventeenth century were bright in colour and very dressy, became the rage among the ladies at Whitehall. They did not want the pretext of a masquerade to don them there. The honest W. Watts charged "Madam Carwell" twice for the same taffety lining for her coat and inexpressibles, which must have eclipsed in spruce elegance the stage habiliments of Nelly.

The heavy pensions and emoluments, as it has been shown, were for Louise, and the small ones for Nell. Below these charmers there was a mob of rampant harlots, bastards, pimps and bawds, who all figure in the Treasury account books. Mistress Chiffinch, for showing ladies of easy virtue up the back stairs to the king's assignation rooms at Whitehall, had a pension of £1,200 a year. Catherine Crofts had one of £1,500. Frances Stuart, the stupid, but it cannot be said very mercenary, beauty, who married the Duke of Richmond, put up with £150 a year. The pretty Bulkely had £400 a year. A crowd of lesser concubines were only given sums of £50 each.

It was French money[1] that Charles scattered with such a loose hand; and England was to pay for it in the arrest of national evolution and development. The valet de chambre, Chiffinch, went to receive the instalments of subsidies at the French Embassy; and his wife, a seamstress by trade, gave the occasional mistresses their allowances. But the cash-box was opened for many others. All Barrillon's account-books have been preserved at the Ministry for Foreign Affairs. One learns in them, at what prices English patriots sold themselves, and under the stress of what temptation austere Puritans betrayed their principles. Algernon Sidney is still in English eyes surrounded with the nimbus of a pure-souled martyr. He received £500 for each parliamentary session, from the King of France.[2] The friends of Government did not stay empty-handed. Lord Berkshire was given £1,000, and Coleman £360. He was also entrusted with £700 to buy members of

---

[1] Not so. The Treasury clerks who paid Louise de Keroualle the vast sums already mentioned, never fingered a stiver of French money. (*Translator's Note.*)

[2] See *Aff. Etr. Angleterre*, tome cxxx., fol. 68; tome cxxxi., fol. 146, for 1678.

the House of Commons, as his receipts and memoranda show. One Scott, a knight, according to his receipt, had £200 for the same kind of work. Barrillon gave into the hands of different persons of note, for the information they communicated to him, one hundred and eight pounds six and eightpence. He furthermore spent four hundred pounds in obtaining secret reports from officers of the army, treasury clerks, and secretaries of state.

Before the year 1678 had expired, Barrillon found it expedient to renew his largesses. He was frightened at the drain on the French exchequer; and yet he did not dare, from a fear of compromising a long-laid scheme of policy, to put a stop to it. No bribe was carelessly given. Sir John Baber[1] was engaged by him to sound Littleton, and bring him and Poole into close relations with the French Embassy. Poole was one of the leaders of the Puritan party, and distinguished himself by

---

[1] This Baber constantly appears in the secret service accounts of Barrillon, who attached great importance to his information. He was doubtless the person whose reserve and reticence Pepys eulogizes in the *Diary*, March 14, 1660.

his virulence against the honest Strafford. Littleton received a bribe, direct from Barrillon. It would be difficult, the latter reported to his Government, to find two men who had more credit for patriotism and austere virtue in the House of Commons. It was impossible to withhold from Montagu fifteen hundred guineas for which he asked to bribe obscure country members, whose votes would tell at a division.

This intervention of Montagu was an odd complication of the ties which bound Louis XIV. to Charles.

Montagu was the brother of Lady Harvey, and had long been ambassador in France. All the political men regarded him as belonging to the French party, when he suddenly denounced the Treasurer Danby as having been for many months engaged in secret negotiations with the Court of Versailles, and that, at a time when frightened by the strong tide of Opposition, he talked in public the loudest against France, and prepared with much noise a treaty of alliance between England and the Netherlands.

Thus, Louis, abandoned by Charles, and betrayed by Danby, at the moment that he was about to enter upon a new campaign in Flanders, found himself obliged, at no matter what price, to paralyse the action of England for at least another summer. He struck out a course with quick decision; and did not hesitate, in paying Charles to adjourn or prorogue Parliament, to employ Montagu to attack Danby, whom he was also bribing. He entered into the game of each of his adversaries, and supplied them with money, on the condition that they were not to make up and unite against France, but to prolong agitation, and reduce England to the condition of an impotent State. By his orders, his worst enemies in Parliament were encouraged by Montagu. Barrillon was delighted at this double intrigue; and, while he egged on the King of England against the Opposition, he seconded the Russells, Lord Holles,[1] and Buckingham in opposing Charles. Louis, in an autograph letter, instructed him to make use of the king's authority

[1] Barrillon was mistaken in his estimate of Holles, who was second son of the Earl of Clare, was created Baron Denzil in 1661, sent as ambassador to France in 1663, as plenipotentiary to the Hague in 1662, and who died in 1680, before he could receive a splendid gift Lous XIV. intended sending him.

and friendly feeling against the House of Commons, and of the Parliament to prevent effect being given to resolutions which Charles might be brought to take against him.

Danby's treaty with Holland reconciled Charles and his Parliament; but party divisions were sufficiently prolonged to enable Louis to strike a decisive blow in his campaign of 1678. He went to war early in that year. On March 12th, Ghent fell into his hands. Ypres yielded a few days later, and Mons was invested. The Dutch plenipotentiaries hastened to sign the peace of Nimeguen. Spain followed their example in the next month, and the German Empire gave in at the beginning of winter. Louis issued triumphantly from his struggle with coalesced Europe. This triumph of France was due to the long neutrality of England. The English people beheld with rage the crippling of Protestant Holland by a Catholic power. They were carried away against the Catholics by one of those frenzies of contagious hatred which sometimes take hold of a nation like an epidemic. When a nation is possessed by a fit of such fury, there is always a statesman ready to pander to it.

Shaftesbury, in this instance, came forward to throw fuel on the raging fire.

Ashley Cooper, Earl of Shaftesbury, had in his youth fought for Charles I. against the Parliament; and turned round to serve the Parliament, when he saw it was the strongest. He flattered the Republicans, by celebrating the fall of the Malignants; and was "the loudest bagpipe of the noisy crew." When monarchy was restored, he cast off the sanctimonious mask, and, to please Charles, postured as a libertine. He played each part so well, as to be successively lauded as a patriot and a God-fearing man by the Puritans, and to deserve being called by Charles "the most vicious dog in England." A daughter of the Protector Cromwell, whom he courted, refused to marry him. He was incapable either of piety or libertinage, because a born sceptic and of a feeble constitution. He had in youth the body of an old man, was ghastly, wrinkled, and his hands shook from palsy. When a minister of Charles, he courted the Opposition, and prepared to avenge himself, not only on Danby, whose head he wanted, but on Charles himself, whom he longed to humiliate.

Shaftesbury was never so humble and obsequious as when he was meditating vengeance. He wrote to the king, that all he wanted was "to lye at his feet, and make publicly, in the House of Lords, any acknowledgment and submission that his Majesty demanded." But while he cringed, he was suborning the crew of false witnesses who were gathered together by Titus Oates. That monster announced that the English Catholics had hatched a plot for the assassination of the king and all the Protestants. The people, who were in a state of frenzied anger at the impunity granted to Louis, swallowed Oates' fable with a credulity which had no parallel in history. They wanted victims to satisfy their rage; and nobody suspected of sympathizing with the Papists was in safety.

The first victim was the knave Coleman,[1] the Secretary of State, whose receipts figure in Barrillon's accounts. The French ambassador wrote coolly to Versailles: "Coleman has sent me word to be in no wise uneasy, because nobody can find in his papers a scrap of writing to testify to his transactions with me."

[1] *Affaires Etrangères*, tome cxxxi. fol. 53.

We now know that Coleman was a traitor to his country. But those who accused him and those who found him guilty had nothing to go upon. He was charged with not having shown horror at the Papist Plot, and with having neglected to keep minutes of the letters that he wrote. "Don't be afraid," said the Lord Chief Justice to him. "There will be no condemnation if your crimes are not brought home to you. We shall not act towards you as you wanted to act towards us, in trying to murder us." Thus, the judge held him morally guilty before his counsel spoke of the crime invented by the perjured informer. It is worth noting that the English people, who are imbued with the notion of fair play, are the most respectful of law, and the most scrupulously observant of legal forms, have produced the greatest number of servile judges, and in their State trials shown the most revolting examples of juridical iniquity. English history, from the time of the Tudors to the reign of George III., is a narrative of juridical murders. Coleman was accused of having incited the Jesuits of St. Omer to assassinate the king, in return for the payment of 30,000 masses. Oates swore that he had learned of this bargain at St. Omer, and the Lord Chief Justice praised him for his courage in giving evidence to this effect. He also swore that Coleman was to pay the Irish £200,000 to rise in rebellion. The miserable wretch had sold himself to Barrillon for £200! The king was to have been either poisoned, poignarded, or shot. Titus Oates, who pretended he had seen Coleman in a Jesuit conclave, was unable to identify him. But the jury were indifferent to this point. The scene described had taken place by candle light, which, every one knew, dimmed the sight. In cross-examination he was asked why he had not been so circumstantial in his early depositions? The answer was, that he gave them standing, and that being on one's legs impairs the memory. The Lord Chief Justice adopted this explanation. Coleman wanted to establish the Catholic religion, by assassinating the king and placing the Duke of York, his friend and patron, on the throne. This could only be done by assassinating Charles. Therefore he planned the assassination. In virtue of this reasoning, the judge summed up against the prisoner, the jury found him guilty, and he was sentenced to be disembowelled, and his intestines burned before his eyes.

This example terrified Charles. His ladies ceased from quarrelling, and gathered round him in dismay. Oates denounced the Duchess Mazarin as the accomplice of all the plots against the Protestant religion. The Duchess of Portsmouth, who had a Catholic chaplain in her household,[1] felt that at any instant she might become the mark for popular fury. She saw that Charles was ready to bend to the storm, and that if it burst over her head it would be idle to hope for his protection. She told Barrillon that she could not help remembering how, three hundred years before,[2] Alice Perrers, the mistress of Edward III., was obliged to appear before Parliament and swear that she would never again see that king. England was a country of precedents. Perhaps she thought her wisest plan would be to return to France. "Madame de Portsmouth," wrote Barrillon to Louis on Dec. 1, 1678, "has had another conversation with me.[3] She is not

---

[1] Courtin to Pomponne, March 25, 1677.
[2] In 1376.
[3] Barrillon to King Louis, Dec. 1, 1678.

sure that she can stay in England. There are many persons who are minded to name her in Parliament, as conspiring against the Protestant religion for the King of France. She thinks it would not be a great misfortune to be obliged to retire to France, especially since your Majesty has assured her, through Lord Sunderland, of your kind protection. Her presence here, she is afraid, must embarrass King Charles, and she would prefer to get away while he preserves some kind feeling for her, than, by staying longer, to expose herself to the rage of a whole nation. Her position would be sad indeed, if, after she lost the king's favour, she was assailed by Parliament and people."

The queen herself was in danger during this hurricane, and clung to the Duchess of Portsmouth.

The Duke of York left England. Charles did not dare to keep his band of French musicians at Whitehall, because they were Papists, and sent word to Barrillon through Louise, to beg that he would shelter the poor fellows at the Embassy. The King of England finally cowered down to the lowest depth of abasement, and abandoned every one whom he was in honour bound to protect. He had not even the courage to defend his wife, who, as a Catholic, was set upon by the Shaftesbury crew.

The libertine in difficult circumstances rarely preserves dignity. The habit of enjoyment lowers every energy. Love of pleasure destroys courage. One sees in a full strong light, in Charles, a common enough character, that of a man of happy endowments who sinks down into a life of slothful ease and luxury, regards every difficulty with dread, loses all self-respect, and, although naturally goodnatured, becomes capable of no matter what bad action, from sheer indolence and cowardice. He got the better of the jealous rages of his mistresses by yielding to them. This habit was brought into his policy; and when the people demanded the heads of Popish plotters, he let them have them, in order to enjoy quietly his epicurean pleasures. He not only sacrificed innocent and estimable persons, but became their persecutor; and he even gave his countenance to the false witnesses. Nobody knew better than Charles what the Catholics wanted. He was a Catholic himself. He was more guilty than any of the suborners, false witnesses, and intriguers, because he not only was chief magistrate, but because, with the money paid for his promise to declare himself a Catholic, he was paying Titus Oates and his band of fellow perjurers. He let them sleep beside him, and surrounded them with his guards; he saw to the preparation of their meals; recruited, with the money he had received from Louis, subordinate informers, and paid limbs of law who were employed to dog Papists and hunt them down. In the bottom of the money-chest, which the mistresses had nearly emptied, he found £10 a week for Titus Oates, whom he boarded and lodged in his palace of Whitehall. The weekly allowance of £10 was augmented to £12. Charles paid for the maintenance of false witnesses in town, he paid spies engaged in discovering Popish plots. The Protestants did not force him to do this. On the contrary, he hid his hand when it made these payments. It was all done out of the secret fund, with money that he obtained from abroad for his seraglio. One Millicent Hanson obtained "£10 for seeking out priests." One Massal got £20 for tracking and arresting a priest. Dangerfield and Oates, besides their stipends, were allowed for expenses and time lost in going to depose; for discovering Papists hidden at Court, and for informing where Jesuits had property concealed. They also received handsome presents.

Among the victims of this shameful panic,[1] was the most respected member of the House of Lords, and the most odiously condemned of all the alleged plotters—the Earl of Strafford. Charles II., who knew his moral worth, incurred the same reproach for weakness as his father earned in deserting the first Lord Strafford. He was guilty, besides, of having paid out of his pleasure fund the perjurers who swore away the second Earl's life. He gave Charles Clare, "for finding witnesses and bringing them into court, £100."

The Duchess of Portsmouth did not descend with the king so low as to court Titus Oates.

---

[1] The popular instinct was right. All that M. Fornenon has brought to light shows that the panic was well founded. But it took a wrong direction—the king being the arch plotter, not so much to destroy Protestantism, as, for the gratification of his shameful vices, to reduce England to the rank of a satellite of France, which then, to obtain the co-operation of the Jesuits in Louisiana, Indo-China, and in the Spanish Colonies, became more Catholic almost than the Pope. (*Translator's Note.*)

But she judged well to make peace with Shaftesbury, and helped him to re-enter the Cabinet. Shaftesbury then became the preponderant minister. Buckingham[1] was discredited in the eyes of every party, and was harassed into his grave by his creditors. Danby was a prisoner in the Tower. Sunderland entirely depended on the support of Louise Keroualle. But this great rise in the tide of his fortune turned Shaftesbury's head. He thought himself able to get rid once and for ever of the real chief of his party,—a man as ailing and ambitious as himself,—the Prince of Orange.

Some other heir to the throne was essential to the perpetuation of Shaftesbury's power. He wanted a docile tool, and made the blunder of setting up as a Pretender the Duke of Monmouth, the eldest of the king's bastards, six of whom were dukes, and brought forward as his sons when he touched for the evil.

/ Monmouth had many natural gifts; but he had been adulated from his cradle, spoiled by his father, caressed by the mistresses of Charles and of the Duke of York, and corrupted by the atmosphere and examples amid which he was

[1] The Zimri of Dryden's *Absalom and Achitophel*.

reared and thrown by all the circumstances of his early manhood into libertinage and nerveless poltroonery. /He was a poor chief to offer to the Protestants during their effervescence. Charles certainly was fond of him; but he had not sunk so low as to wish him to be accepted as his heir.

The king, in his embarrassment, sent word by the Duchess of Portsmouth, that he would be glad to have some talk with Barrillon at Whitehall, as soon as the company she usually received there in the evening had retired. When the ambassador went, Charles told him that the King of France might, if he chose, preserve to him his crown, and attach him for the rest of his life to his interests. It was not a time for compliments and empty words, but for rapid action. The King of France would have to decide whether England was to remain a monarchy or become a republic. Things had come to such a pass that his majesty would have to make up his mind to support Royalty. Unless he did so, nothing could prevent the Parliament from absolutely disposing of questions of peace, war, and alliances. Finally, Charles urged Barrillon to repeat all that he said to his sovereign, and to conjure the King of France, in his name, to help a course which for the rest of his life would make England dependent upon him, and attach the Crown indissolubly to his interests.

Barrillon profited by the opportunity to tax Charles with paltering conduct; and with some sharpness reproached him with the Princess Mary's Dutch marriage. He reminded him that, notwithstanding the heavy pecuniary sacrifices which the King of France had made, he had always reason to complain that English neutrality was insecure.

Charles asked for the favour of another conversation, an account of which, along with that of the one just cited, is given on July 13, 1676, in the Foreign Affairs archives. The King of England owned that the reproaches of Barrillon were well founded, and yet not quite just. How was it possible to resist the Duke of York and the Lord Treasurer, who wanted to fish for popularity in crying out against France? Secretly he stood out against them as far as he could; but there were resistless fatalities that dragged him on. Charles admitted that he erred in not foreseeing what the Dutch match would lead to. But his bitter experience would be a guarantee of his future conduct; and the King of France might credit him when he declared that, in future, nothing in the world would detach him from his interests. He saw with pain and deep grief the shedding of innocent blood. But if he had stood between the accused Catholics and the national fury, he would have risked everything.

Meanwhile, young Monmouth,—and particularly in the evenings after supper, when excited by wine,—claimed through his mother, Lucy Walters,[1] descent from Edward IV. and the

[1] Charles, who seems to have had a taste for Celtic beauty had among his concubines a Breton (Louise de Keroualle), two Welsh women (Lucy Walters, or Barlow, and Nell Gwynn), and an Irish woman (Peg Hughes). Lucy Walters, Monmouth's mother, was,—in 1649, when she was with him at St. Germains en Laye, where Evelyn first saw her,—a beautiful, brown, bold, and insipid creature. She was the daughter of Richard Walters, of Haverfordwest in Wales, a gentleman of little means, and she came to London to seek her fortune. Algernon Sidney, when a colonel in Cromwell's army, meant to have her, and gave her fifty broad pieces (as he told the Duke of York), but missed his bargain, he having been hastily sent away with his regiment. She fell into the hands of his brother, Colonel Robert Sidney, from whom Charles II. got her in his

rights of the House of Plantagenet. This, Barrillon thought, might be regarded at Versailles as chimerical. But chimeras were less ridiculous in England than elsewhere.[1] There was a general taste for romantic improbability, which would serve the ends of an impostor; and the common people liked the fables they saw played in the theatres, about mysterious marriages being cleared up, and true heirs in the end, coming by their own.

Louis stopped supplies, and drily wrote, that until a positive engagement was made that Parliament would not be again convoked, no further subsidy would be given. Charles accepted his humiliation, and, at the Duchess of Portsmouth's rooms, told Barrillon that he had resolved to follow the course proposed by Louis, and not to let Parliament assemble until

wanderings. The world had cause to doubt whether Monmouth was a Stuart or a Sidney. He had the countenance, complexion, stature, and even the wart on the face of Robert Sidney. However, the king owned him. Lucy Walters called herself Mrs. Barlow. She led such a loose life during the campaign of Charles, ending in his escape at Worcester, that he would have nothing more to do with her; and she became a woman of the town in Paris, where she died miserably. (*Translator's Note.*)

[1] Barrillon to King Louis, July 6, and July 13, 1679.

the King of France judged that it might be convoked without inconvenience to him. The ambassador recriminated on the sovereign, and asked him how he could reasonably hope that the French Exchequer could afford to subsidize Charles with unstinted generosity, if he played into the hands of the enemies of the King of France, and by doing so helped European coalitions to make war upon him. The last war he sustained against Spain, Holland, and the Empire, was a wasting one. If Charles had an intelligent perception of his own interest, he would try to spare France every kind of military expense. But instead of that, the last war had been begun by the King of England. He made peace certainly with reluctance, and under the constraint of the House of Commons, which forced him to make it on a separate footing, and to leave France single-handed to fight Europe. This misfortune drained the French exchequer. It was no longer possible to give heavy subsidies unless for serious services. Formerly they had been given out of brotherly friendship, and this might have been continued had Charles proved staunch in cleaving to the French alliance, and enabled Louis to dispose rapidly of his enemies. However, as Louis did not wish to see Charles distressed for want of money, he would give him a proof of his desire to see him free from pecuniary embarrassments and his authority restored. To this end he had ordered Barrillon to offer him an advance of £20,000 if he would engage not to convoke Parliament before the month of March.

Charles expressed great surprise at the offer of so inconsiderable a sum, and spoke warmly about the alternative which was imposed on him of either being reduced to dependence on Louis or of letting the House of Commons act according to its impetuous hatred or caprice. He got the Duchess of Portsmouth to plead for him, and submitted to her in everything. She had the skill to direct the Government through the medium of Sunderland. What little energy remained to Charles he showed in defending her. Two young courtiers, Jarret and Dunquot,[1] set her little blackamoor drunk, and gave him money to tell them things derogatory to the ladies, and in particular to the one most

[1] Probably Duncomb. English names are sometimes mis-spelt by Louis's ambassadors. (*Translator's Note.*)

honoured by the attentions of the King of England. When the slanderous tittle-tattle which they based on what they heard from the blackamoor came to the king's ears, he forbade them to appear at Court. A cause of fresh and deep annoyance to him was, to find that his secret conferences with Barrillon were revealed by Sunderland's wife, who feared her husband might be compromised by his relations with France. She vowed to every one that she was in a state of constant hostility to the Duchess of Portsmouth, and that that "designing jade" brought about interviews between the king and Barrillon, gave the latter his cue, and that he repeated what she told him like a prating starling. The Countess protested, that all she asked was to extricate her husband from dangerous intrigues.[1] At the same time, Algernon Sidney[2] beheld with irritation the favour which the Frenchwoman

---

[1] *Henry Sidney's Diary of the Times of Charles II.*, ed. 1843, vol. I, p. 232, the Countess of Sunderland to H. Sidney, Jan. 13, 1676.

[2] *Algernon Sidney's Letters to H. Saville in the Year* 1679. London: 1742. See letters from Feb. 20 to April 28, 1679. I do not know what value is to be attached to these letters on the score of authenticity.

enjoyed, and the want of energy of the House of Commons, which, when her name was mentioned in a debate, did not seize the opportunity to attack her. To prevent herself being attacked, she adroitly looked for support in Monmouth. There was in her following a confidential servant, one Mistress Wall,[1] who cried on the house-tops about Louise's passion for him, and of her disinterested tenderness in trying to further his pretensions. This Mistress Wall was given, as a recompense, the privilege of furnishing body-linen to the queen, and promised the secret function of Mistress Chiffinch whenever she might die.[2] These tricks came out, and were made a theme for satirical lampoons. The pamphleteers published "intercepted letters" from Madam Carwell to the Duke of Monmouth. They taxed their ingenuity to place her, to the nation, in the most odious light, by holding her up as the sheet-anchor of the Catholics and of France. She was made to say to Monmouth, "All these English hate me, but that does not trouble me, since the king tells me everything, and my friends alone have influence."

[1] *Henry Sidney's Diary*, vol. i., p. 170, Nov. 17, 1679.
[2] *Ibid.*, vol. ii., p. 22, April 2, 1680.

The Duchess renewed her instances with the French ambassador on behalf of Charles.

"I saw yesterday," wrote Barrillon,[1] "Madame de Portsmouth, from whom the King of England keeps nothing hidden. She came to tell me that if your Majesty would give him four millions of livres a year for three years, he would enter into any engagement your Majesty might propose. But without this sum he could not avoid assembling Parliament. The king himself told me later in the day, that he was mortified to be reduced to driving a bargain with your Majesty."

While these negotiations were going on, the hopes of Monmouth and Shaftesbury were raised. But Charles was taken with a malignant fever, and seemed on the verge of the grave, when his doctors gave him up and allowed him to take the Chevalier Talbot's quinine specific, which was then a novelty and known as Jesuits' bark.[2] This illness

---

[1] This letter should be regarded as of doubtful authenticity. It is not in any of the French State records, and is only found in the MS. of the British Museum.

[2] The disease, according to Evelyn, was ague; and quinine, or *quinquina*, had been brought into vogue, not by Talbot, but by Tudor, the king's apothecary. The physicians would

brought about Shaftesbury's and Sunderland's disgrace. The Duchess of Portsmouth and the Duke of York united to get Monmouth sent from London. He was saved from exile by Louis, who feared such a stretch of authority would give rise to a situation that would force Charles to make concessions to Parliament. He also pointed out to Barrillon that the, for him, cheapest manner of proceeding, was to foment quarrels between the king and Opposition, by giving subventions only to members of both Houses; and he continued his largesses to the Country party.

To this end Barrillon paid Algernon Sidney[1]

not, out of envy of Tudor, give it to Charles, until the king secretly obtained the opinion of Dr. Short, in whom he had confidence because he was reputed (falsely) a Papist, and was told that it was the only thing that could save him. (*Translator's Note.*)

[1] It is due to the memory of Sidney, to say that his Republicanism was thought sincere by the different agents of Louis, and that they classed him among the political Englishmen of his time who were not bereft of moral sense. There is no direct evidence in the French records to show under what pretext or through what agency the French Embassy got round Sidney, and induced him to be a pensioner of Louis. But from much in them the inference may be drawn that he thought any stick good enough to beat down such

the 500 guineas that he wanted; to Baber, the Presbyterian leader in the Commons, 500 guineas; to Littleton, 500 guineas; to Powels, 500 guineas; to Herbert,[1] 500 guineas; and "to maintain Bulstrode in his employment at Brussels," 400 guineas.

Notwithstanding these *gratifications*, Parliament continued unmanageable. Monmouth came back triumphantly to London. Barrillon informed Louis that an event had just taken place "which would have appeared most extraordinary in any other country."[2] It was the return of Monmouth, "who every night," Barrillon added, "sups with Nelly, the courtesan who has borne the king two children, and whom he daily visits." Nelly set up to place a vile thing as the English throne had become; and made up his mind to accept aids which Barrillon artfully led him to hope for. Sidney spent a good deal of money in trying to get up a Republican movement. (*Translator's Note.*)

[1] Probably the Herbert who became Lord Herbert of Cherbury in 1678, and was grandson of Herbert the author. He married Catherine, daughter of the Earl of Bradford. The other Herbert was William, Earl of Powis, Marquis of Montgomery, who, being a Catholic, could have no influence. Herbert Earl of Pembroke, Louise Keroualle's brother-in law, was never in the House of Commons.

[2] Barrillon to Louis, Dec. 14, 1679.

herself at the head of the Protestants, which did not prevent her subsequently from going over to the Catholic Church.¹ Parliament demanded the removal from Court of the Duchess of Portsmouth and Sunderland, against whom the heads of an impeachment were drawn up. It was proposed to execute them both, with Danby and the Catholics who were in the Tower.

Charles at last resolved to prorogue Parliament. As the treaty of which this step was a condition remained a secret, it was attributed to " Madam Carwell." She, it was said, feeling herself exposed to an impeachment, made the king prorogue for a long period. She was alarmed at the rumours to this effect, and fell ill from sheer fright. She spoke of dismissing all her Catholic servants, and prepared to retire, herself, to France.

¹ Letters in the Verney collection at Claydon House.

CHAPTER IX.

SUNDERLAND AND SHAFTESBURY.

THE sudden blow which Charles struck deferred the danger in which Louise stood, without suppressing it. Popular hatred of France ran higher than ever; and the judges were as abject in pandering to the animosity of the nation, as they had been servile to the Government. The Duchess of Portsmouth, by boldly standing up in this crisis for the French alliance, became the object of general hatred, and was not sure that the king would persevere in defending her, or of the sincerity of the Duke of York when he sought to unite with her. The king had again found another mistress, who was the daughter of a nobleman.[1] His brother sought to make his peace with the Protestants, and offered as a holocaust the

[1] Thought to be the daughter of Rochester, who, in 1683, married Lord Ossory.

Duchess of Portsmouth.[1] She had therefore to manœuvre with extreme dexterity in keeping all her friends, and in not exasperating her enemies. She entered into the closest union with Sunderland. In this she scandalized his beautiful wife, who wrote: "So damned a jade as this would sell us without hesitation for 500 guineas." Louise and Sunderland drew towards them, and brought into their orbit the supple, adventurous, and clever Godolphin, who was coquetting with the Prince of Orange. The latter was becoming uneasy at the pretensions of Monmouth. The efforts of the Duchess of Portsmouth and Sunderland in 1680 were directed towards keeping alive the uneasiness of the Prince of Orange, husband to the presumptive heiress to the throne; not letting the Duke of York, whom they knew to be cold and selfish, play them false, and avoiding to stir the bile of Shaftesbury, or to wound Monmouth's vanity. The Frenchwoman took the audacious course of declaring openly for the Prince and Princess of Orange; and was so explicit in declaring she preferred English to

[1] Barrillon to Louis: "I believe each wishes to save himself at the cost of the other."

French interests as to seriously alarm Barrillon and make him lose his temper, which was further tried on his hearing that she sought to be on good terms with the arch-enemy of France. But she re-assured him somewhat, by coming privily to tell him that the king at bottom was what he always had been, and that he wished to preserve the friendship and alliance of the King of France.[1] The French ambassador, however, could extract nothing from her regarding the conclusion of the treaty.

Barrillon did not attach at this time much importance to the services of the Duchess. He knew that public opinion had risen against her with a violence which he thought irresistible. He overheard tipsy bloods in the theatre[2] speak in abusive terms of her and Lord Sunderland; and on the same day the Duke of Monmouth's health was drunk by the wild young men about town, in all the taverns and coffee-houses.[3] Barrillon thought he might by

---

[1] Barrillon to King Louis, to whom, after Pomponne's disgrace in 1679, he addressed most of his letters.

[2] Barrillon to King Louis, Jan. 15, 1680.

[3] May 20, 1680. It was in this letter Barrillon said of the future Duke of Marlborough: "He is wholly inexperienced in public business."

his efforts create a cross current of opinion which would take from the tumultuous force of the one that was growing up, and that he might get the better of intriguers by corruption. He moreover thought it of the highest importance to retain Montagu by his sister, Lady Harvey, who had power over his mind, and who could render many useful services. She might be secured by a nice present; and the snuff-box intended for Lord Holles, not having been given to him, might go to the lady. If his Majesty thought it too considerable, a sum of less value than it represented would do as well, for she was not above taking money. Her rapacity might be stimulated by insinuating that she might expect further gifts from France. As her aid could be most valuable, Barrillon was anxious to secure it. He also, he said in the despatch on this subject, had gained two Nonconformist preachers.[1] His aim was to form a solid group of agents from the different parties, and to use alike Republicans and courtiers. To well understand this policy, his "list of persons to whom gratuities may be offered"[2] should be read.

[1] July 1, 1680.   [2] July 24, 1680.

In the letter which accompanied that document he says: "The Duke of Monmouth is now more considerable than anybody else. He might perhaps not relish being offered money; but I think that, under the pretext of enabling him to withstand the machinations of courtiers, a sum might be offered for him to dispose of *as he thought well*. In gaining him, all his partisans would be gained as well, and he would be placed in a situation in which he could never more be reconciled with the Court, or the Prince of Orange. However, it should be made clear to him that he was to prevent Parliament voting the king any money, because, if his majesty Charles II. does not feel his dependence, he will give us the slip. I think the Duke should be offered £4,000. This would be more efficacious than if we spent twice as much in bribing the Parliament. Shaftesbury directs all the attacks against the Court, and is at the head of the malcontents. If money is given him, and he thinks he has France behind him, he will be more daring. £4,000 is the least that could be offered to him. The members of the House of Commons who might be usefully bought are: Algernon Sidney, for

500 guineas down, with the promise of 500 guineas more; Powels, 1,000 guineas; Herbert, 1,000 guineas; Baber, 1,000 guineas. All the other members named in the annexed list were tested in the Danby affair, and were very useful. Baber is not in Parliament, but he mixes a good deal with Parliamentary men and with the Presbyterians, and he has their confidence. He is a man from whom I have much profit, and it is to him that I owe my intimacy with Lord Holles. There are other members of the House of Commons who could be made, according to opportunities and conjunctures, to serve our ends. Vindington,[1] who has been Solicitor-General; Colonel Titus, Burnet, Bernard, and Eslon and Papilion, who are all merchants of the City of London, and highly respected Presbyterians; Player, treasurer of the Corporation of London; Sacheverell,[2] and Harley, the ex-governor of Dunkirk. It is

[1] Probably Sir T. Widdrington, who was Speaker under Cromwell, but very old in 1680.
[2] Not the preacher who obtained for himself prominence in Anne's time, but an M.P. who was rabid against the second Earl of Strafford. Player was the City Chamberlain, and the "railing Rabsheka" of Dryden's *Absalom and Achitophel*.

hard to say what might be offered to each of them. But there might be a fund of 20,000 crowns placed at my disposal, which could be employed according to the utility and facility that there would be in gaining them. It is indispensable to begin with a payment of 1,000 guineas to Montagu, who is industrious, capable of continuous application, and enjoys the entire confidence of the Duke of Monmouth. This money ought to be remitted to him before the end of September, when I promised that he was to have it." Louis XIV. wrote in pencil on the margin of the letter: "M. Colbert will give an order for 4,000 pistoles. Instruct M. Colbert to have a letter of change sent to M. Barrillon for 100,000 francs."

Barrillon insisted that, in his judgment, France should not have a secret bias for any party,[1] but set them all on, one against the other, and keep them at daggers drawn. Thus the King of

---

[1] It is to be gathered from the correspondence between him and the Court of Versailles, that he was reproached with having encouraged Sidney to appeal to his old Ironside comrades against Monarchy. The warmth with which he insists that the King of France should be indifferent as to means, Republican or other, in a degree clears Sidney's memory. (*Translator's Note.*)

France, who was destined to revoke the Edict of Nantes, was led to support the Presbyterians, because the Prince of Orange, whom he hated, was drawing close to Charles. His ambassador only thought of preventing these sectarians falling into pits dug for them by the Court; and with this object made the acquaintance of their chief orators. He so gained Powels[1] that he was able to write: "This person is entirely with me, and will follow all my instructions. I have taken the same steps to bring Herbert into my hand. Nobody made himself so useful in the Danby affair. He stayed a whole day when the impeachment debate was going on,[2] and only allowed those whom he thought favourable to the Court to go out, and prevented the others leaving, almost by force.[3] He is a strong, vehement, hot-tempered, and selfish fellow. I have much intercourse with Sidney. He is greatly opposed

---

[1] Poule.   [2] Oct. 4, 1680.
[3] The English historians never seem to have suspected the real cause of Danby's impeachment. They regard it as due to political rivalry or patriotic indignation. It was simply owing to the rancour of Louis, and to all the money he spent in hunting down Danby, whose fall, he thought, would serve as a warning to Charles. (*Translator's Note.*)

to the Court. But I have reason to fear that Sunderland, who is his nephew, is getting round him for the Prince of Orange. I know that Sidney has a strong leaning towards the Republic. Baber continues to work the Presbyterians. It is through him that I have gained two popular preachers, who can insinuate things which it would never do to say openly. I know they have spoken in the pulpit of a matter which would not count any where else, unless here, but which in England is no trifle. It is, that the Prince of Orange hunts on Sundays."

The Duchess of Portsmouth had no cause, at this time, to be afraid of Nell Gwynn, whose eldest son[1] had just died. She had recruited to her side another actress, Mary Davis, whose daughter she was bringing up under her own eyes, with the intention of giving her in marriage to Sunderland's son. She even suffered the queen to receive some little marital atten-

---

[1] James Beauclerc, died in 1680; the second son, Charles, born May 8, 1670, was created Duke of St. Albans on Jan. 10, 1684, and married, in 1694, Diana de Vere, the last of the Oxford de Veres. He was the ancestor of the present Duke of St. Albans.

tions from her indolent husband. He went to inform Catherine of what had taken place at a debate in the House of Lords,[1] and, as a mark of extraordinary kindness, sat for some time in her chamber after dinner, and then took a long nap there—a thing he was only in the habit of doing in the rooms of the Duchess of Portsmouth.

The apoplectic Charles had allowed Parliament to be convoked at the end of 1680, when it discussed a bill to exclude his brother from the throne. Barrillon redoubled his efforts to destroy the chances of the Prince of Orange.[2] He was obliged to go to work through agents. To have treated directly with him, would have been to expose life and fortune. Montagu and his sister, Herbert, Algernon Sidney, and Baber were his best auxiliaries. Mrs. Harvey was bold and enterprising, and was intimate with numerous courtiers and members of Parliament. She recruited Hampden[3] and Haber—both men of weight in the Opposition. Algernon Sidney, Barrillon reported as a man of great views and designs, which all made

[1] Nov 28, 1680.   [2] Dec. 5, 1680.
[3] Son of the patriot who stood out against Charles I.

for the establishment of a Republic. He belonged to the party of the Independents and other sectarians who carried all before them in the anti-Popish disorders. They were not strong in Parliament, but were powerful in the City; and it was owing to Sidney's management that Bethel[1] was elected Sheriff. The services that Sidney rendered were not apparent, because he had to deal with obscure and hidden men. Herbert was a friend of Montagu, and vigilant, active, pushing, and wanted to make his fortune in obtaining payments for services rendered to France. He often brought information of great value to the French Embassy. Baber was a link between Barrillon and the Presbyterians. Louis instructed Barrillon to persevere in keeping England weak by internal divisions. He was to prevent, at any cost, the reconciliation of the Court and Parliament. It is probable that the King of France found it cheaper to bribe members than to go on bribing Charles. The expense of doing the former, for the session which ended on January 16, 1681, was not so

[1] Slingsby Bethell, Sheriff of London in 1680, and the Shimei of *Absalom and Achithophel*.

heavy as the smallest subsidy to the king. Hampden and Herbert received 1,000 guineas each; Haber, Titus, Hermstrand, Baber, Hill, Boscowen, and Algernon Sidney, 500 guineas each; Bennett, Hodam, Hicdal, Frankland, Tompton, Harvey, Garowan, Sacheverell, Tolen, and Bide, 300 guineas each; one Ducros, residing in Holstein, and a friend of Lord Sandwich, 150 guineas, "for furnishing good information"; one Le Pin, a clerk of Sunderland, 150 guineas, "who sometimes gave valuable hints;" to Baron de Witt, a Spanish agent, 100 guineas, also "for hints and news;" and 1,000 guineas to Montagu.[1]

Louis was working to oblige Charles to indefinitely prorogue Parliament. He knew to what degree he was unnerved by pleasure, and how lazy his mind had become. Louis also feared a reconciliation at his expense. He stirred up, therefore, the king against the Commons, and egged on the Commons to aggress upon the king. As the force of Opposition lay in the most intolerant Protestant

---

[1] See *Les Etats de Barrillon*, inserted in *Affaires Etrangères, Angleterre*, tome cxl. fol. 338, and tome cxlii. fol. 170, from Dec. 5 to Feb. 13, 1681.

sects, he subventioned the preachers who led these fanatical bodies to attack the Crown.

The Duchess of Portsmouth was not in the secret of this Presbyterian and Republican policy, which was begun when Louis was commencing to persecute his own Protestant subects. She imagined she was pleasing him when she intrigued to restore the authority of Charles, and was astonished to find herself often thwarted by Barrillon. To find out how things really stood between the French Embassy and Versailles, she pretended to him that she had been sent a warning from France, that Louis was not satisfied with her conduct, and that yet, as the ambassador well knew, she had done her utmost to restore good intelligence between the kings of France and England.[1] But Barrillon, while acknowledging that the French favourite was holding her own and was not shaken by the downfall of her ally, Sunderland, preferred acting without her and winning his way by the sheer force of money. She, however, affected to ignore his change of tactics, continued to tell him everything,[2] and did not appear to suspect the too great sim-

[1] Feb. 27, 1681.   [2] August 28, 1681.

plicity with which he opened his mind to Lord Montagu. He gave to this nobleman a second bribe of 2,000 guineas, and was soon after, under a clumsy pretext, asked for a third.[1] Indeed, in a vague elucubration, having a cock-and-bull flavour, Montagu told the ambassador of Louis that he would soon be able to render his Majesty the King of France services of not less importance than those he discharged when the interests of that sovereign demanded the impeachment of Danby. But he could bind himself to do nothing more, if full and entire payment were not guaranteed. What his proposed services were, he refused to say, because, if he disclosed them prematurely, he would risk to seem frivolous in the eyes of the King of France. Nevertheless, they were of a nature to place England in a situation which would long prevent her injuring France.

On finding that she was no longer utilized as a secret service agent, Louise de Keroualle struck up a friendship with the Duke of York. She had a percentage on the Irish taxes, and got the grant, in virtue of which she derived this income, confirmed. She also leant with

[1] Sept. 22, 1681.

one arm on the king, and with the other on the Duke of York, his brother. Meanwhile Barrillon and the Prince of Orange[1] worked, each on his own behalf, the House of Commons. Shaftesbury and Monmouth fancied they could trust in their partisans, and the Republicans hoped to deceive their corruptor.

Finding himself unable to deal with the complicated web of intrigue woven around him, Charles II. submitted himself without reserve to Louis XIV. He prorogued Parliament indefinitely, and turned into his own coffers by his docility all the French money that came into England and which would, if he had not obeyed, have gone on losing itself in a number of pockets. The calm his submission produced, was sudden and complete. The Duchess of Portsmouth soon recovered her serenity of spirit.

It was during this lull that she summoned

---

[1] To understand to what extent English patriots were corrupted by the Prince of Orange, see Barrillon to the king, July 7, 1681: "The Earl of Arran (Duke of Hamilton's son) has not yet accepted the 500 guineas which your Majesty permitted me to offer him, because he wished first decently to decline offers made him by the Prince of Orange." Perhaps he wanted to see whether he could not get more out of the Prince.

to London Henri Gascar,[1] a French painter. Another French artist, Ramboury, was authorized by Louis XIV. to go and execute at Windsor[2] paintings which his Britannic Majesty wished him to do. No mark of confidence and satisfaction was spared by the King of France, who was already preparing the campaign in which he meant to take Courtray and Luxembourg, and who wrote, by the hand of his secretary Rose (who was authorized to imitate his writing, so that it would pass for his autograph), to proffer a request which, in the place of Charles, he would have never granted. It was to ask the King of England to exert his authority to put a stop to the prosecution of Count Kœnigsmarck.[3] This affair throws a

---

[1] Gascar, born in Paris in 1635, died in Rome in 1701. There are two portraits by him extant of the Duchess of Portsmouth. One represents her with a Portuguese headdress; the other, which has been engraved, shows her defending against a cupid a bird that is in her lap. Gascar painted also Henriette de Keroualle. The oldest portrait of the Duchess is by Anthony Cooper. It must have been done soon after she first arrived in England, Cooper having died in 1670. There are also portraits by Kneller and by Lely. Gascar's is at Hampton, and Mignard's at Kensington.   [2] Oct. 26, 1681.
[3] Barrillon to Colbert de Croissy, Nov. 24, 1670.

strong light upon English manners in the reign of Charles II.

Lady Elizabeth Percy, daughter of the last Earl of Northumberland, had been married at the age of twelve to Lord Ogle, and was a widow in the following year. Her husband was hardly in the grave when she was abducted. She had set sail for Holland with Lady Temple, and Sidney had escorted her to a yacht which he had obtained for her. The old Countess of Northumberland and the youthful widow's guardian, a Mr. Bret, forced her to marry Mr. Thomas Thynne,[1] of Longleat, who had an estate worth £10,000 a year. But he was in no haste, for a cogent reason, to consummate the marriage. Lady Ogle was told the legal consequences of this; and as she knew she had been deceived and sold, she availed herself of them to try to get the marriage declared null, or at least to escape from Thynne. Miss Trevor appeared at her side when she went to give evidence, and swore that she and Thynne were solemnly engaged. But three months later, Thynne[2]

---

[1] The Issachar of Dryden's *Absalom and Achithophel*.

[2] Barrillon to the King, *Affaires Etrangères, Angleterre*, tome cxlvi., fol. 343.

being in London, was, when riding along Pall Mall, at seven in the evening, attacked by three armed men. One of them fired at him six musket-balls, which entered his body and killed him. Count de Kœnigsmarck was one of the murderers. He had aspired to marry Lady Ogle,[1] and wanted to be avenged on Thynne for snatching her up. The Count was the lover of Sophia Dorothea, Electress of Hanover, and aunt of the second wife of the Duc d'Orléans, *née* Princess Palatine, with whom the Electress kept up an affectionate correspondence. This fact explains why the King of France interfered to save an assassin, whom it was, once that monarch interfered on his behalf, impossible to hang. The prosecution was so managed by the Attorney-General that, though he was notoriously guilty, no proof of guilt was produced, and he was acquitted. The heiress who, at the age of fourteen, was twice widowed, married the Duke of Somerset when she was scarcely fifteen.

[1] Swift, in doggerel verse, accused her of complicity in Thynne's murder. She avenged herself by, on her knees, imploring Queen Anne not to give him a bishopric. That dull but amiable monarch said, a good man could not have such a bitter enemy, and refused the see to Swift. (*Translator's Note.*)

The dream of Louis was accomplished. He held England in the web he had woven round her. Charles became more and more attached to his even-tempered mistress, who had weathered out with him the storm of the Popish Plot. She was sure henceforth of exercising undisputed authority, and was no longer obliged to conceal that she headed the French party and was the connecting link between the kings of France and England. She had such confidence in her force, that she did not fear to absent herself from Charles for several months. It had been her dearest wish to return to the French Court, the scene of her early humiliations, to shine there as the favourite of the King of England. She desired to tell Louis by word of mouth all she had done to reduce the British nation to be the satellite of France, and to a state of durable subjection. The period of her visit to France was one of splendid triumph and gratified pride. She triumphed in the most brilliant Court in the world, and among those satirical French ladies who had known her poor, humble, and blown upon.

CHAPTER X.

RETURN TO FRANCE.

CHARLES and the Duchess of Portsmouth separated from each other for some months at the beginning of March, 1682, the king going to Newmarket, and the Duchess to her native country. But before she set out she was careful to draw in advance the quarter of her pension which was to fall due at the end of the month.[1] She moreover provided herself with letters from the King of England and Barrillon, one of which asked and the other advised Louis to grant her the favour enjoyed by the Duchess of Cleveland at Versailles, namely the right to sit on a *tabouret* when she went to pay her respects to the queen.[2] She also wished for more solid favours; and Charles did not shrink from speaking about them to Barrillon.[3]

[1] Money for secret services, fol. 68.
[2] March 5, 1682.
[3] Barrillon to King Louis, March 16, 1682.

"He has charged me to supplicate your Majesty to accord to her your protection, for the arrangement of her private affairs in France. I turned the conversation to another subject, when he spoke about her wish that your Majesty should withdraw the domain of Aubigny from the Crown to give it to her. But I made him hope that your Majesty would give her other marks of kindness. The truth about her is, that she has shown great, constant, and intelligent zeal for your Majesty's interests, and given me numberless useful hints and pieces of information. She believes that the King of England wishes to further your Majesty's interests. The enemies of the Duchess of Portsmouth give out that she is going to France to settle there."

The Duchess embarked at Greenwich on board a yacht, that was fitted up purposely for her, and landed at Dieppe.[1] She was received as a sovereign at the French Court and invited to all the *fêtes* at St. Cloud.[2] She wrote to

[1] Barrillon said, at Dieppe; Godolphin said, at Calais. See Godolphin to Bulstrode, in a letter preserved at Keele Hall by the Rev. W. Sneyd.

[2] See correspondence of Preston, the English ambassador to Louis XIV., which is at Netherby Hall.

inform Charles of her triumphal reception, and he hastened to address to Louis "his best thanks for the kindness he had shown to the Duchess of Portsmouth."

"There has never been a parallel for the treatment she meets with," St. Simon bears witness. "When, on a high holiday, she went to visit the Capucines in the Rue St. Honoré, the poor monks, who were told beforehand of her intention, came out processionally to receive her, with cross, holy-water, and incense. They received her just as if she had been the queen, and threw her all in a heap, she not expecting so much honour."[1] On the 29th of April she left St. Cloud for Aubigny, where she spent some days, because she was to take the waters of Bourbon in the middle of May. At that watering-place she met her sister the Countess of Pembroke, stayed with her about three weeks, and then traversed Paris again, towards the middle of June,[2] probably to revisit Brittany. She showed herself at Court a month later, and busied herself with investing the

[1] *Ecrits inédits de St. Simon*, t. iv. p. 485.
[2] See the Preston correspondence, at Netherby Hall and at Keele Hall.

fortune which she had amassed in England. It was usual at the English Court to invest money in foreign securities. The Duke of York trusted for this purpose £160,000 to Father Gaufre, a French Jesuit,[1] on learning of whose death he was much concerned. Barrillon had advised him to lodge the money in la Chambre des Emprunts, in the name of the honest Courtin.

The victorious progress of Louise Keroualle in France had its reflex action in London, when she reappeared there at the end of July, 1682. "She has never been previously," Barrillon wrote to Louis,[2] "treated here as a person of high quality and great consequence. She and the Duke of York are very intimate."[3] He spoke some months later of "the homage paid her by Louis XIV. being like sunshine, gilding and glorifying an insignificant object." It dazzled the Court of England; and the dazed eyes there no longer saw her imperfections. Her power became incontestable, and her coolness of head and intriguing dexterousness seem to have been favourably judged by the

[1] Barrillon to Colbert, May 14, 1682.
[2] July 27, 1682.   [3] Oct. 18, 1682.

political men in France, for Louis himself sent her word that he had the fullest confidence in her judgment, and that no blunder could be committed so long as she was his medium. He thought it was due to her tact and discernment to consult her on everything relating to the Court, and that there was to be no suspicious hanging back from any step that she recommended. It became dangerous to cross the path of the woman who was to be henceforth the link between two kings of great nations. The Dutch minister, Vanbeunengen, learned to his cost how ill-advised he was to stand in her way. He thought well to call attention to her familiarity with Barrillon,[1] whose access to her at all hours showed a confidence and a close intimacy which could hardly fail to give umbrage to the King of England's allies. Louise took offence at his remark, and complained to the king of his want of respect for her. Vaubeunengen offered formally to beg her pardon, and to give her any explanation that would show how far he was from wishing to offend a lady for whom his Britannic Majesty showed such great regard. He was even will-

[1] Oct. 20, 1682.

ing to go to the rooms of the Duchess at Whitehall and to apologise there.

The queen herself obliged her ladies to be deferential towards the favourite. One of Catherine's maids of honour, Philis Temple,[1] had the boldness to speak ill of the Duchess before Lady Conway, who meanly and humbly ran off to denounce her. The Duchess, who had the gift of tears, wept and complained to the queen, who deprived Miss Temple of a quarter's salary.

The Duchess Mazarin was too observant to remain unconscious of the meridian height to which Louise's star had mounted, and descended with a good grace to a secondary rank in the seraglio. She sought a compensation in a gay life with persons of easy morals. There were only two things which disturbed her epicurean serenity. Her income was not equal to her expenses; and, her husband having withdrawn her pension, she depended entirely on Charles's generosity. The King of England preferring that M. Mazarin should join in the expense of maintaining the lady, the King

---

[1] Letter in Sir H. Verney's possession at Claydon House, dated, Oct. 23, 1682

of France was again pressed to make him give her an annuity. Charles supplicated Barrillon[1] to tell his master what an obligation he would confer on him, if he exerted his authority in behalf of the Duchess Mazarin, who had not received any remittance for two years from France. She almost simultaneously assured the ambassador that she had not craved the good offices of Charles, because she placed all her hopes in the bounty and protection of Louis.

The other cause of trouble to the Duchess Mazarin, were the importunities of her gallants. She so wonderfully retained the charms with which she was gifted, that her situation of king's mistress did not inspire awe, or prevent her from being the object of the most romantic and passionate adoration. After the Prince of Monaco, who had come to spend two days in London, and remained two years, absorbed in her worship—after the Portuguese Vasconcellos,[2] who did not see that the blindness of his love made him an object of ridicule—after Montagu, who neglected for her sake the

---

[1] Feb. 9, 1682.
[2] Dom Luis de Vasoncellos y Souza, who had been in London from 1667.

political intrigues on the success of which he staked his head—there appeared among her worshippers a Swedish hero, and a young Frenchman, her own sister's son, who was destined to humble the pride of Louis.

The Chevalier de Soissons, better known as Prince Eugene de Savoy-Carignan, came to London and fell in love with his aunt. Baron de Bainer, son of one of the generals of Gustavus Adolphus, was also captivated by her. They had both attracted attention by their hectoring airs and the great length of their swords, which dragged on the pavement as they strode along. They grew jealous of each other, and fought a duel in which Bainer was killed. The combat amused the Court of Versailles,[1] where lords and ladies wondered at the eyes of a grandmother doing such execution. Madame Mazarin, when Prince Eugène killed de Bainer, was the mother of a son and three grown-up daughters. The second daughter was Abbess of Lys; the youngest had married the Marquis de Bellefonts in 1681; and the eldest, whom the father wanted, in spite of her aversion to a religious life, to take the veil, got

[1] DE SÈVIGNÈ, Nov. 26, 1684.

the Marquis de Richelieu to run away with her from the Convent of Ste. Marie of Chaillot, and was still running about Switzerland and elsewhere, while the young lady's father was consulting monks and other Churchmen at Grenoble, la Trappe, and Angers, as to whether he should consent to the marriage of the fugitives. Both families were for letting them get married. But the Duke Mazarin went on asking theological consultations; and the runaway couple would have been obliged to go on as lover and mistress, if the king had not interfered.[1] At the end of two years the scrupulously pious father was forced to give his consent to marriage, but showed his reluctance by refusing to give a dowry of more than 100,000f. The king signed a pardon—the first ever granted for the abduction of a novice from her convent.[2] But the habits of wild liberty contracted when she was an outlaw prevented M. de Richelieu's wife from settling down quietly. Her husband, forgetting how he had taught her to use scaling-ladders, confined her in

---

[1] Jan. 1683.
[2] DANGEAU, Sept. 5, and Oct. 17, 1684.

the English nunnery in the Faubourg St. Jacques, from which she got away, by climbing over the wall.[1]

The mother was mortified at her daughter's adventures and at Prince Eugene's duel. She talked of embracing a conventual life, and of her salutary sadness and disgust with everything. Saint Evremond, in elegantly turned stanzas, painted her black melancholy, from which she eventually found a solace in drink. Meanwhile the passion for gambling took possession of her, and was a cause of chagrin to her poetic adorer, who speaks of 1682, as the year in which the preponderance of the Duchess of Portsmouth became definitive, and her rival's love for basset got to an incurable height. She passed her nights at the card-table, where she held the bank, and forgot Maurice her buffoon, Chop her dog, Pussy her cat, and Pretty her parrot. Of Roman origin, she was accused of ancient Roman vices, which she mixed up with modern French and English modes of sinning. In the daytime, she searched for Oriental curiosities in the ships that had freshly arrived from India. At Newmarket, she was up and

[1] DANGEAU, April 1, 1703

out on horseback, at five in the morning. On racing days there were the excitements of betting, and of being jostled in the crowd which rushed to see the horses on the course. In the evening there was the theatre and Shakspeare's plays, which, as well as the English drama of the period, Saint Evremond thought tedious. After the play came the oyster supper, and then basset. Madame Mazarin had at Newmarket her regular court of ladies. Besides Lady Harvey, she was watched with admiration by Mademoiselle Beverweert-Nassau,[1] whom she called Lotte, and employed to serve at her toilette. The other fair followers were Mesdemoiselles de Bragelone, Grenier, and de la Rocheguilliem, the novelist. This group of women did not attempt to cross the path of Louise de Keroualle after her return from France. Her power was thenceforth undisputed and indisputable.

[1] Daughter of Prince Louis of Nassau, the Dutch ambassador to Whitehall.

CHAPTER XI.

END OF THE REIGN

THE Duchess of Portsmouth also held gambling tables and a bank in her rooms. But the excitement of cards did not entirely absorb her. She played at the more dangerous pastime—amorous intrigue with Philippe de Vendôme, Grand Prior of France.

This French nobleman was grandson of Henri IV. and la Belle Gabrielle, and son of the Duke de Vendôme and Laura Mancini, sister of the Duchess Mazarin. He came to London in 1683, when he was twenty-eight, had a bright wit, was singularly handsome, but did not pass for being brave. He slipped out of a duel about the Duchess de Ludre with M. de Vivonne by riding off to the country, and slid out of the army on the eve of the battle in which Turenne was killed. This descendant of Henri IV. was received and retained in London by the Duchess of Portsmouth with a tenderness so undisguised as to excite the raillery of the whole Court.

The watchful and crafty Barrillon did not like this.[1] He saw that the king took umbrage at Louise's fondness for the Grand Prior, and that now and then he showed himself suspicious and ill-humoured about him. But these fits did not last long. Prudence should have made the Duchess of Portsmouth order the Grand Prior to return to France. But she was so happy to have him with her that none of her friends had the courage to tell her what she ought to do. To advise her to separate from de Vendôme would have displeased her. Sunderland feared that the king's suspicions would become angry convictions, and bring on a rupture. Nevertheless, although she did not banish the Grand Prior, she continued to find favour in the eyes of Charles.[2] The leading ministers kept in close intimacy with her. Her enemies were alert to do her mischief, but she was no less so to defeat their malignity. Sunderland, in spite of the fears he expressed to Barrillon, took care to be on good terms

[1] Barrillon to Louis, June 17, 1683.
[2] *Ibid.*, June 28, 1683.

with M. de Vendôme, whom he asked to dine at his house. The suspicions that Louise was playing the wanton with her countryman, did not prevent Louis from keeping up with her an autograph correspondence, and charging Tilladet, his Lieutenant-General and Captain of his Cent Suisses, when he sent him on a mission to Charles, "to remain in constant relations with Madame de Portsmouth."[1]

That envoy informed the King of France[2] that, on reaching London, he called on the favourite, and informed her that he had been ordered to tell her in what high regard his Majesty held her, and to assure her that he desired to give her proofs of his friendship in all sorts of occasions. She received the message with signs of the deepest respect, and prayed the Lieutenant-General to say to his Majesty how unfortunate she esteemed herself in not having been so far able to prove to him her gratitude, and how sorry she was that his Majesty had been obliged to content himself with good intentions only.

[1] July 29, 1683, tome cl., fol. 124.
[2] Autograph letter of Tilladet to Louis, *Affaires Etrangères, Angleterre*, tome cl., fol. 163.

Charles beheld, with no unmoved countenance, the Grand Prior's visits. Not that he dared voluntarily to show his displeasure. His will was flaccid, and he was too conscious of that limp state which throws worn-out epicureans under the domination of their mistresses. He, however, tried by peaceable means to get rid of Vendôme's odious presence.

To this end he asked Barrillon, through Sunderland, to forbid the Grand Prior to visit the Duchess of Portsmouth, in whose rooms the grandson of Henri IV. and the Beautiful Gabrielle did not appear for four or five days.[1] But this absence made her irresistibly attractive to him, and he renewed his attentions. The king, finding this out, thought it a reason for expelling the Grand Prior from England. Barrillon undertook to break to him Charles's intention in the gentlest way possible, and thought to make him go away quietly. But M. de Vendôme declared he would only leave when the king himself ordered him by word of mouth to go, and requested the ambassador to demand for him an audience. Barrillon, to prevent a storm, obtained, after much suppli-

[1] Barrillon to Louis, Nov. 21, 1683.

cation, leave for the Grand Prior to speak to his Majesty in his chamber. There he attempted to justify himself; but the king declined to hold conversation on the subject, and would not rescind his decision. The Grand Prior did not make any preparations for leaving, wanted Barrillon to refuse to intimate to him the order to quit England, and, although menaced with the displeasure of Louis, refused to tear himself from Whitehall.

Charles sent for the French Ambassador, who prayed him not to impose on him the harsh necessity of telling the Grand Prior that he must quit the country. After letting the matter drag some days, Lieutenant Griffin, of the Household Guard, intimated to M. de Vendôme that if he did not leave in two days he had orders to arrest him and put him on board a packet which was to sail for Calais. The distracted lover still held out. He offered to go to the country, or to go to France, provided he were allowed to come back to England. At the secret entreaty of Louise, who wanted to avoid a scandal, Barrillon communicated these proposals to Charles. But he remained firm to the message he had sent by

Griffin; and so the Grand Prior sailed at the end of November for Holland.

The friends of the Duchess of Portsmouth breathed again freely, and she found relief in the absence of the fancy lover. She had been in terror lest the Grand Prior should think she was playing a double game, and show the letters he had received from her. He was as much stimulated by ambition as love to stick to her, he hoping to derive great advantages and consideration from a *liaison* with her. Up to the moment that the ship in which he sailed left her moorings, the Duchess of Portsmouth was in dread of a public scene.

Louis XIV., of whose foreign policy the Duchess was still a necessary agent, helped her through this scrape. He ordered the Duc de Vendôme to write to the Grand Prior to inform him that he was free to return to the Court of France, where he would meet with a better reception than his bad conduct in England had given him a right to expect.

The Grand Monarch himself instructed Barrillon to let Madame de Portsmouth know how he had sent Croissy to warn her lover, that if ever he said a word to her disadvantage, he would incur his resentment.[1] He spoke to the same effect to the Duc de Vendôme, so that the lady might feel assured she would not be in France an object of raillery or slander. Indeed, Louis expressed his will so clearly, that the Grand Prior never opened his lips about his Whitehall adventure, which was kept so dark that the Duc d'Orleans, who obtained some inkling of it, either from the king his uncle or the De Vendômes, fancied the object of the Grand Prior's passion was one of Charles's minor concubines. He would not have paid any attention to the matter if he had not been amused at the audacity of a foreigner in braving a king in his own State and at his own Court.

The Duchess of Portsmouth, in her relations with the Grand Prior, had formed such a low opinion of him that, notwithstanding the threats of Louis, she feared an ill use might be made of her letters. What strengthened her uneasiness was, his persistence in remaining at the Hague, and saying he would return to London. An order, at her instance, was sent to him from

[1] Dec. 21, 1683. The Duke of Vendôme was eldest brother of the Grand Prior.

Versailles, to proceed there forthwith; and the French ambassador was instructed, that if he showed himself in England, King Charles was to be encouraged to use his authority in having him arrested and expelled,[1] so that the Duchess of Portsmouth was to be exposed to no further annoyance. In due time the Grand Prior appeared at Versailles, and thus ended noiselessly an affair which had been a cause of deep anxiety to Louise de Keroualle.[2]

Charles, during this period of his reign, received £60,000 a year from Louis. The receipts were signed by Rochester, who alone, with the Duchess of Portsmouth, was in the secret of this transaction. He was a brother of the Duke of York's first wife. The Duke of Rochester and Louise were on the best understanding with each other, and they three directed all the affairs of the Royal family. When the Duke of York was looking for a match for his second daughter, the Princess Anne, he consulted the Duchess of Portsmouth on the choice of a husband. She was charged to ascertain the opinion of Louis Quatorze on Prince George of Denmark, and to send the

[1] Feb. 14, 1684.   [2] Jan, 1684; Feb. 18, 1684.

likeness of the Princess to Copenhagen.[1] The King of Denmark replied by sending his miniature set in brilliants to the Duchess.[2] In London the gift was estimated at 1,500 guineas. When the ambassadors of Morocco came to London, it was not the Queen or Duchess of York, but the Duchess of Portsmouth, who entertained them. She received them, surrounded by all the mistresses who were admitted to the Court. These dames,—the accomplished Evelyn spoke of them as "cattle,"—were as splendid as flowered tabby dresses, point lace, and jewels could make them. They blazed in diamonds. Chocolate was served to them all. When Louis Quatorze ordered the Marquis de Preuilly[3] to sail up the Channel without deigning to send a notification to Charles, it was she who undertook to show the king that this was not to be taken as a sign of want of respect or friendliness, and that his best course was to make believe it was concerted between the two sovereigns. Otherwise those who wanted to detach him from France

---

[1] Barrillon to Colbert.
[2] *Affaires Etrangères*, *Angleterre*, tome cxlix., fol. 401.
[3] Barrillon to King Louis, June 21, 1683.

would see in it an opportunity to weigh upon his determination to lean on that country. Barrillon, who was so adroit and crafty, treated her as a colleague. When the Princess Anne was married, she asked him whether the Court of Versailles would not send a special envoy to the wedding? He answered: You and I will suffice to pay all the compliments, and it would be a mistake for persons in our situation to ask for a special Embassy to be sent."

The good understanding between the two monarchs was heightened by a favourable turn in public opinion, which was brought about by a blundering plot. Some old Ironsides of Cromwell, and fanatical preachers, burning with shame and indignation at the debauchery of king and Court, and the contempt in which England was held abroad, conspired together to assassinate Charles, who, they discovered, was the Man of Sin and the Son of Perdition. The iniquities of him and his Court were rotting the fibres of the nation, and bringing God's displeasure upon it, as shown in severe winters, prolonged east winds, the great fire, the plague, small-pox, and the disrespect into which the name of England had fallen. /That there was a plot, is established. But the names of the plotters are not so well known. The Court had the adroitness to implicate the principal members of the Opposition; and the judges, with their habitual servility, summed up against them. Shaftesbury disappeared from the political scene, and Algernon Sidney was beheaded. The arrest of Monmouth relieved the partisans of the French alliance from a strong rallying-point for its adversaries. Charles had turned against his eldest son, and spoke cynically about him.[1] Lord Grey had been among those tried, attainted, and condemned to death. After his execution the King's heart melted, and he wanted to restore his confiscated estates to the children of the unfortunate nobleman. But the intervention of the Duchess of Portsmouth prevented the desired act of restitution; and she was able to obtain for herself and her friend Rochester[2] a grant of all that had belonged to Lord Grey. Rochester and Godolphin were in utter subjection to the Duchess, who judged well to apprise the latter of the secret treaty with France, and of the different subsidies which

---

[1] Barrillon to Louis, July 12, 1683.
[2] *Ibid., Affaires Etrangères, Angleterre*, tome clvi. fol. 30.

Charles had received from Louis XIV. She ventured to do herself the honour to write to the King of France to answer for the intentions and conduct of Godolphin as she would for her own.

Barrillon sometimes grew restive under her yoke. But neither Charles nor Louis XIV. showed impatience under it. One day Charles called aside the French ambassador,[1] and told him that the Duchess of Portsmouth and her son, the Duke of Richmond, were the persons above all others in the world whom he loved the most, and would be deeply obliged to the King of France if he agreed to reconvert the estate of Aubigny into a duchy for her, with the reversion to her son and his future issue. "Is not this outstepping all bounds?" wrote Barrillon.[2] "As an English duchess, she has by courtesy the same honours in France as a French duchess. But that does not satisfy her. She must have them in virtue of letters patent, and as a *right* sit on a *tabouret* whenever she may go to pay her respects to the queen at Versailles." Louis did not regard the application in the same light. Barrillon

[1] Barrillon to Louis, Jan. 14, 1684. [2] Jan. 21, 1684.

was informed by return of post that the letters patent to revive the Duchy of Aubigny were being made out.[1] This news was received with the utmost gladness at Whitehall. When Barrillon brought it to Charles there, he was delighted, and ran across the room to tell it to the Duchess of Portsmouth, who was overjoyed; and when it got out, she received the congratulations of the whole Court. From that hour she held so completely England in her hands, that she was the real sovereign. When she fell ill, in November, 1684, public business came to a full stop.[2] The king was never out of her room. Inquiries were made constantly about her state by the different ambassadors; and Barrillon was constantly asking how she was, in the name of the King of France. Her malady was an opportunity for him to grant her fresh privileges. She was uneasy[3] lest her son, he being a foreigner, should not be able to inherit the money she had invested in France. Without delay, Louis

---

[1] The King to Barrillon, Jan. 21, 1684. The letters patent are in *Les Archives Nationales*, tome xxviii. fol. 150.

[2] Barrillon to Louis, Nov. 15, 1684.

[3] Barrillon, Nov. 30, 1684.

issued letters of naturalization in favour of his very dear and well-beloved cousin Prince Charles Lennox, Duke of Richmond, who, as well as his mother, was to enjoy all the privileges, franchises, and liberties to which gentlemen were entitled in the kingdom of France.[1]

The riches heaped up in the apartments of the Duchess at Whitehall, scandalized the English. She was always building and pulling down her rooms at extravagant expense. On rising in the morning she received in her loose undress gown, surrounded by young girls; and sitting before her toilet mirror she gave audiences to courtiers. She had that gift of nature to Bretons of both sexes—a splendid head of hair, which a maid combed out when she was receiving visitors. Her sanctuary was reached by galleries and saloons hung with exquisite French stuffs, and with Gobelins tapestries, then newly invented, representing the twelve palaces of the great king. Inlaid cabinets, tables, desks, and buffets, Japan screens, finely carved timepieces, massive

[1] Registered Jan. 22, 1685. See *Aff. Etr. Angleterre*, tome cli., fol. 230.

pieces of silver in profusion, ornaments and rare pictures, at first delighted and dazzled, and then surfeited the eye. This magnificence stirred the bile not only of Puritans, but of men of the world who still retained some honest feeling. They reflected that it was not only the wages of a wanton, but of a traitress, who, whenever her Royal paramour embraced her, compassed how she might bring him and the country he ruled into utter servitude to France. / The queen's rooms seemed plain, compared to those of "Madam Carwell," whose wardrobe was as fine as her other belongings. The bills run up by her sister, the Countess of Pembroke, whose luxury was on an inferior scale, give some idea of the style in which Court beauties at Whitehall dressed. They were incurred in part for gloves, ribbons, and other haberdashery furnished by one Lesgu, a shopkeeper of Paris, and Jaquillon Laurent, his wife, and are in the French national archives. In the last three months of 1682 this couple sold to Lady Pembroke "twenty eight pairs of openwork white gloves, with orange and amber scent, and one pair of gloves costing thirty-three *livres*, trimmed with ribbon, gold and silver at the arms, and herring-boned in gold and silver on the back of the hand; seventy pairs of gloves embroidered and fastened at the arm, opening with strings and bows of *point de diamant* ribbons; twenty sashes and fringed ends, in various embroideries and brocades." The Earl of Pembroke dying, the gloves are no longer perfumed with orange and amber, but violet and hyacinth. All the fans are mourning ones; and gold clocks are worked on black silk stockings, which are fastened up with *feuille morte* and silver garters. The *fontanges* in golden crape are falling cravats. They were called after a favourite of Louis XIV., who enjoyed his admiration for nine months, and died giving birth to the fruit of the amour. At the end of the twelve months' mourning, flame-coloured bows of ribbon are placed over the button-holes of some of the gloves. On others there are flame and silver, or gold and blue. Some of the gloves are to match with a rose-coloured *tablier*, or front breadth of the skirt, surrounded with "silver clouds." When the Countess quitted her all-powerful sister, to live permanently in France, several ships were chartered to transport the booty she was taking with her from England. One bill of lading speaks of chests filled with silk moiré, with Indian stuffs flowered with silver, with Welsh flannel, with cabinets, gueridons, looking-glass frames. And such small haberdashery as a hundred pounds weight of pins and needles; a hundred pounds of best wax tapers, and several chests of dip candles, with five pounds of iris-root scent. Another bill of lading mentions: Seventeen dozen gloves, thirteen pairs of silk stockings, thirty pounds of Moka coffee, four bales of soap, a chest of chocolate, a large chestful of Greek currants, wax candles, a large chestful of spices, including cloves, mace, ginger, nutmeg, and cinnamon. In the bill of lading of the ship in which the lady herself sailed, we find a pearl necklace worth twenty thousand francs; ear-ring drops and clasps, *idem*, a miniature of King Charles set in brilliants, a basin and ewer in carved silver, worth respectively 12,000, 20,000, and 4,000 *livres;* several dozens of massy silver plates and dishes, with salvers, bowls, candlesticks, snuffers and snuff trays, goblets, chocolate mugs, spirits of wine heaters, dish covers, dish heaters. The Countess's bed is of crimson Genoa velvet, hung in brocade, with a white ground to the red pattern, and satin linings for the curtains, head-board, and canopy. The coverlet is of needlework point. The other bedchamber furniture is composed of a grand cabinet in old Chinese laquer; a Chinese incense-burner in old silver; twenty rare and precious tapestries; a very rich and grotesque screen; many teapots; Chinese and Japanese curiosities; much other household furniture; coaches, chaises, Sedan chairs; a whole set of kitchen utensils, with pewter platters for the servants' hall.

Voluptuousness reigned at Whitehall, where, listening to the French melodies of François Duperrier, or to erotic songs sung by children, the sleepy Charles was to be seen in the grand gallery, reclining between his three favourites, who were in the full bloom of womanhood. He was decrepit and aged although but fifty-two. The ladies with whom he toyed and chatted were dazzlingly fresh and magnificently attired; and gold flowed with a soft chink on the basset tables, which were lighted up with wax candles. It was in the Whitehall gallery that he passed his evenings with the Duchesses of Portsmouth and Mazarin, in the winter of 1684-85. There had been premonitory signs of a break-down of constitution, and a more than ordinary aversion to mental effort. His Breton mistress more than ever spared him the trouble of transacting State business, by managing it all with Barrillon and the corrupt intriguers who at last accepted her as queen in all but name. She held the reins of such government as there was; and the King of France no longer felt that Great Britain was an obstacle to his ambitious plans. He was to strike another blow in the end of March, which would give him solid supremacy, not only in Europe, but in Asia, Africa, and America. It seemed that in a few months more Holland was to be a French province, and all the Dutch colonies to pass under the dominion of Louis. But the work of a single statesman, however industrious, politic, and powerful, is always fragile, and at the mercy of an accident. On the evening of February 12, 1685, Charles, in rising to withdraw from the grand gallery and its dissipations, suddenly lost consciousness, and fell. His face was contorted, and he gave no sign of recognition to the courtiers who pressed around him. Blisters were clapped on his head, his arms, and his legs. He was cupped between the shoulders, bled, and emetics were poured down his throat; but nothing roused him from his torpor, and he remained still unconscious until one o'clock on the next day. A hot warming-pan was then placed on his head, and his jugular vein was opened. He was again bled at four o'clock in the other arm, and the blood flowed abundantly.

Nobody was prepared for the catastrophe, and great were the tumult and confusion. The Portuguese queen was clamorous in her distress; and the courtiers were fussy and officious. The Duke of York coolly summoned the leading statesmen who were not his open enemies, to prepare to assert his rights to the Crown. Servants ran hither and thither, not knowing what to do, and having no one to direct them. As for the French, they were in consternation. The only person who showed any head, or heart, was Louise de Keroualle, who at once sent for Barrillon.

"I found her," he said, in the account he transmitted to Versailles of this blow of destiny, "in great grief. But instead of bemoaning her own sad and altered position, and her impending fall, she took me into a little room and said : " Monsieur l'Ambassadeur, I am now going to tell you a secret, although its public revelation would cost me my head. The King of England is in the bottom of his heart a Catholic, and there he is, surrounded with Protestant Bishops! There is nobody to tell him of his state or speak to him of God. I cannot decently enter his room. Besides, the queen is now there constantly. The Duke of York is too busy with his own affairs to trouble himself about the king's conscience. Go and tell him that I have conjured you to warn him that the end is approaching, and that it is his duty to save without loss of time, his brother's soul."

The motives of Louise probably were mixed. Bretons are religious Catholics; and then, in showing that she was anxious for Charles to die in the arms of the Church of Rome, it may be supposed that she hoped to win the esteem and kind regard of the Duke of York, to whom the Crown was on the point of devolving. Be this as it may, Barrillon hastened to the queen. A priest was discovered who had found favour in the eyes of Protestant Royalists for the sword-cuts he had inflicted on Roundheads in the civil war. He was taken to Chaffinch, the minister of the king's amorous affairs, and introduced by a back stair and secret corridor to the bedside of the dying monarch. He took for granted everything the Church required of the king, and gave absolution. On the fifth day of his illness, Charles died. An hour after his decease, his brother, now James II., went to see the Duchess of Portsmouth, and assured her that she might trust in his friendship. He had in doing so but one simple object in view —to get Louis XIV. to continue the subvention that he paid the late king. The Duchess also placed her hopes in Louis, who, in answer to a prayer transmitted by the medium of Barrillon, that she might hope to be honoured by his protection, wrote that it would be continued to her. This promise was the only bright spot in her overclouded prospects. She had sore need to ask for his assistance, which he was prompt in giving. "I have learned with surprise," he wrote to[1] his ambassador, "that

[1] March 2, 1685

the new King of England had deprived the Duke of Richmond of the office of grand equerry, notwithstanding the manner in which the late king recommended this son of his to his brother." As Louis held the purse, James humbled himself before Barrillon, and multiplied his visits to the Duchess of Portsmouth. He openly declared[1] that what was said in Holland about her would only have the effect of making him pay her greater attention and go more often to see her. It is true, added Barrillon, that he has been twice to her rooms within the last few days, and has given her numerous marks of confidence and esteem. I am happy to find that she is beginning to think her prospects less dark. She has accepted the reasons put forward by King James for not leaving the place of grand equerry to a boy of thirteen, who cannot fill it for many years. In thus yielding, she hopes to be well used in the settlement of other affairs of major importance. She is now trying to get herself confirmed in the income of £19,000 allowed her by King Charles. Lord Rochester is well disposed towards her. She has pressed me

[1] Barrillon to Louis, March 8, 1685.

to let your Majesty know that a mark of your esteem would be, in the present conjuncture, of decisive importance to her, and that she would thereby secure incomparably better treatment. I have told her that I am commanded to render her every good office in my power, and that I have even defended her interests warmly in speaking to the king; that your Majesty has given her and the Duke of Richmond the highest dignity that you can confer; and that her past services would be remembered, even though your Majesty had never promised in writing not to forget them. I can see that she does not, apart from your Majesty's protection, hope for much more from France, than for a sum of money to pay her debts and to buy a dwelling-house in Paris. The King of England has told me that he had obtained the promise of the Duchess of Portsmouth not to rear her son a Protestant, although he must be classed as one, and that if she keeps it he will do everything in his power for him.

The power of the purse was the uppermost one at this juncture. James and Louise were hungering and manœuvring to obtain French money. She knew herself to be held in horror by the English, and that the pensions which remained to her, and her share of the revenue duties, could not be paid for a long time.

"It is generally rumoured," said Barrillon, "that the Duchess of Portsmouth and Lord Sunderland were the principal agents in bringing your Majesty and the late King of England into a close understanding. This is why they are both hated by the whole country. The Duchess apprehends attacks on her in the next Parliament, and she wishes therefore to hasten away from England before it has time to meet, and to retire to France. She is not satisfied with the treatment she has met with, and makes no great secret of her discontent.[1] His Britannic Majesty allows her a pension of three thousand guineas for herself, and two thousand for the Duke of Richmond. She sent him word to give all the five thousand to her son, because she would not trouble him on her own account. She has, besides, two thousand a year from a part of the confiscated estate of Lord Grey, which, however, is to belong to the Duke of Richmond when he is of age.

[1] Barrillon to Louis, August 13, 1685.

She claims the right to go on drawing from twenty-five thousand to thirty thousand pounds a year from the Irish taxes; but she has not yet been able to get herself confirmed in the enjoyment of this income, which was granted her by the late king. The disgust so caused, along with the withdrawal from her son of the post of grand equerry, has provoked her into using plain speech; and she complains that the services rendered in obtaining money for the expenses of the Crown of England from your Majesty have been forgotten."

Whether James was too ungrateful or the Duchess too greedy, it is hard at this distance of time to say. But each had a well-accentuated vice. The Duchess returned to France with an English estate worth £5,000 a year, exclusive of the money she had invested in France, or of her furniture, her jewels, her £2,000 a year during Richmond's minority out of the confiscated Grey lands, or the 250,000 francs in gold that she drew the instant Charles had drawn his last breath. The poor Breton soldier's daughter, the humble maid of honour of Madame Henriette, assuredly was not to be pitied. When the day of her departure was fixed, she had the pleasure of receiving a visit from the new king, who told her he would befriend her and her son. He allowed her to keep her rooms at Whitehall, spoke kindly to her son, and exhorted him to embrace the true religion. This she wished him to do; and she hoped that the King of France would, later, find occasion to complete the work of conversion begun by King James. Her adroit mode of thus flattering both monarchs, rendered her interesting to them. She embarked in August, 1685, and on landing proceeded to Versailles.

When she quitted the English shore, England issued from its fifteen years of degrading and dangerous moral torpor and servitude to France. Not that James's palm itched less for Tournois *livres* than that of Charles. But his narrow and fanatical mind and his base spirit brought his reign to a speedy close, and afforded the opportunity to the arch-adversary of Louis XIV. to ascend the throne of England. The disasters which his diplomatists had apprehended, and which Louise de Keroualle had skilfully averted, overwhelmed France.

The diplomatic strategy which so marvellously succeeded for fifteen years in paralyzing England, and placing its government in a foreign woman's hands, does not seem to have been often repeated. Villars, however, boasted of having been its imitator. Remarking[1] that the Elector of Bavaria was brought into the orbit of the Court of Vienna by the Countess Von Kaunitz, he egged on that prince to draw the young Countess Von Wilin, a lady of the Empress, to Munich. She came, but she was so stupid that the Marquis de Villars soon found she would not help him to break the chain in which the Countess Von Kaunitz had bound the Elector. A young Italian named Canossa took her place. This enchantress had studied gallantry in Venice, and was more beautiful than she had need to be with her great cleverness and experience.

[1] *Mémoires* of Comte de Vogüé, published in 1687. See analogous intrigues in the 18th century, in *Le Secret du Roi*, par le Duc de Broglie, tome i., p. 368, and *Louis XV. et la Czarine Elisabeth*, by Albert Vandal, p. 62.

CHAPTER XII.

IN RETIREMENT.

THE Duchess of Portsmouth had still fifty long years of life before her. She survived Charles half a century; and, after outliving most of her contemporaries, died in the reign of Louis XV., amid a generation who knew her not, and whose eyes were turned towards other horizons than those on which the courtiers of Louis XIV. gazed. Monmouth was the first to go down for ever. He plotted against James II., and was coldly beheaded. His widow married Lord Cornwallis. James II., dethroned by his daughter, found a refuge at St.-Germain en Laye. The Duchess of Cleveland, grown old, and continuing irascible and a gambler, became a widow in 1705, and married a second time, in her sixty-fifth year, Beau Fielding, who played false to her and ruined her. She died in 1709. Her son, the Duke of Grafton,[1]

[1] Henry, Duke of Grafton, born in 1663, created duke in

was allowed to keep her pension, which has been handed down to his posterity. He was killed in fighting for King James against Marlborough, his mother's paramour, at the siege of Cork. Nell Gwynn for a short time was outlawed by her creditors. But James, who had promised Charles not to let her starve, paid her debts, often made her presents, cleared off the mortgage on her residence of Bestwood Park, and paid for her funeral and grave. She was buried, in 1687, in St. Martin's-in-the-Fields. Her son, Charles Beauclerc, was the ancestor of the present Duke of St. Alban's.

The blood of Charles II. runs in the veins of many peers of the realm of Great Britain.[1]

1675, with,—for a youth with a bar sinister on his arms,—the strange motto of: "*Et* decus et pretium recti." Married Lady Isabella Bennet, Arlington's daughter.

[1] Of the children whom Charles II. owned, the following grew up: James, Duke of Monmouth and Buccleugh, son of Lucy Walters; Mary, daughter of Lucy Walters; Charlotte Boyle Fitzroy, daughter of Viscountess Shannon; Charles FitzCharles and a girl, children of Catherine Peg; Henry Fitzroy, Duke of Grafton; George, Earl of Northumberland, and Charlotte Fitzroy, Countess of Sussex, the children of the Duchess of Cleveland; the two Beauclercs, sons of Nell Gwynn; the Duke of Richmond, son of Louise de Keroualle; Mary Tudor, daughter of Moll Davis, and

The Duchess Mazarin shed floods of tears for that monarch, to the astonishment of Saint Evremond, who compared her to Artemisia, and wondered why she troubled her head more about him than for any of her other lovers. She survived him fourteen years, and died in 1699 without ever having quitted England. Bacchus consoled her as she descended towards the grave. Her husband claimed her corpse, and was overjoyed to obtain it. He took it about with him for a year, from one estate to another, and gave it temporary sepulture at Notre Dame de Liesse, where the country folks treated it as the remains of a saint, and touched the coffin with their chaplets. He ended by placing it in the same tomb with her famous uncle in le Collége de Quatre Nations, now the Palace of the Institute. The Duchess transmitted her sovereign charms to her five granddaughters the De Mailly-Nesles, who, with the Mancini blood, received the power to captivate kings. The eldest was declared the mistress

married to the Earl of Derwentwater; and Benedicte Fitzroy, Prioress of the Hôtel Dieu de St. Nicolas at Pontoise. There was another Benedicte, who was said to be an early fruit of the amour of Henrietta Maria and Lord Jermyn.

of Louis XV. in 1735, some months after Louise
de Keroualle's death, and was a little later
cut out by the second, who was eclipsed by
the third, who had in turn to make way for
the fifth.[1] Barrillon become the inseparable
friend of Madame de Sévigné, and died, rich,
fat, and old, in 1691.

The Duchess of Portsmouth had the mortification, on arriving in France, to find her sister
in an interesting state, and forced to own that
she had privately married the Marquis de
Thois, governor of Blois.[2] The young Duke
of Richmond entered the Catholic Church, but
was not for that the less corrupt and vicious.
He relapsed to Anglican Protestantism, or
rather lived and died a godless life, and was to
its end plunged in drunkenness and debauchery.
From being one of the handsomest young men
in England he became the most hideous old rake.

The Duchess of Portsmouth went back to
England a year after she left it. Whether this
journey appeared suspicious to Louis XIV., or

---

[1] The five granddaughters of Madame Mazarin were the Duchesses de Mailly-Nesles, de Vintimille, de Lauraguis, de Flavacount, and de la Toumelle.

[2] See Dangeau, t. i., Feb. 5, 1685.

whether, as Saint Simon avers,[1] she dared to talk too freely of Madame de Maintenon, an order was given to Louvois to draw up a *lettre de cachet* for her exile. The minute of this letter was on Louvois' desk when Courtin entered his cabinet. He took up the paper, and on reading it protested. No doubt she had been in fault, but even so, it would be a mistake to go further than to warn her. To exile her after the services she rendered, would be to dishonour the king. Louis, to whom Courtin defended her, burned the *lettre de cachet*, and admitted the Duchess to a long conversation, from which she issued greatly satisfied.[2]

Her interests obliged her to be in constant relations with England. In July, 1688, she made up a match between her niece, the daughter of the Earl and Countess of Pembroke, and the son of Jeffreys, the hanging judge. Her correspondence with English kinsfolk and friends was often denounced; and the denuncia-

---

[1] Saint Simon's notes on Dangeau.
[2] Dangeau and Saint Simon differ in some points on this interview; and Saint Simon is not in full agreement with himself, in the *Papiers Inédits* recently published by Hachette.

tions obliged her to make humiliating explanations. On January 1st, 1689, the young Duke of Richmond presented himself at the king's *coucher*, to speak in favour of his mother. Louis told him that he knew both of them too well to have suspected them for a moment. However, to draw certain revenues, they were obliged to pay their court to William of Orange. The Duchess of Portsmouth got Henry Sidney, Algernon's brother, to remind him of the evenings he spent at her rooms at Whitehall, and how she intrigued for him, against Monmouth. But the Revolution of 1688 had upset many of the fortunes granted out of the revenue by Charles II. Even her income out of the Post Office returns, which the Duchess of Portsmouth thought so sure, was suspended. She was informed simultaneously that none of her English pensions would be paid until further orders; that her apartments at Whitehall, with all her sumptuous furniture, had been burned; and that her father was dying. The Duke of Richmond absconded from her to England, without letting her know where he was going. She sent word to Louis, that she could not doubt of her son's folly; and that, believing he had gone over to the Prince of Orange, she was ready to die of despair.

This despair was all the more real, because Louis had granted the young scamp a pension of twenty thousand *livres*—which, in a degree, consoled his mother for the loss of her English emoluments. But whilst misfortunes were crowding on her, the King of France did not abandon her. He transferred to her a part of the pension which her son had abandoned.

From this time she devoted herself to the management of her estate of Aubigny, and exerted for the benefit of her serfs what influence remained to her. Owing to the persistent patronage of Louis, her position in France remained a good one. The collections of portrait engravings of the principal Court ladies[1] always included the likeness of the

[1] Five engravings of the series, executed at this period, represent the Duchess of Portsmouth as Venus, and her son as Cupid, against whose arrows a Sphinx protects her, *Chez Marriette, Rue St. Jacques;* in a loose undress on a couch, *Chez Barry, Graveur, Rue St. Jacques;* an imitation of the preceding, *R. B. del., chez N. Bonnart, Rue St. Jacques;* toying with a glove and perroquet, *Chez H. Bonnart, au Coq;* with a cane (the most charming of any), in which the Duchess's back is shown, with her head turned round, *Chez Trouvain, Rue St. Jacques,* 1695.

Duchess of Portsmouth. But her income fell off rapidly. William of Orange grudged her the smallest sum. In 1697 she obtained leave to go to London, and Louis spoke with much kindness on the subject.[1] William, who divined the object of her journey, and had no wish to let her fill her purse with guineas, sent her word that he would prevent her landing.

So, she was obliged to face her creditors. Procurators' pens ran on slips of parchment, which bailiffs served on her; and her chattels were on the point of being seized and sold. Louis again saved her. By a decree signed in Council, he ordered her creditors to desist from pursuing her for a year. When that period elapsed, there were fresh writs, followed by fresh petitions to the king to intervene, "The state of the Duchess of Portsmouth's affairs," it was set forth in an order of Council, "does not allow her at present to discharge the debts that she has contracted, for which cause, her creditors harassing and pursuing her, she is obliged to have recourse to his Majesty's authority, and humbly to supplicate him in his good pleasure to stay these pursuits; and whereas, in con-

[1] Dangeau, t. iv. p. 207.

sideration of the said Duchess's petition, his Majesty in Council has prorogued and prorogues for a full year, ending September 9th, 170c, the effect of the writs obtained by such creditors, or any which may be within that time taken out; and his Majesty forbids all the creditors of the said Duchess during that period to make any seizure of her furniture, equipages, or other chattels belonging to her, under pain of nullity of proceedings, the payment of all costs and damages."

Year after year the petition was renewed, and always received with favour. To protect this woman in the enjoyment of her ill-gotten gains, Louis suspended the course of justice, ruined tradesmen who sold in good faith, and shook the security of commercial transactions. She had only to write to him, that the present state of her affairs did not allow her to pay her debts, and the sovereign's hand was stretched out to drive away her creditors. There were identical orders of Council in 1699, in 1700, on Oct. 5, 1701, on Oct. 2, 1702, and 1703, and on Dec. 10, 1704, and Dec. 30, 1705.[1] In

[1] *Archives Nationales de France*, E. 1917; E. 1924; E. 1929; E. 1933.

1706 the unfortunate tradesmen were able to find protectors, and began to defend themselves before the Council from abuses of the royal authority. The Sieurs Galpin, Pillet, and Lefevre presented balances coming to a total of 130,926 *livres*, 16 *sols*. The Duchess had put them off by paying an instalment on a total of 160,000 *livres*, recoverable in eight years on the rents of Aubigny, in the proportion of 20,000 *livres* annually. The order of Council did not deign to look into this contract. It only took cognisance of the distressed lady's prayer. The wars between France and England having, she represented in 1706, withdrawn from her during fourteen years a pension of 150,000 *livres*, accorded her by the late King Charles, she was, to keep up her rank, obliged to borrow money, and often to live on credit." "But," pleaded the creditors, "it cannot have been the intention of his Majesty to place the said lady in the enjoyment of an income which she has assigned them."[1] The Council decided that the creditors to whom the rents of Aubigny were conveyed, in the propor-

[1] *Archives Nat.*, E. 1934, du 20 Juin 1703.

tion of 20,000 *livres* a year for eight years, were not to be meddled with; but that the others, who claimed as large a sum, were to get nothing. This order of Council, as inconsistent with French law as with natural justice, was made "in order to ensure facilities to the said Duchess for the payment of her debts." There was another similar order granted for two years,[1] beginning on April 28, 1710.

The gratitude of Louis for the services rendered such a long time previously only died with him. The Duchess was not only protected against her creditors, but against the States of Brittany and the administration of the Crown Domain.

The Duchess had, in the beginning of the last century, the rare piece of good fortune to be "evicted for reasons of public utility." The poor manor house of her father, overlooking the port of Brest, was comprised in the evictions which the creation of arsenals, ropewalks, and naval stores would necessitate. But Louis XIV. had decided that the price of the properties situated at Brest, in the borough of the Recouvrance, was to be paid

[1] *Arch. Nat.*, E. 1937; E. 1952, fol. 57.

for, on the eviction of the owners, by the States of Brittany. They tried not to pay, and then contested the valuations. The Duchess of Portsmouth, whose paternal manor was in the borough of the Recouvrance, applied to the Comptroller-general of Finances, and obtained an order of the Council granting her 56,122 *livres*, payable by the Exchequer of the States of Brittany. Only the half of it was paid, and a new order was petitioned for and obtained.[1] The treasurer of Brittany was commanded to pay it on the king's authority, which covered his responsibility, and not to be impeded by anything which the States might have determined. But this functionary had not faith in the validity of the command he received. He fell back on the petitions of other landowners near Brest, who stood out against any one claimant being paid in full while the other creditors were only partially satisfied. This difficulty was settled by a further order to pay every one in full.

The Duchess had a sharp appetite for public

[1] For all the proceedings in this affair see *Archives Nationales*, Feb. 26, 1704, E. 741; 242; July 6, 1704, E. 1927; July 1, 1704, E. 746.

money. When the governor of the province in which Aubigny was situated offered for sale the functions of surveyors and valuators of land, with liberty to sit as royal notaries, she entered a protest, and claimed the exclusive right, in virtue of her seigneurial privileges, to sell these functions.[1] The Council, to which she appealed, ruled in her favour.[2] But if she was so keen in defending any old usage that helped to swell her income, she was equally ready to evade all seigneurial obligations. The Château of Aubigny fell out of repair. She pleaded that it was for the Crown to keep it up, inasmuch as it was an appanage which, in the event of her posterity becoming extinct, would revert to the Royal Domain. She could not, therefore, be bound to make any great and necessary repair. Now, the roof was falling in, the chapel had gone to ruin, and the forests had to be replanted. The plea was accepted.

Towards the close of the Great King's reign the Exchequer was impoverished, and the Duchess's allowances fell into arrear. She

---

[1] *Arch. Nat.*, July 1, 1704, E. 746.
[2] Arrêt du 20 Janvier, 1707, *Arch. Nat.*, E. 776

again applied, and not in vain, to the Comptroller-general.

After the death of Louis XIV., begging supplications were sent up to the Regent, who augmented her pension from 12,000 to 20,000 and then to 24,000 *livres*.[1] She was then wholly converted—a penitent, in debt, and obliged to live entirely in the country. The services she rendered to the French cause when she was the all-powerful mistress of Charles, were still remembered. However, she had learned by hard experience not to trust to pensions. When she saw the financial crash of the Regency coming on, she proposed that her pension should be commuted into a government debenture, and prevailed upon the Regent to sign the following order.

"M. Pierre Gruyn, the keeper of the Royal Treasury, is hereby ordered to pay in ready money to Madame Louise Renée de Penancoat de Keroualle, Duchess of Portsmouth and Aubigny, the sum of 600,000 *livres*, which have been accorded to her by the king, to be employed in buying a life-annuity, payable out of his Majesty's Exchequer, and to replace the pension of 24,000 *livres* which was partially granted her by the late king and partially by his present

---

[1] *Dangeau*, June 20, 1718, t. xvii., p. 329.

Majesty, in consideration of the great services she has rendered France, and to enable her to support her rank and dignity. Signed on 28th October, 1721.—

PHILIPPE D'ORLÉANS."[1]

The Duchess of Portsmouth's son, the Duke of Richmond, died in 1723. Two years later her sister Henriette, Countess of Pembroke and Marquise de Thois, felt that her end was near,[2] and had a notary fetched to her house in the Rue de Varennes, on May 12, 1725. There "seated in an arm-chair in a ground-floor room, looking on the garden of the said hotel, she dictated her will, and died on May 24. Louise survived her nine years, and in that time never quitted Aubigny.[3] She there founded a convent of hospital nuns, who equally divided their time between the education of the young and the care of the sick. She also spent freely in decorating churches. In October, 1734, she went to Paris to consult a doctor, and died on November 14, at the age of eighty-five. She was buried in the church of the Barefooted Carmelites, where there was a chapel of the

---

[1] MS. *Bibl. Nat.*, t. 50417.
[2] *Arch. Nat.*, t. 152 ; 6.
[3] *Mercure de France*, Nov. 1734, p. 2533.

Des Rieux, who still were proud of being of her kindred. Louise's English descendants, who lived in England on the wages of her double iniquity, neglected body and tomb, but made haste to enter into possession of the fief of Aubigny. Its Château, in the reign of Louis XVI., was lent to the Duchess of Leinster by her brother, the Duke of Richmond. That lady was then the wife of M. Ogilby. She took with her to Aubigny her son, Lord Edward Fitzgerald, who spent some years there in his boyhood, in ignorance of the story of how it came into his relative's hands. Aubigny was taken from the Richmond family, when fiefs were abolished by the Revolution. But the pension the grasping Duchess of Portsmouth extracted from the unpatriotic Charles II., and which was sequestrated by William of Orange, was restored to her son; and the British Parliament, which thinks £1,200 a year enough to relieve the distressed families of authors, artists, scientists, and other benefactors of their country, continues to pay the Duke of Richmond £19,000 a year in virtue of the secret services rendered to Louis XIV. by his ancestress Louise de

Keroualle. While thus Great Britain heaps wealth on her descendants, France has suffered her memory to fall into oblivion, and still owes her the statue which she so well earned, for enabling the most brilliant of her monarchs to conquer Flanders, Alsace, and le Franche Comté, and to bring Holland for a short time within his grasp.

Letters of the
DUCHESS OF PORTSMOUTH.

F LETTER

ESS OF PORTSMOUTH.

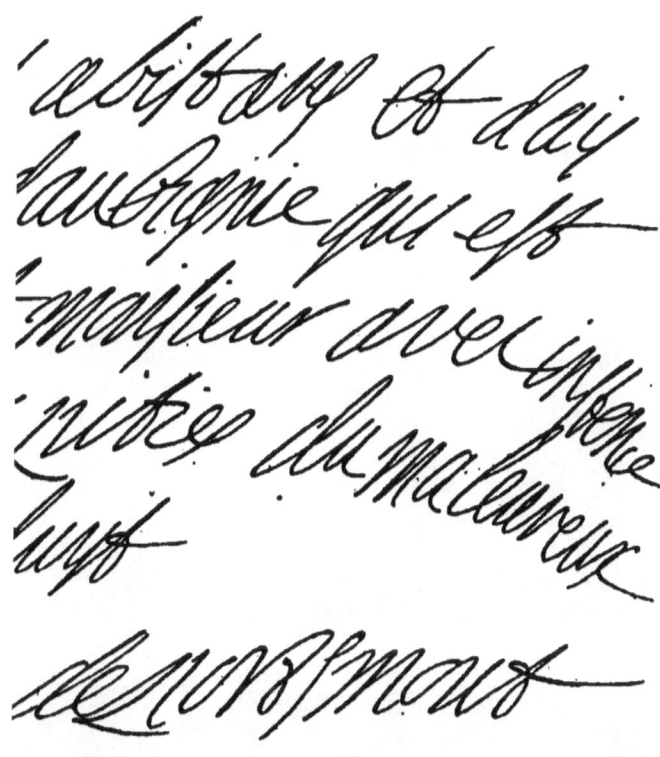

(National Archives, (G⁷ Contrôle général des finances).

In giving the following letters, the Translator thought better not to attempt a translation, because all that shows a total absence of education in them is untranslatable. "*Le style, c'est l'homme;*" and, perhaps in a greater degree, *le style, c'est la femme.* Louise de Keroualle has no style whatever. She spells like a serving-wench who has taken to gallantry, and, apt to write love letters, is not mistress of her pen, and shows in the inability to say plainly what she wants to express, a disposition lacking frankness. Although orthography was not fixed in her time, there was a current mode of spelling among men and women of good breeding. Well-bred women, in the seventeenth century, were well read and were admirable letter-writers. Nobody knew better how to say just what she wanted, without surplusage or baldness, than Madame de Maintenon. And who was ever more skilled in using elegant language for the purpose of saying nothing, when she had to write a good deal and appear effusive? This is shown in her letters to the Princesse des Ursins, when that diplomatic lady was directing Philip V. and his wife, or later, trying to inveigle that king into making her his second wife. Madame de Sévigné was so spontaneous and frank that one can almost see the workings of her heart and brain in her letters. Madame de Montespan gave the clear, sharp stamp of a coin to the ideas that circulated around her. The Princesse des Ursins and the Comtesse d'Aulnoy were at the court of Madrid what Lady Wortley Montague long after was at Stamboul. These women were prepared by severe mental drill in youth to be the bright and unconscious chroniclers of their time; and belonged to sets priding themselves on scholarly taste, which then took a tinge from Spain and a strong colour from Italy. Madame de Sévigné was at home in the Italian poets, which she read in their own tongue, and in the Latin authors; and she was at once a bookish, a brilliantly sociable, and a business woman. She called ignorance, by which she meant non-acquaintance with the standard books, ancient and modern, of her time, an "ugly beast." The library of Hortense Mancini, Duchess Mazarin, was, when she was a refugee in London, one of the subjects of table talk at Whitehall and St. James's. Ninon d'Enclos, the enchantress of three generations, divined in her old age the part Voltaire was likely to play in the world, and gave the first impetus to his literary career by leaving him her books.

The brilliant French women of Louise de Keroualle's time, save Mdlle. de la Vallière, were *maîtresses femmes*—a term for which strong-minded women is not quite an equivalent. They were women of initiative and of genius, which is always an independent thing, and bears trammels uneasily. Madame de Sévigné's genius was governed by her maternal passion, and strengthened by good sense. Mesdames de Montespan and de Maintenon were, in the bottom of their hearts, merely ambitious of governing the ablest and most self-willed monarch of their time; and they succeeded—one by her wit and her imperious temper, and the other by her strength and coolness of head, and her reposeful, simple, elegant conversation, and her craft.

A little later, two of the illegitimate daughters of Louis the Fourteenth turned out to be the most accomplished rhyming lampoonists that ever used the French tongue for a ribald and malignant use. They possessed the spirit and the form of the *chanson* in a no less degree than Béranger. But they polluted all they touched, graceful and light as their muse was, for they went in the way of the old Princess Palatine in grossness, and had a pruriency of feeling for which their origin accounted. Their grand position was, I may here remark, due to the example set by Charles II. and its action on the court of Versailles. Those accounts given by French ambassadors for the private reading of their King, of the goings on in the seraglio at Whitehall, and of the English king's prodigality in giving pensions and duchies to the children bred therein, doubtless helped to break down that respect for what was seemly, which Evelyn and other Englishmen so much noticed in Louis the Fourteenth, and contrasted with the disregard for decency of the merry monarch in saddling his ladies and their offspring on the nation. May not the desire that Louis so often showed, to hear all about the corruptions of the English court and the shamelessness of Charles in giving dukeries to these children, have arisen from a secret wish to find in his bad example a pretext for legitimizing and enriching the offspring of Mademoiselle de la Vallière and Madame de Montespan? The existence of the sons and daughters of both ladies was kept long a mystery. Madame de Maintenon took charge as governess of the Montespan lot, which were hidden away at Issy. Evelyn, when in France, noticed the care taken to keep them out of sight. It was only when the mind of Louis was saturated with letters about Whitehall that he thought of legitimizing and heaping appanages on his illegitimate sons and securing the most brilliant matches in France for the daughters. To do him justice, he did not seek so much to enrich them at the cost of the country as at the cost of his elderly and eccentric cousin la Grande Mademoiselle, or rather, at that of M. de Lauzun, a Gascon who made fascinating the fair the business of his life, and had infatuated the princess in question. The evil communications of the French ambassadors in London corrupted, there is room to believe, the good manners of their master.

The mission to which nature called Louise de Keroualle, was to be a conscious tool; and her main ambition, to be *la courtesane la mieux entretenue en Europe.* She had much subtlety and social tact, but little or none of that sympathy for ideas which made some of the most brilliant Frenchwomen of her day revel in the lofty ethics of Corneille, and quit cards and other dissipations to hear Bossuet discourse on "*la vie cachée en Dieu*," or Bourdaloue exert his penetrating eloquence in teaching those whom he exhorted to strengthen themselves for a higher life by prayer. The big sprawling handwriting of the woman is as full of significance as her spelling. A facsimile of the former is given in this volume. It is that of a child who has hardly got beyond writing m's and n's in large copy-book characters. This is to some extent a sign of an inactive mind and a poor heart. An affectionate woman must have scribbled often and at length to friends and relatives whom she left behind in quitting her home-country. She would have packed a deal into small space, letter-paper and postage between France and England being very dear, and the opportunities for sending letters from one country to another being rare and irregular. Use would have made her mistress of her pen. The fact of Louise de Keroualle being in a foreign and a hostile country, the tongue of which she never mastered, ought to have been a stimulus to the epistolary faculty. We must conclude that this gift was altogether wanting in her, and that she was one of those characterless women whom Pope best liked. An independent and an active intellect would have been in her way. It was her business to take cues from the French Embassy, and she did this with docility, and, because of her lazy brain, *sans trop de zèle*. This laziness is shown in her handwriting. The pen snails along laboriously because the thoughts shape themselves slowly. Wealth and luxury were the grand objects of her life. She wanted them both for herself and her son, and certainly succeeded well in getting them. It is not to the credit of England that this woman, whose courtesan-level of mind would have withheld her from attaining distinction at Versailles, directed the policy of Charles II. for so many years.

G. M. C.

I.

TO HENRY SIDNEY.

Letter published in the diary of Henry Sidney, vol. ii., p. 307.

Paris, 8 mars 1689.

Je sais toutes les bontés avec lesquelles vous avez parlé de moi, Monsieur, dont je vous suis infiniment obligée. Vous savez combien toute ma vie j'ai été dans vos intérêts de vous et de vos amis. De mon côté je ne suis point changée, et l'on ne peut prendre plus de part à tout ce qui vous regarde que je fais. Que mon absence ne me nuise donc non plus auprès de vous, et veuillez, en ce qui dépendra de vous, de bonne foi protéger mes intérêts. Vous savez qu'ils sont si attachés à ceux du duc de Richmond que l'on ne les peut séparer. Je ne doute point que le souvenir que vous avez de qui il a l'honneur d'être fils, ne vous porte davantage à nous continuer votre amitié que je souhaite trésfort et pour l'un et pour l'autre. Vous voulez bien que je vous supplie d'avoir un peu de bonté pour M. Hornby qui est celui qui vous rendra cette lettre. Il est tout à fait dans mes intérêts et de mes amis. Ce me seroit un grand plaisir si je pouvois autant compter sur vous. Il est sûr, mon cher oncle, que vous ne pouvez jamais être des amis de qui que ce soit qui soit plus des vôtres, ni qui vous honore plus parfaitement que

L., duchesse DE PORTSMOUTH.

II.

TO THE COMTE DE PONTCHARTRAIN.

Letter preserved in the National Archives, G^7, contrôle général des finances, and published in the *Musée des Archives*, n° 897, p. 540. Original autograph document.

Paris, 4 octobre 1692.

L'extresme misere dais abistans et dais paysant à l'antour d'Aubignie, qui est ma duché, me fait, Monsieur, avec instence vous conjurer d'avoyr pitiés du malheureux estat où il sont réduyt, tams par la grande charge de taille et des ustensille qu'ils ont tous les ans, que par le malheur qu'ils ont eu d'une grelle qui les a tous grellé st'anné. Ils sont sy accablé et sy peu annestat de payer qu'ils abandonnent et la ville et la taire. C'est ce qui fait, Monsieur, que j'ose vous conjurer par pitiés d'an avoyr pour eux, et de vouloyr mander à M. de Ceraucour, intandant de Bourge, de les vouloir exsanter de jens de guerre st'anné, et de vouloyr leur diminuer la taille, estent apsollumant une taire ruynée, sy vous n'avés ste bontés-là pour moy. Monsieur, ne me la refussé pas, estent une vrais charisté, et la misere y estent au dellas de ce

que vous pouvés vous ymaginer. Pardonés moy
mais fréquantes inportunistés, vous m'avés permis de
conter sur vos bontés esssentiellement : ainsy, Monsieur, ge m'adresse à vous avec confiance.

L., duchesse DE PORTSMOUTH.

III.

TO CHAMILLART.

Letter preserved in the British Museum, Ms. Add^nl 18675, f° 74.
Original autograph document.

De Paris, ce 2 d'avril 1701.

Sachant et connessant, Monsieur, lais anbarras
d'afaire que vous avez, je n'ê ossê tous se tems cy
vous trop presser et vous conjurer de vouloyr pancer
à moy comme vous m'avés fait la grasse de me le
promestre. O nom de Dieu, Monsieur, ayés assês de
bonté pour moy et de pitié pour ma triste sirconstance
pour vouloyr m'accorder le payeumant dais quinsse
mille franc que vous m'avés dist que le Roy ordonest
que je touchasse à pressant, et acordés moy l'expêdission de mon arrest pour le surplus ; que je me flate,
Monsieur, que vous ne me ferés le tord de mettre cy
bas mais interais que M. Pelltier les a réduyts ; que
je vous aye donc la sansible obligassion, Monsieur,
que je ne perde poînst moytié par moytié, de considérer qu'estens sur les estats que je seré ancore bien
du tems sans toucher mon arjent. Ainsi, Monsieur,
ayés l'umanisté d'antrer dans mon malheureux estat

Y

et que la liquidassion que vous voullés bien avoyr la
bonté de faire soyt en ma faveur et la plus avanta-
geusse qu'il vous sera possible ; car de vostre bonté
an sesy despand tous le bonneur et l'arengemant de
mais afaire ; je charge mon homme d'afaire d'avoyr
l'honneur de vous présenter sette lestre. Vous orés
la bonté de luy ordonner lais pas que vous treverés
bien que je fasse auprais de vous pour la terminesson
de sette afaire ycy ; donnés luy donc, s'il vous plest,
vos ordres avec autems de bonté que vous m'avés
permis d'espérer que vous oriés pour moy. J'osse
vous an conjurer très-instammant, Monsieur, et de
vouloyr bien croyre que vous n'an pouvés avoyr pour
personne qui estoyt plus vesristablement sansible ny
qui vous estimme et honnore cy parfaitement que
moy.

L., duchesse DE PORSTMOUT.

IV.

TO CHAMILLARD.

National Archives, G., 7.   Original autograph document.[1]

De Paris, ce 5 daoust 1702.

Permestez moy, Monsieur, dosser ancore vous demander une grasse qui est seullement de me vouloir
faire mestre sur la feuille de distribution ; vous nan
pesrez pa plus tot sy vous ne le voullez, mais si vous

---

[1] This letter, and the eleven following, were discovered by
M. A. de Boislisle.

me voullez bien faire ce plesir la je treve le moien de macosmoder avec mais jens dafaire, sy vous me donnez ceste marque de bonté. Ne me la reffusé pas, Monsieur, je vous an conjure, car par là vous me donerez le moien de sortir davec dais arabe qui me tiranisse de toute maniere. Soufré donc, Monsieur, que je vous conjure de me donner ce secours et de vouloir bien vous donner la penne de me faire savoir sy vous orez ceste bonté pour moy. Je natems que sella pour partir disy et finir et sortir absollument dafaire, sy je suis assé heureuse pour que vous veillez bien me donner ce secours que je vous demande instamment avec la justisse, Monsieur, de me croyre la personne du monde qui vous estime, ayme et honore le plus parfaistement.

L., duchesse DE PORTSMOUTH.

V.

TO DESMARETS.

Letter preserved in the National Archives, G., 7, 543. Original autograph document.

De Paris, ce 20 mars 1708.

Ne pouvant avoyr l'honneur de vous voir, Monsieur, par le grand abattement qui me reste d'une violente fiesvre et une etresipelle que jé eu dans la taite et sur tout le visage, je prant la liberté de vous escrire sais lignes pour vous suplier devouloir bien vous resouvenir de la promesse que vous avez eu la bonté de me faire auprès de M. Nicolle, qui anagist le plus mal du monde avec moy car, depuis castre moy, je nê pas pus parvenir a tirer un soult de luy pour ma subsistance. Il a ma belle tapisserie dont il se sert et qu'il gaste toute, et je me treve pis que je nettais avec Thévening, car au moins me payès til rêgulliêsrement tout lay moy ; mais tapisserie ne servoient poingt et estet fort soigneusement conservé ; je ne luy donnè que huit pour cent, jendonne dix à icelluy cy, il touche mon revenu et il ne me payen poingt et me lesse manquer de tout ; enfin s'yl ne luy parest pas que vous macordyé une forte protection, je n'en vienderé jamais about. Ne me la refussé pas, Monsieur, je vous ansupli, et donnez-vous la penne de luy parller comme luy marquant voullant estre obéys. Josse espérer cet ésantiel servisse de vous, Monsieur, et que vous serez persuadé que personne dans le monde ne vous peut estimer et honorer sy parfaitement que moy.

L., duchesse DE PORTSMOUTH.

Je prie Monsieur de de ce doner la penne de vous rendre cette lettre, et de vous dire ce dont je lé chargé ; soutenez-moi, je vous ansuplie.

VI.

To DESMARETS.

Letter preserved in the National Archives, G., 7, 543. Original autograph signed document.[1]

De Paris, ce 12 avril 1708.

Ma santé ne me permettant pas encore d'aller à Versailles, Monsieur, je vous envoy le sieur Pinson pour vous porter un mémoyre ; il vous expliquera, sy vous voullez bien macorder le plésir de luy doner un mosmant dodyance, la conséquance que ce mest de macorder la grasse que je vous demande ; jê lieux de me flater de vos bontés et desperer de vous tous lais secours qui sont a vostre pouvoyr ; selluy cy est antiesremant, acordèlle moy donc, Monsieur, je vous an conjure, la pronte expédissions mest importente, et vous le connesterez parce quil aura l'honneur de vous dire. Josse espérer que vous macorderez cette marque de l'interait que vous me foite l'honneur de prendre an moy comme à la personne du monde qui sertennemant vous honore, ayme et estime le plus parfaitement.

L., duchesse DE PORTSMOUTH.

---

[1] Some of the letters of Louise de Keroualle in the National Archives are unsigned.

VII.

TO DESMARETS.

Letter preserved in the National Archives, G., 543, Original document with the note, "Par le sieur de Lonchant."

De Paris, ce 9 juillet 1708.

Comme vous m'avez permis de conter sur vos bontés, Monsieur, josse prandre la liberté de les inplorer non an chosse qui vous peuvent estre a charge, car sait ce que jé visteré toujours, mais comme vous mavez fait l'honneur de me dire dans le cosmancement que vous avez esté controlleur général[1], que vous ne trouvesriez pas movais que je vous présantasse autems dafaire que on man donnerest qui parussent résonnable, je mosse flater que vous avez assé de bontés pour moy pour aymer autems et j'espère mieux me faire du bien de cette maniere cà des personnes indisférente; vous connaissé mais besoings et le malheureux estat ou je suis et de quelle conséquance me peut estre un secour comme selluy sy qui ne fait tort a personne et qui notte rien dais coffre du Roy; ne me reffusé donc poingt vostre protection. Vous m'aviez paru sy rempli de bonté, d'amitié et de bonne vollonté pour moy devent destre

---

[1] Desmarets only became contrôleur général in the month of February this year.

dans le poste ou vous este, que josse me promestre, Monsieur, que dans dais chosse comme celle-cy vous me voudrez bien proqurer tous lais secour à ma môvesse situassion qui despenderont de vous. Vous voullez donc bien me permettre de vous faire souvenir par ce mémoyre, que je joingt à ma lettre, des deux affaires que jus l'honneur de vous présenter la surveille de vostre despart. La personne qui a l'honneur de vous présanter ma lettre est le sieur de Longchant qui me les a donné et qui est un homme fort industrieux dans sait chosse là ; anfin, Monsieur, josse espérer que je trevesré an vous dans dais chose qui ne vous seront pas plus anbarrassante ny plus disficille que selle sy, une vraie protection et un veristable et essantielle ami, et que vous me feré la justisse destre fortement persuadé que personne ne vous aynie, ne vous estime et honore sy parfaitement que je le fais véritablement.

     L., duchesse DE PORTSMOUTH.

Permettez-moi de vous suplier de vous souvenir de me faire mestre sur l'estat de distribussion pour ma pansion eschue depuis le commancement de juin.

VIII.

TO DESMARETS.

Letter preserved in the National Archives, G, 7, 543. Original autograph document.

De Paris, ce 18 juillet 1708.

J'osse espérer, Monsieur, que la grasse que vous avez bien voullu accorder à monsieur le marquis de Thoye *an parllant au sieur Volland pour luy, ne seras pas retraite par vous comme monsieur le marquis de Vallance ce le promest et quil la fait entandre au sieur Vollant an luy demandant six ou sept jour* pour anployer sait sollicitassion auprais de vous. Je me flatte, Monsieur, quelle noront nulle lieux et que vous orez la bonté de nous continuer vostre protection, monsieur de Thoye ayant toute lais suretés à donner au sieur Volland. Ne me refusez donc poingt ceste marque de bonté et de consideration que josse vous dire, Monsieur, que je mériste pas lais santimants d'amitiés et destime que jé pour vous comme pour un des plus honneste homme du monde et qui a le plus de mérite et que j'onnore le plus parfaitement.

L., duchesse DE PORTSMOUTH.

Permettez-moy ancore, Monsieur, d'osser vous suplier de vous voulloyr souvenir de moy pour ma pansion qui est eschue depuis le cosmancement du moy passé.

IX.

TO DESMARETS.

National Archives, G, 7, 543.   Original autograph document.

De Paris, ce 8 daoust 1708.

La maniesre obligente avec laquelle vous me fiste la grasse, Monsieur, dantrer dans mes interais quant jus l'honneur de vous parller de ceste grande afaire des billiey de monoye manhardy de vous importuner de sais ligne-sy, pour vous représenter quelle doyt parestre a un homme aussy escléré que vous, sy aventajeuse pour le servisse du Roy quelle mériste que vous y donniez toute vostre atantion, afin de la conclure insesemmant et que ceux qui l'entreprennent puisse travailler à s'arenger là dessu. Ainsy j'espère, Monsieur, que vous leur manderez insesamment de vous aller trever a Fonteneblaux. Monsieur Nicollas man a entretenue à fond et dans mon peux de jugement, je treve qui la possede sy bien que rien ne peut manquer de leur part a l'exéqution. Il m'a paru quil a fait de sérieuse réflecsion sur tous lais événemens et quil ne craing auqun inconvénient pour vous ny pour eux. Je ne voye an luy qu'un très grand selle pour vostre service et une franchise qui lobligerest d'abandonner lafaire, syl nestet persuadé que vous y orez de grands aventages et baucoup donneur dedans et dehor du royaume, et cy je nestais pas persuadé je ne prandrais pas, Monsieur, cette liberté. Sertennement personne ne s'interessant plus vivement anvous que moy, sait ce qui me porte à vous marquer quil faudra que vous mandiez monsieur Nicolla et un associé et puis retenir Nicolla tout seul pour vous instruyre a fon et vous mestre en estat toute lafaire pour la conclure ; jê de nouvaux de luy sa parole quil fera pour moy tout au monde ce que vous voudrez. Mais ne croyez pas s'il vous plest, Monsieur, que sy je nanvissajest pas la chose glorieusse et utile pour vous, que l'interais que il peux avoyr me fit vous representer la chose sy vivement, ne trevez donc poingt movais, Monsieur, la liberté que je prand et soyez persuadé de mon atachement et de ma saingsere amitié pour vous, personne ne pouvant vous considérer avec une plus parfaite estime et vous honorer plus infisnisment que je le fais.

L., duchesse DE PORTSMOUTH.

Trevez bon que je vous supli aussy de vous resouvenir de ma pansion et d'ordonner que je soye payé.

X.

TO DESMARETS.

National Archives, G, 7, 543.   Original autograph document.

De Paris, ce 14 aoust 1708.

Je resoy, Monsieur, dans le mosmant la lettre que vous m'avez fait l'honneur de mescrire; je charge monsieur Niscolla davoyr lhonneur de vous rendre selle ycy, qui san retourne a Fontenneblaux pour attendre vos hordre contems et croyant estre sûr et an estat de lever toute lais difficultés que vous pouvez trevez dans stafaire, sy vous voullez bien luy faire la grasse de luy an parler. Ne refusez pas je vous pris la liberté que j'osse prandre dantrer dans stafaire comme présumant de vous exsiter et persuader contre vostre propre jugement et vos grandes lumières ny maime par un esprit davisdisté et d'interais desrésonnable, car je ne la souette quantems quelle vous pouras estre agréable et utile. An ce cas là jeanresantiré un sansible plaisir puisque vous pourez estre mon bien faiteur sans qu'il vous an coute rien dauqune manière que quelque parolle. Ainsy quant josse vous suplier de voulloir aprofondir la chosse avec le sieur Nicollas, se nest que pour que vous an ayez un parfait esclercissement et lesprit satisfait làdessus pour vous desterminer comme vous le jugerez le plus apropos. Il serest resté pour atamdre vos hordres et vostre tems sans quil avest ysy eune a faire de conséquance. Aujourdhuy je vous suis infiniment obligé, Monsieur, de la bonté que vous me faite espérer que vous hordonnerez le payement de ma pansion ; soyez persuadé, je vous suplie, de mon parfait atachement pour vous et que personne ne se peut intéresser avec plus d'amitié à tousse qui vous regarde, ny vous estimer et honnorer plus parfaitement que moy.

L., duchesse DE PORTSMOUTH.

XI.

TO DESMARETS.

National Archives, G, 7, 543. Original autograph document.

De Paris, ce 16 octobre 1708.

Je viens d'aprandre, Monsieur, que quelque hun de messieurs les intendant de fisnance avest antrepris doptenir de vous pour un ostre compaigny que celle de monsieur Vollant et sais assossiés dont vous trevesrez les noms sy joings, lafaire de latribustion de la noblesse. Josse espérer, Monsieur, que vous n'avez pas oublier que je vous la proposé sainc ou six jours aprais que vous fuste nomé controlleur général et que vous me fiste l'honneur de m'assurer que vous ne la feriez que pour moi et vous la renvoyatte à monsieur Couturier que vous an avez chargé pour vous an faire souvenir. Sait un bien que vous me ferez, Monsieur, et dont je mosse flater que vous aymerez mieux que je profitte que quelques amis de messieurs lais intendant de fisnance. Comme vous mavez fait la grasse de me donner vostre parolle, je suis persuadé que vous orez la bonté de me la tenir et de voulloyr préférer la compaigny du sieur Vollant à tout offre et de leur permettre de vous faire leur soumission. Lextresme craincte, Monsieur, de vous importuner a fait que je nè pas ossé trop souvent vous an parller pour vous an rafréchir la mémoyre non plus que de l'afaire de la banque, mourant toujours de peur de vous estre trop incosmode ; cependant, Monsieur, se sont dais plésir et dais grasse quil faut que vous fassiez à quelquun ; vous savez la cruelle situation de mais afaire, par sais deux que jè eu l'honneur de vous proposer vous me proqurez un repaux esternel et vous devennez sertennemant mon bienfaiteur et hor destat de vous devoyr à la venir trop importuner. Accordez moy donc, Monsieur, sais deux grasse et ansella une marque de vos bontés et de vostre amitié et de vouloyr bien me faire savoir le tems a peu prais que vous trevesrez a propos de les fisnir pour que je prenne lais mesure nécessaire pour la suretté de ce que les uns et les ostres mont ofert tant pour la faire de la banque que pour selle de la noblesse ; je natems que vostre dessision pour manaller à ma campaigne, mettent de conséquance de ne poingt quiter que je nay eu mais sûretés pour proficter du bien et de lavantage que josse espérer que vous voudrez bien me faire et me proqurer dont je vous orez une esternelle obligassion, car, Monsieur, sertennement vous ne ferez jamais de plésir ny de bien à pérsonne qui lais ressante avec une plus parfaitte reconnessance ny qui vous estime, ayme vesristablement, Monsieur, et honore plus parfaitement que moy.

L., duchesse DE PORTSMOUTH.

The following is the list mentioned in the letter:

Monseigneur aura la bonté de se souvenir de la proposition de l'attribution de noblesse aux commissaires ordinaire des guerres, à ceux de la marine, galleres et artillerie dont Sa Grandeur a chargé M. Le Cousturier pour la travailler avec les proposant qui sont : Rolland, Lantage, Accault, Caquet, Vollant, Montmarqué, Durbec, Vannelle, Mérite, La Bussière, Saint-Léon, Imbert Nicolas, Lacombe, Le Vasseur.

XII.

TO DESMARETS.

National Archives, G, 7, 543.   Original autograph document.

De Paris, ce 25 janvier 1709.

La bonté que vous avez eu, Monsieur, de me promestre quan fessant l'*afaire consernant la noblesse dais 8 cosmissere vous agrériez la compaignie que jorais l'honneur de vous présanter*, dont le sieur Volland est à la taite et qui a esté travaillé par le sieur de la Combe, me fait espérer, Monsieur, que vous voudrez bien vous an souvenir, ce qui fait que je prand la liberté de vous inportuner de sais ligne sait que je me suis lessé dire que monsieur Poultier voullest vous an parler pour loptenir pour un otre compaigny; mais jé tems de foy an vous, cas moings que ce ne soyt pas un oubli, je mosse assé flater de vostre amitié, pour me persuader que vous voudrez bien man continuer lais marque et ne rien changer asse que vous mavez faist l'honneur de me promettre. Je vous ansuplie tres instamment et vous demande la justisse, Monsieur, de croyre que personne ne peut avoyr plus de recosnessence et de sansibillité de vos bontés ny ne vous peut estimer, considérer et honorer plus parfaitement que

     L., duchesse DE PORTSMOUTH.

Je vous envoye si joingt, Monsieur, les noms de ce qui compose la compaigny: Rolland, Lantage, Acco, Oiseau, Vanelle, Le Vasseur, Caquet.

XIII.

TO DESMARETS.

National Archives, G, 7, 543. Original autograph letter.

De Paris, ce 24 juillet 1709.

L'estat où je me treve, Monsieur, me forsse a prandre la liberté de vous importuner de sais lignes pour vous demander an grasse très instenmant de vouloyr bien mordonner le payement de ma pansion. Si vous trevez la disfisqulté de me faire donner quelque espesse qui me ferest pour tems fort grand plésir, au moings accordez-moy la marque de protection et d'amitié de lordonner an billais de monoye. Ne me refussé pas, Monsieur, je vous suplis, ce secour essentiel ; je natems que ceste marque de vostre considérassion et damitié pour partjr pour la province. Josse, Monsieur, me flater que vostre bon cœur et vostre pitié pour moy vous portera à macorder mon instente priesre comme à la personne du monde qui y sera la plus sansible et quy vous ayme, estime et honore, Monsieur, plus parfaitement que je ne le puis exprimer.

L., duchesse DE PORTSMOUTH.

Oserés je espérer un mot de réponse de vous ? Quelle soyt je vous conjure favorable.

XIV.

TO DESMARETS.

National Archives, G, 7, 543. Original autograph document.
Noted with these words : *A. M. de Vaubourg.*

Daubigny, ce 5 octobre 1709.

Je ne sais, Monsieur, sy vous avez la bonté de remarquer par mon sillance la craingte que jè et que je vous ay toujour marquer de vous estre importune. Tems que jé pus, jé suyvis ansella mon goust et la veritable considération que jé pour vous ; mais an veristé, Monsieur, je me treve dans un sy rigoureux estat, que je me treve forcé d'implorer vostre secours et vostre amitié. Jestay venue isy contems dy trever quelque douseur et quelque essance ; mais la misère y est sy afreuse que l'on ne sorest tirer un soult car lon a pas seullement de coy acheter du graing pour semer, et sy vous navez pitié de moy, mais taire ne seront pas ancemancé, car, sy je ne lais fait pas faire moy maime, lay fermier sont hors d'estat et cassy tous à la mandiscité ; trevez donc bon, Monsieur, que je vous supli instamment de me donner une marque de distingtion et de bonté partiqulliesre, an me fessant hordonner le payeumant de ma pansion, ce seras une obligassion esternelle que je vous orez, car je suis o non plus. Ne me refussé pas, Monsieur, je vous an suplie, et laissé vous toucher aux besoings d'une amie qui vous honore autems que je fais. Trevez ancore bon, Monsieur, de resevoyr un plasset de ma part qun homme à moy ora l'honneur de vous presanter sur le sujest de mais boys. Ce plaset vous instruyra ; ayez, syl vous plest, atantion. Que je treve donc, Monsieur, en vous, un essentiel ami dans mes vrais besoings, josse me le promestre et man flater et que vous serez bien persuadé que personne ne peut estre avec une plus parfaite estime, Monsieur, vostre tres umble et tres obéissante servante que je la suis.

L., duchesse DE PORTSMOUTH.

XV.

TO DESMARETS.

National Archives, G, 7, 543. Original autograph document.

Daubigni, ce 27 novembre, 1709.

J'us l'honneur, il y a deux mois, de vous faire présanter un plasset, Monsieur, par lequel je demandais qu'il vois plut ordonner que lais vente dais boys de mon duché Daubigny fussent remise a l'année prochenne dans lespérance que j'avais quelle serest porté à un plus hault pris que stannée, et nayant poingt este statué sur ce plassait, lon a exéqusté laroit du conseil qui an hordonnait la vente. Lay boys furent vandus le sainc du présent moy pour la somme de dix-huit cent livres, et mestent par moy maime fait informé, lon ma raporté qu'ils estet porté a leur juste valleur tems par raport à leur caslité cà leur situassion, estant esloingné de neuf lieux dais rivière. Cependant comme monsieur Thiton grand mestre ma fait voyr lordre que vous luy avez envoyé le quinsse novambre pour la remise de l'adjudication, josse vous suplier de vouloyr bien luy ordonner quil nanpesche poingt l'adjudicataire de jouir puisque sait une chose conforme et que le retar me serest tres préjudissiable ; josse ancosre, Monsieur, vous conjurer davoir pitié de ma triste situassion qui est plus rigoureuse que vous ne pouvez vous l'imaginer. Je suis très persuadé que le Roy qui nignore pas depuis fort longtems mon malheureux estat, que si vous aviez la bonté de le luy ancosre représanter an bon et véritable amie, que ny luy, ny vous, ne pouvez pas trever auqun desrengemant pour dix mille franc de plus ou de moings dans lais afaire. Dautant que sait la seulle grasse et le seul bienfait dont il mest jamais honoré et mayant fait l'honneur de masurer quant jé pris la liberté de luy andemander dautre qu'il ne le pouvest pas, mais qu'il me ferest payer régulliesrement et préférablement. Onon de dieu, Monsieur, veillez antrer avec un cœur umaing et tandre dans mon rigoureux besoing. Josse espérer ceste marque de vostre amitié et de vostre bonté comme la justisse, Monsieur, destre persuadé que de toute lais personne qui ont toujour fait profession destre de vos amis il ny en a auqune qui vous aime et honore aussy parfaitement que moy.

L., duchesse DE PORTSMOUTH.

XVI.

TO DESMARETS.

Letter preserved in the British Museum, Ms. Add^{al} 18675, f° 75. Original autograph document.

De Paris, ce 22 septembre 1711.

Comme vous aviés eu la bonté, Moniseur, de m'assurer que vous donneriés ordre de me faire resevoyr une anné de la pansion dont le Roy m'onore, jê esté au trésor royal chê M. Groing et chez M. de Turmenis ; il m'ont assuré que vous n'an aviés donné auqun à ma faveur, et comme je ne doute poingt que vostre intansion ne soyt de me faire resevoyr les neuf mille, et tems de livre que vous m'avez fait la grasse de me promestre, et que comme vous avés l'esprit auqupé de chose très-importente vous pouvés avoyr oublié de pancer à moy, trevés bon ste lestre pour vous an faire souvenir et pour vous suplier instanmant de vouloyr bien anvoyer vos hordre possitive pour que je puisse profister de vostre promesse, an ayant, je vous assure, Monsieur, un bessoings infisnis. Ayés donc cette bonté pour moy, je vous an conjure instanmant, comme de m'accorder la justisse d'estre bien persuadé, Monsieur, que personne ne vous estime, considère et honore plus parfaitement que moy.

L., duchesse DE PORTSMOUT.

Trevés bon, Monsieur, que dans cette mesme lestre j'ose vous suplier, sy sella ne vous ayt pas désagréable, de vouloyr bien an ma recosmandassion accorder au sieur de Mongela, fils enné du sieur Grimaux, un des fermiers généraux, une souferme dais ayde, soyt dans le Lionnays ou de Chaslon an Champaigne ou dans le Bourbonnay. Se sont dais jens très solvable et qui peyront bien, et qui sont persuadés que vous m'onorés d'un peux de bonté et d'amitié, et qui ont crus que vous leur acorderiés par raport à moy plus tot cette faveur là que par d'autre voye. Comme je leurs ay obligassion, je né pas refussé de vous an faire ma trèsumble priesre; ne le trevés pas movais, je vous an suplis, Monsieur. Et permestés moy de vous demander an grasse un most de réponce, et s'yl ce peut qu'elle me soyt favorable an tout.

XVII.

TO DESMARETS.

National Archives, G, 7, 543. Original autograph document.[1]

De Paris, ce 2 février 1713.

Je suis bien mortifié, Monsieur, de me trever obligé par la cruelle situation de mais affaire et mon malheureux estat de vous inportuner sy souvant pour

---

[1] This letter and the following one were discovered by M. de Boislisle.

vous conjurer davoyr la bonté de me faire au moing payer une année de pansion sur selle qui me sont dus. Accordez moy donc, Monsieur, sette marque de bonté et d'amitié de vouloyr bien antrer dans mon extresme besoing et de me faire mestre sur l'estat de distribution de dimanche et avec un ordre positif d'estre payé et sanrien qui ne me fasse pas languir. An véristé, Monsieur, ma considération pour vous et mon atachement à vous honorer depuis le moment que jé eu l'honneur de vous cosnestre, meryterest un peux de protection et de secours dun ceur aussy bien fait et aussy juste que le vostre ; ne me refussé donc pas, Monsieur, la grasse et la justisse que je vous demande instammant, non plus que la justice destre tres fortement persuadé que vous ne lacorderez à personne qui vous souette plus de bonheur, qui vous honore plus parfaitement, ny qui soyt plus vesristablement, Monsieur, vostre très umble et très obéissante servente que moy.

L., duchesse DE PORTSMOUTH.

XVIII.

TO DESMARETS.

National Archives, G, 7, 543. Original autograph document.

De Paris, ce 9 mars 1713.

Je resge toujours, Monsieur, assé malheureuse pour que vous ne veillez jamais antrer avec un peux de bonté et dumanisté dans ma cruelle sytuassion et dans mais extresme besoings. Je vous avourez, Monsieur, que la sirconstance ou je me treve me mest au desespoyr, et se qui maflige an caure le plus griesvement, sait de cecasprais mestre ossé flater d'un peux de part dans l'honneur de vostre amitié jé la doulleur de nan pas resevoyr la moindre petite marque ny de ne vous trever jamais dispossé a entrer dans aucune considérassion pour moy ny de sou¹ager mon malheureux estat et mais extresme bessoing, mestent dus troys années de la pension dont le Roy ma honoré. An véristé, Monsieur, par lestime et la considération que jé toujour eu pour vous depuis que jé l'avantage de vous cosnestre, je mestais cru androyt despércr une marque de vos bontés et de vostre justice. Je vous la demande, Monsieur, avec toute lais instance qun très présant besoing le peut exsiger et que vous veilliez bien au moings mordonner une année. Vous mé laviez fait espérer devant le voyage de Fonteneblaux : ne me refussé pas, Monsieur, je vous ansuplie, et veillez vous souvenir que je suis une dais personne du monde qui ayt toujour plus pris de part a vos avantages que qui que se soyt. Ainsi, Monsieur, par umanité, sy je ne le puis optenir de vostre amitié, compastissé à ma triste conjoncture an ma cordant la grasse que je vous demande ysy et la justisse an maime tems de me croyre avec toute la considération possyble vostre tres umble et très obéissante servente.

L., duchesse DE PORTSMOUTH.

XIX.

TO THE CONTROLEUR GENERAL OF FINANCE.[1]

Signed letter ; collection of M. de Barberey.

A Aubigny, le 10 décembre 1731.

Permettez-moi, Monsieur, de vous prier cette année, comme j'ay fait l'année dernière, de m'estre favorable auprès de M: le Cardinal dans la demande que je luy fait de la grattiffication annuelle qu'il m'a jusqu'à présent fait accorder par Sa Majesté, et d'une petite augmentation, si cela est possible. Vous trouverez cy-joint, Monsieur, la copie du mémoire que j'ay fait présenter à M. le Cardinal ; comme il vous

[1] Philibert Orry was contrôleur général from March 1730 to December 1745.

sera apparemment renvoyé, je vous prie de voulloir bien l'appuyer de votre crédit auprès de Son Eminence, et de l'engager à m'accorder ma demande. Je me flatte par l'amitié que vous m'avez témoignée que vous voudrez bien me rendre service en cette occasion, et que vous êtes bien persuadé de l'estime et de la considération avec laquelle je suis, Monsieur, votre très-humble et très-obéissante servante.

L., duchesse DE PORTSMOUTH.

On the margin is written in a handwriting resembling Orry's: "Bon pour 5,000. Répondre en conformité à madame de Portsmouth." The copy of the following memorial and of the petition to the King are appended to Letter XIX.:

To Monseigneur the Cardinal de Fleury.

MONSEIGNEUR,

Vous avez eu la bonté de faire donner à la duchesse de Portsmouth en l'année 1726 une ordonnance de grattiffication extraordinaire de dix mil livres; en 1727 une de six mil livres, et les années suivantes cinq mil livres seulement. Et cela en considération des services importants qu'elle a rendus autrefois à l'État et à cause de la perte qu'elle a fait de presque tout son bien dans le papier; la réduction qu'elle a souffert sur quelques rentes viagères qu'elle avoit, et dont jusqu'à présent elle n'a pu obtenir le rétablissement, ayant encore rendu sa situation plus fâcheuse.

Elle supplie très-humblement Votre Éminence de voulloir bien luy accorder pour la présente année 1731 une ordonnance de cette grattiffication un peu plus forte que celle de l'année précédente et la proportionner à ses besoins et à son âge de plus de quatre-vingt-deux ans.

Note subjoined:

Madame la duchesse de Portsmouth
Supplie Sa Majesté de lui continuer la même grâce qu'elle a la bonté de luy accorder depuis plusieurs années, en luy faisant donner une gratification pour la présente année. La réduction qu'elle a soufferte sur quelques rentes viagères qu'elle avoit, et dont elle n'a point demandé le rétablissement, ayant rendu sa situation encore plus fâcheuse.

Sa Majesté luy a accordé :

 En 1726 . . . . 10,000 liv.
 En 1727 . . . . 6,000 —
 En 1728, 1729 et 1730 . . 5,000 —

FINIS.

www.ingramcontent.com/pod-product-compliance
Lightning Source LLC
Chambersburg PA
CBHW032028220426
43664CB00006B/401